THE GUINNESS BOOK OF

ODDITIES

GEOFF TIBBALLS

GUINNESS PUBLISHING

Editor: Anne Marshall

Design: Keith Pointing

Picture Editing and Research: Alex Goldberg/Image Select

Cover illustration: Rob Judges (see p. 98)

The Work copyright © Geoff Tibballs, 1995

The right of Geoff Tibballs to be identified as Author of this Work has
been asserted in accordance with the Copyright, Design & Patents Act 1988.

First published in 1995 by Guinness Publishing Ltd
Reprint 10 9 8 7 6 5 4 3 2 1 0

This publication copyright © Guinness Publishing Ltd 1995
33 London Road, Enfield, Middlesex, Great Britain

Typeset in Great Britain by Ace Filmsetting Ltd, Frome, Somerset

Printed and bound in Great Britain by The Bath Press, Bath

A catalogue record for this book is available from the British Library

ISBN 0–85112–661–8

CONTENTS

INTRODUCTION 5
ACKNOWLEDGEMENTS 5
1 ECCENTRICS 6
MONARCHS   WEALTHY ECCENTRICS   ECCENTRICS OF THE ARTS
HERMITS AND RECLUSES   INTELLECTUALS   ANIMAL LOVERS   THE MILITARY
RELIGIOUS ECCENTRICS   SPORTING ECCENTRICS   STYLISH ECCENTRICS

2 THE HUMAN MIND 31
CHILD PRODIGIES   DREAMS AND PREMONITIONS   MIRACLE HEALING
OUT-OF-BODY EXPERIENCES   SUPERSTITIONS

3 ENDEAVOUR 40
CURIOUS EVENTS   ODD FEATS   SPORT

4 ARTS AND ENTERTAINMENT 64
ART   SCULPTURE   LITERATURE   MUSIC   CINEMA   THE STAGE
TELEVISION AND RADIO

5 BUILDINGS AND STRUCTURES 82
CASTLES, PALACES AND STATELY HOMES   CHURCHES AND CATHEDRALS
COMMERCIAL BUILDINGS   FOLLIES   HOME FROM HOME   PRIVATE HOMES

6 HISTORY 102
BATTLES   CHARACTERS IN HISTORY   LAW AND ORDER   TRIALS

7 TRANSPORT 118
AVIATION   BICYCLES   MOTORCARS, CARRIAGES, BUSES AND TRAMS   RAILWAYS
SHIPS AND CANALS

8 SCIENCE AND TECHNOLOGY 132
INVENTORS AND INVENTIONS   METEOROLOGY   NUMBERS
SCIENTIFIC CURIOSITIES   SPONTANEOUS HUMAN COMBUSTION
STRANGE EXPERIMENTS   THE UNIVERSE

9 THE NATURAL WORLD 152
ANIMAL KINGDOM   PLANT KINGDOM   PLACES

10 COINCIDENCE 175
THE ARTS   CRIME   DISASTERS   PAST COINCIDENCES   SPORT   TWINS

BIBLIOGRAPHY 186
INDEX 188

INTRODUCTION

What is an oddity? Almost daily, we have experiences which we might consider odd. It need not be something as dramatic as seeing a UFO hovering above the supermarket, but could be something odd like running out of petrol when the gauge shows there is a gallon left in the tank, or discovering a mislaid letter in an unlikely place. There is usually a perfectly rational explanation for such occurrences – you probably have a faulty petrol gauge or a hyperactive puppy.

But some things defy explanation – cases of spontaneous human combustion or sixth sense and out-of-body experiences – while others are remarkable departures from the norm. They may contradict the laws of science and nature such as the woodpecker which hits the bark of a tree with such force that, by rights, its head should fall off, the great bustard, which, according to the laws of aerodynamics, should be too heavy to fly, or the male seahorse which gives birth. They may be wonderful eccentrics like Princess Alexandra of Bavaria who throughout her life remained convinced that as a child she had swallowed a full-size grand piano, or the French King who thought he was made of glass. They could be bizarre events such as the World's Shortest St Patrick's Day Parade from America, Australia's Henley-on-Todd Regatta (a boat race run on a dry river bed) or Scotland's World Flounder Tramping Championships. And they could be just unusual sights, such as the sausage tree, the house with a fibreglass shark embedded in the roof or the building that is shaped like a pineapple.

Oddity is in the eye of the beholder. To some people, the Sydney Opera House is a monstrous example of modern architecture – a true oddity – to others it is a building of considerable beauty. Many would consider Victoria Herberta of Houston, Texas, who regularly shared her bed with a pig to be a shade eccentric. But to her, it was just an expression of porky devotion. Thus, by its very nature, this book has to be a personal interpretation of oddity. It is designed to be browsed through and dipped into and contains only a selection of the vast range of oddities that exist and indeed arise every day of our lives.

ACKNOWLEDGEMENTS

The author would like to thank the following for their kind assistance in the compilation of this book: Nottinghamshire Library Services, BBC, Leicestershire Constabulary, Harber, Masson & Associates (Durban, South Africa), Rollerworld of Derby, the organizers of the World Gurning Championships, and Stephen Adamson at Guinness for coming up with the original concept.

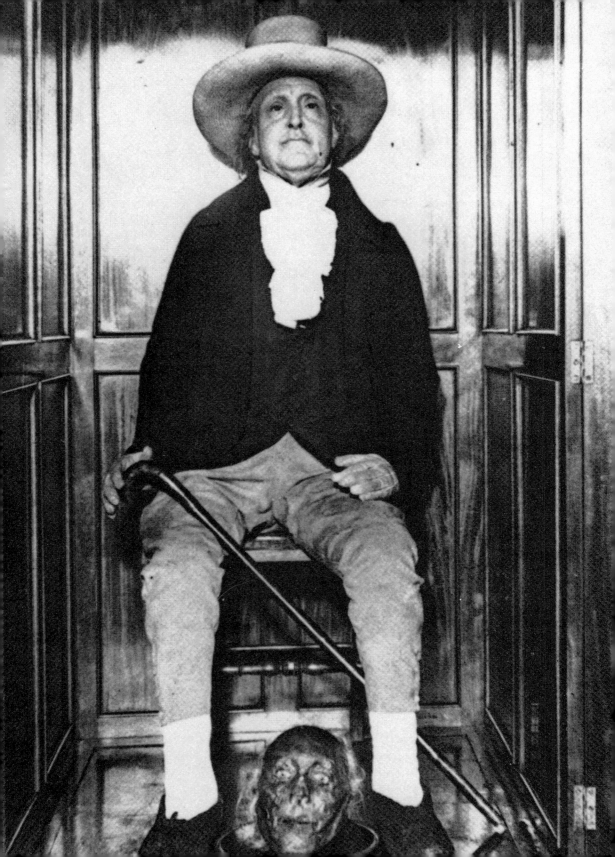

1
ECCENTRICS

MONARCHS

● When **Catherine the Great** of Russia (1729–96) discovered that she was suffering from dandruff, she imprisoned her hairdresser in an iron cage for three years to stop the news from spreading around the royal court. Catherine was as devoted to nature as she was to hair. Gazing from her window one spring morning, she spotted the year's first primrose and, to deter anyone from picking it, posted a sentry to guard it day and night. The sentry and his descendants continued to patrol the lawn long after the death of both Catherine and the primrose, simply because nobody had countermanded the order. It was some 50 years before Count Bismarck finally uncovered the folly and decided that the manpower could be more gainfully employed elsewhere.

● **King Charles VI** of France went through the majority of his life convinced that he was made of glass. Consequently, he abhorred travelling by coach for fear that the vibration would cause him

to shatter into a thousand pieces. Charles came to the throne in 1380 at the age of 12 but began to deteriorate mentally from 1392. It was then that he started prowling the corridors of the royal palace, howling like a wolf. Not unreasonably, his Queen, Isabeau, decided that she no longer wished to sleep in the same bed as her husband and came up with a lookalike, Odette de Champdivers, to take her place. The daughter of an impoverished horse trader, Odette was only too pleased to acquire the trappings of royalty. Thus, wearing Isabeau's clothing, she was dutifully placed in the King's bed each night until his eventual death in 1422. Such was his mental state that he never once spotted the deception.

● The vanity of **Ferdinand II** of Sicily (1810–59) knew no bounds. When postal officials suggested that Sicily should have its own postage stamps, Ferdinand agreed on one condition – that his portrait was never to be marred by an unsightly franking mark. He furthermore pronounced that anyone disobeying this edict would be guilty of treason. The terrified officials sought every possible solution, eventually designing a special franking mark which fitted around the royal head like a frame. Principally because of the delays caused

---

Left The mummified body of Jeremy Bentham – 'present, but not voting' (see p. 20)

by the King, the new stamps were not issued until 1 January 1859. Ironically, they were withdrawn less than five months later when Ferdinand died.

● **George III** (1738–1820) first showed signs of impending madness one day in 1787. He was being driven by carriage through Windsor Great Park when he suddenly ordered his driver to stop. The King got out, walked over to an oak tree, shook hands with one of its branches and talked to it for some minutes. He was under the impression that he was talking to the King of Prussia. At first, George suffered only temporary fits of insanity but his condition worsened over the years. It was not helped by royal surgeon Dr Francis Willis who prescribed that hot mustard plasters be placed on the King's legs, stomach and chest to 'draw out the evil in his body'. George spent his last years locked away in Windsor Castle. He was often kept in a strait-jacket for 24 hours at a time and when he was released, he made a pitiful figure, shuffling around in a tattered dressing-gown. From 1811, his son, the future George IV, acted as Regent. George III finally died in 1820, aged 82.

● **Henry Christophe**, King of northern Haiti, came to power in 1807 at the age of 40. One of his first deeds was to order his subjects to build him a castle on top of a high mountain. Henry Christophe had a penchant for cannons and demanded that his new castle be guarded by 20. This necessitated parties of 100 men hauling the heavy cannons up the steep mountainside. When one party gave up through sheer exhaustion, the King had half of them executed on the spot. In total, over 20 000 men died of strain and fatigue. When the castle was finally completed, the King had one more test of devotion. He ordered his personal brigade of guards to prove their loyalty to him by marching over a 200 ft (61 m) high cliff. Those who obeyed plunged to their deaths; those who refused were tortured and executed. By 1820, his subjects could take no more and they stormed his mountain fortress. Henry Christophe saved them the trouble of killing him by shooting himself.

● **Queen Juana** of Spain, the daughter of King Ferdinand V and Queen Isabella, worshipped her husband Philip whom she married in 1496 when she was 17 and he was Archduke of Austria. Thus Philip's death in 1506, aged just 28, came as a bitter blow – so much so that she refused to allow his body to be buried and had it embalmed instead, declaring: 'We must remain together for eternity'. Thereafter, wherever Queen Juana travelled throughout Spain, she was accompanied by Philip's coffin. She sat next to it at dinner and lay beside it on her bed at night. Eventually, her father, fearing for her reason, had her locked away but, even in confinement, she wore a black mourning dress and continued talking to her late husband. She remained in a darkened room for almost 46 years before dying at the age of 76. She was buried in the Royal Chapel of Granada Cathedral in the same tomb as Philip.

● Given his family history it was hardly surprising that **Ludwig II** of Bavaria (1846–86) should veer towards the eccentric. After all, his aunt,

Left Charles VI of France was convinced he was made of glass (see p. 7)

Princess Alexandra, was convinced that as a child she had swallowed a full-size grand piano. And nothing could ever shake her from this belief. Ludwig's grandfather, Ludwig I, had rashly fallen in love at the age of 60 with a woman he thought was a Spanish dancer called Lola Montez. Her real name was Mrs Eliza Gilbert. The smitten monarch proceeded to squander vast amounts of Bavaria's national fortune on her. When Alexandra's brother, Maximilian II, died in 1864, his 18-year-old son Ludwig became King. Ludwig II had a novel interpretation of life – he decided to reverse night and day, to the point of having a moon painted on the ceiling of his bedroom. As a result, most of his activities took place in the dead of night. These included going on winter drives through the mountains in a golden rococo sleigh, accompanied by coachmen and outriders who were forced to dress in the style of Louis XIV. Another of Ludwig's moon-light escapades involved riding on horseback round and round his riding school for up to seven hours at a time, pausing only to change horses. The object of the exercise was to simulate the distance of heroic journeys such as that from Munich to Innsbruck and the riding time was calculated accordingly. Known as the Dream King, Ludwig hated warfare and all things military, preferring to inhabit a world of fairy tales and legends. To realize his dreams, he arranged for the building of fairy-tale castles, notably Neuschwanstein (see p. 84), which was never completely finished. For in 1886, Ludwig, having been declared unfit to rule, had an accident and drowned in nearby Lake Starnberg.

● The ill-fated **Marie Antoinette** (1755–93) was so modest that she always wore a gown buttoned right up to her neck – even in the bath. Still taking no chances, when she climbed out of the bath she insisted that the servant present should cover her eyes lest she caught so much as a glimpse of royal flesh.

Marie Antoinette was also fastidious about food. On her arrival in Paris from Austria, she refused to eat anything but chicken, and the only liquid which ever passed her lips was water.

● **Ludwig II** (see above) was succeeded as King of Bavaria by his younger brother, 38-year-old Otto, an equally unstable character. Eleven years prior to becoming King, Otto had made his mark by bursting into a crowded church during High Mass, wearing a shooting jacket and deerstalker. He proceeded to hurl himself face down at the altar and confess to a long list of sexual misde-meanours involving pageboys. Otto harboured a deep mistrust of the medical profession (it was they who had declared his brother insane) and came to the conclusion that the best way to preserve his own sanity was to shoot a peasant every morning. His motto, quite simply, was: 'A peasant a day keeps the doctor away'. So he started taking pot shots at the peasants working in the royal garden. Otto refused to be swayed from this course of action and so his family took matters into their own hands. Each morning, before Otto awoke, a servant would creep into the royal bedchamber and load the King's pistol with blank cartridges. Simultaneously, a guard, dis-guised as a peasant, would station himself in the bushes beneath the King's bedroom window. On waking, Otto would reach for his gun and fire at the fake peasant who would dutifully pretend to be dead. The King thus spent the rest of the day safe in the belief that he had shot his daily peasant. This curious ritual was repeated every morning until 1913 when Otto was finally deposed.

● **Peter the Great** of Russia (1672–1725) estab-lished the Museum of Curiosities in St Petersburg where he assembled anything which he considered to be a freak of nature. Items on display included a man without genital organs, a child with two heads, a sheep with five feet, and a deformed human foetus. Peter enjoyed nothing more than wandering among the jars of abnormal speci-mens, all of which were pickled in alcohol, and his provincial governors were offered lucrative re-wards for sending in suitable exhibits. Appropri-ately, the caretaker of the museum was a dwarf who had only two fingers on each hand and two toes on each foot and who knew that when he died he would be stuffed and put on display in the gallery. Peter was obsessed with dwarfs. When two of his favourite dwarfs got married, he invited

Peter the Great of Russia may have been kind to dwarfs but he was by no means the world's most compassionate ruler. He saw a beheading, carried out personally, as the ideal way to work up an appetite

72 more to come from the farthest provinces of his empire. The wedding feast was held at the royal palace, at which Peter provided small tables for the dwarfs and large tables for the other guests. When one of the same dwarfs died, Peter staged a lavish funeral ceremony. The tiny coffin was placed on a tiny hearse, drawn by small horses with black trappings. At the head of the procession walked a priest, selected for his unusually short stature. All of the choristers at the ceremony were children but, as a striking contrast, Peter had the procession flanked by 50 tall grenadiers. Peter was also attracted to giants. He had returned from a trip to France with a 2.28 m (7 ft 6 in) colossus called Nicolas Bourgeois and married him to a Finnish woman of similar proportions in the hope that they would produce huge children. The plan failed but Peter continued to pay the couple an annual salary of 600 roubles and to include Bourgeois in his weird ceremonies, often dressed up like a baby and paraded on strings by a team of dwarfs. When Bourgeois died, he too was stuffed for inclusion in the Museum of Curiosities.

MEN WHO WOULD BE KING

✴ On 1 April 1977, bespectacled 38-year-old bookseller **Richard Booth** proudly declared himself to be King Richard I of Hay-on-Wye, at the same time pronouncing independence for the small country town from the rest of Britain. To mark the glorious day, a single gunshot was fired from a ramshackle old boat on the River Wye, the Free State flag flew over Booth's bookshop and a single-engined plane, hired from a local flying club, performed a ceremonial fly-past. He had passports printed and planned selling them for 25p to anyone crossing the Wye. He did sell dukedoms for £25, earldoms for £15 and knighthoods for £1.50, all of which were eagerly snapped up by tourists. He made his gardener the Minister of Agriculture while a neighbour who travelled to Hereford each day became Minister for Foreign Affairs. Booth's own horse, Waterton, was appointed Prime Minister. King Richard's royal regalia consisted of an orb made from a ballcock and a sceptre constructed out of copper wire. There was method behind Booth's madness. He had decided that the town's small firms were being driven out of business by big companies. With independence, he announced his intention to abolish the Central Electricity Generating Board and instead have locals build wind- and water-powered generators to supply Hay's electricity needs. He wanted to remove all bureaucracy and on 5 November, for some years afterwards, his supporters set fire to a symbolic wooden figure who held a bundle of forms in one hand and a cup of tea in the other. Needless to say, the local council disowned Booth, and old ladies were known to attack him in the streets of Hay with their umbrellas. But he remained undeterred and in 1978 invited 200 Gujarati Indians from Leicester to the town and declared Gujarati to be Hay's official second language. King Richard is now a local councillor himself.

✴ **Joshua Abraham Norton** (1819–80) was a bankrupt ex-businessman who lived in a 50 cents-a-day boarding house in San Francisco. One evening in September 1859, sensing that his country was drifting into decline, he called on the editor of the *San Francisco Bulletin* and left a document proclaiming himself Imperial Highness Norton I, Emperor of the United States of America. The editor duly printed the document on the front page. Over the next 21 years, Norton carried out his role as Emperor. As promised, he declared the abolition of Congress – he claimed it was riddled with corruption – and proceeded to print his own bonds (which bore his portrait) and levy his own taxes which he collected personally. Small shopkeepers were charged 25 cents, bigger businesses $3. Few had the heart to refuse him. He marched around San Francisco in a pale blue army uniform, a tall black hat with a bright green plume and a pair of outsize boots slit at the sides to allow for his corns. Beside him clanked a heavy sabre, purchased from a local blacksmith. People he met in the street bowed and curtsied and his popularity was such that he was often able to dine and travel free of charge. He took his duties seriously and would regularly pause to inspect drains or to discuss the crime rate with the city police. When he was arrested for vagrancy one night, he received a profuse apology from the chief of police the following morning. Norton saw himself as a true statesman. He declared himself Protector of Mexico and, at the outbreak of the American Civil War in 1861, he sent letters to both President Lincoln and Jefferson Davis, President of the Confederacy, demanding that they attend talks with him in San Francisco. Neither replied. When Norton died in 1880, newspaper headlines announced: 'The King is Dead'. Some 10 000 people filed past his coffin to pay their last respects. For all his eccentricity, the self-styled Emperor is credited with one good idea – he was the first person to suggest building a suspension bridge across San Francisco Bay.

POWER CRAZY

✳ In 1982, Wyoming rancher **Pat McGuire** decided to run for the post of State Governor on a Democrat ticket. His attempted break-through into politics was prompted, he maintained, by a fleet of aliens who had landed on his ranch. Apparently, the alien visitors had shown him how to dig a miracle well in barren soil. He was so impressed that he took their advice to go into politics. The basis of his campaign was that unless the United States and the Soviet Union left the Lebanon to its own devices, the aliens would be obliged to kick both countries out. His party threw their hands up in horror. 'Why does he have to be a Democrat?' despaired one member. At the primary election, McGuire managed to poll over 10 per cent of the vote but still lost by a vast margin. Seasoned observers attributed his heavy defeat to his 'unusual campaign style'.

✳ **Glenn Wilbur Voliva** was a disciple of the religious fanatic **John Alexander Dowie** who, in the late 19th century, had set up the township of Zion City on the shores of Lake Michigan. Dowie, who had denounced sex, oysters and life assurance from the pulpit, became the victim of a power struggle with Voliva, the latter taking over as Chief Administrator in 1905. Allegations of fraud saw Dowie banished from the community and he died insane two years later. Voliva, who firmly believed that the earth was flat, imposed even more bizarre rules on the 16 000 residents of Zion City. Lipstick, scanty clothes, high heels and swimming costumes were all strictly forbidden, as were cigarettes and alcohol. There were no theatres or cinemas and no butcher, chemist or doctor was allowed to practise within the city precincts. Nobody was permitted to whistle or sing, or drive a vehicle in excess of 8 km/h (5 mph). And Voliva imposed a 10 p.m. curfew every night. Transgressors were subject to arrest by Voliva's Praetorian Guard, a regime whose helmets were inscribed with the word 'Patience' and who carried miniature bibles instead of truncheons. Punishment included a one-hour lecture from Voliva on sin. Voliva maintained his stranglehold over the populace for 20 years before his religious beliefs were discredited by the Depression.

WEALTHY ECCENTRICS

● The death of **William Beckford**'s father in 1770, leaving an estate worth one million pounds, made his son just about the wealthiest 10-year-old in England. William Beckford (1760–1844) used the money to satisfy his own excesses. Wherever he travelled, he was accompanied by his personal doctor, cook, valet and baker, plus two dogs, three footmen, 24 musicians and a Spanish dwarf. It is said that for one trip to Portugal, he even took with him a flock of sheep – in order to improve the view from his window. Wherever he stayed, he supplied his own bed, cutlery, crockery and wallpaper. Indeed he would not occupy any bedroom until it had been redecorated to his taste. But possibly his greatest eccentricity was the building of Fonthill Abbey in Wiltshire (see p. 91).

● **Hannah Beswick** of Cheetwood Hall in Lancashire lived in fear of being buried prematurely. Upon her death in 1758, she left the sum of £25 000 to her doctor (a man named White) on condition that he regularly examine her corpse for signs of life for a period of one year after her demise. Accordingly, Dr White had her body embalmed and encased in a grandfather clock at the top of the stairs, a small curtain affording a degree of privacy. For the remainder of his life, the doctor visited the body twice a year, accompanied by a friend as witness. When Dr White died, Hannah's remains were transferred to the Manchester Museum of Natural History until finally, 110 years after her death, the trustees decreed that there could be no dispute as to the fact that she really was dead. And only then was Hannah Beswick given a proper burial.

● Known to all as 'Cap'n Tommy', **Thomas Gibson Bowles** was once the owner of *The Lady* periodical. In 1887, he was widowed and left to raise four young children. He laid down curious rules, particularly for his two daughters, Sydney and Dorothy. Both were required to wear sailor suits until they were 17, whereupon they were sent out to purchase 'one grown-up gown' which had to conform in style to those worn at the Court of Versailles some 150 years earlier. For his part, Cap'n Tommy never took a bath at home, preferring to enjoy a steam bath at his London club. Occasionally, his work forced him to leave the capital but he still insisted on carrying out his ablutions. He would take with him a number of dog kennels which were set out in a line some 45 m (50 yd) long. The smallest kennel was lined with bricks to serve as his steam chamber. He would spend 15 minutes in there before emerging and running along the course past the remaining kennels, from the roofs of which his footmen emptied buckets of ice cold water over his head. Tommy was prone to acting on impulse. One morning, he suddenly told Dorothy (by then the only offspring not to have flown the nest) of his intention to emigrate to China 'on Thursday'. With remarkable speed and efficiency, Dorothy succeeded in putting the furniture into storage, dismissing the servants and packing – all in the space of three days. Come the morning of departure, she was sitting in the carriage ready to depart for the railway station when her father, descending the steps of the house, held out his hand, palm upwards, and announced: 'My dear child, it's raining. We won't go.'

● The founder of the Ford Motor Company, **Henry Ford I** (1863–1947) developed some curious habits in the later years of his life, particularly regarding health and food. He took to leaving old razor blades to rust in water in which he then washed his hair because he thought rusty water acted as a hair restorer. Ford believed in reincarnation. Once, when driving along with one of his employees, he pointed out some chickens which had been scattered by the approaching car and announced that they had been 'hit in the ass in a previous life' and had thus learned a lesson they were using in this one. Ford had long banned tobacco from his car plant and had spoken out against the evils of alcohol after his friend Thomas Edison had told him that these substances destroyed the brain cells. Now with Edison dead, Ford's theories flowed unchecked. He refused to eat chickens because they ate bugs; he campaigned for synthetic milk, insisting that cows were on the verge of obsolescence because they were unhygienic; and he claimed that eating sugar was tantamount to committing suicide since its sharp crystals would cut a person's stomach to shreds. This phobia persisted even after a scientist had made him view the dissolution of sugar crystals by water under a microscope. He also took to eating weed sandwiches every day for lunch after hearing that black scientist George Washington Carver did the same.

● **Henrietta (Hetty) Howland Green** (1835–1916) was one of the richest women in the world. She inherited a six million dollar fortune from her Quaker father and set about multiplying it at an alarming rate. Money lending was her business which she conducted from a desk in the foyer of the Seaboard National Bank, New York. She was so successful that she later kept a balance of over $31 400 000 in one bank alone. Yet she was the meanest woman alive. She never gave a cent to charity and her son had to have his leg amputated because of her delay in finding a free medical clinic. She never bothered to wash and lived in a seedy Brooklyn apartment in which the heating remained firmly switched off – even in the depths of winter. Her lunch was a tin of dry oatmeal which she heated on the bank's radiators. She invariably wore an old black dress, which had begun to turn green with age, and tied around her waist with string was a tatty handbag containing an additional food supply of cheap, broken biscuits. Towards the end of her life, she became convinced that she was about to be kidnapped and began hiding in doorways and doubling back on her tracks. She died following a stroke and left an estate worth $95 million.

● American financier **George A. Kessler** had a passion for unusual parties. On 30 June 1905, he threw a party at London's Savoy Hotel to celebrate his birthday. Selecting Venice as his theme, he had the hotel courtyard flooded with blue-dyed water to simulate a canal. Painted backdrops were added and the whole scene was lit by 400 Venetian lamps. His two dozen guests sat inside a vast silk-lined gondola on his specially constructed 'canal', served by waiters dressed as gondoliers and entertained by opera singer Enrico Caruso. The latter was obliged to perform an aria while a baby elephant with a 1.55 m (5 ft) high birthday cake strapped to its back was led across a gangplank to the gondola. Simultaneously, 100 white doves were released overhead. The only blot on the proceedings was the absence of the swans that had been meant to swim around the gondola. They had been poisoned by the dye in the water. Four years later, Kessler returned to the Savoy for a party to celebrate Robert Peary reaching the North Pole. This time he converted the hotel garden into an Arctic wilderness, covering the ground in plaster snow and importing a huge metal nail to represent the North Pole.

● Shropshire squire **Jack Mytton** (1796–1834) was a larger-than-life character. The infamous Squire of Halston regularly drank eight bottles of port or brandy a day and was apt to go duck-hunting stark naked. He was said to have fought dogs and bears with his teeth and once rode a bear into the dining-room to shock his guests. It presumably had the desired effect. His pride and joy was a one-eyed horse called Baronet and, during inclement weather, Mytton would knock on a cottage door and ask whether Baronet could dry off by the fire. Since the cottage invariably belonged to the squire, he was seldom refused. He gave another of his horses, Sportsman, a bottle of port on cold days. Sportsman soon dropped dead.

Mytton came up with an interesting cure for hiccups – it was to set fire to his own night-shirt. His friends arrived in time to save his life but he suffered serious burns. However, his hiccups were cured, no doubt justifying the action in what passed for Mytton's mind. Having gambled away the family estate, he died in a debtor's prison at the age of 38.

● Few have been as obsessed with their health as the **Comtesse de Noailles** (1824–1908). Despite her Gallic-sounding name, the Comtesse, or 'Madame' as she liked to be known, was English and lived near Eastbourne for almost 20 years before moving to France later in life. Wherever she lived, the Comtesse went to great lengths to ensure her continued well-being. She always kept a herd of cows tethered near the windows, believing the methane gas they produced to be beneficial to her health. At night, she would wrap a pair of socks stuffed with squirrel fur around her head and cover her chest with the skin of a Norwegian wild cat – to ward off germs. When staying in hotels, she always insisted that a string of onions be hung outside her bedroom door to keep away infection. She also refused to travel anywhere if the wind was blowing in an easterly direction and was liable to call the train to a halt and return home should she notice the trees blowing the wrong way. She was equally fastidious with her adopted daughter Maria. Sending the girl to an English convent school, the Comtesse arranged for a cow to live in the school grounds in order that Maria might drink only pure milk. She also demanded that the nuns drain a pond in the grounds less the stagnant water should be harbouring any nasty bugs. The poor girl was also forced to wear Grecian tunics and handmade sandals instead of the school uniform, to allow the air to circulate freely around her body. There was no respite when Maria was married. If the Comtesse came to stay, all the trees in the vicinity would have to be felled in case she caught some disease from the bark. And during Maria's pregnancy, the Comtesse instructed her to drink only water in which the tips of pine branches had previously been boiled. This could have presented a problem with no trees left standing. No matter how odd her behaviour

Bear-back rider Jack Mytton shocked guests at a dinner party

seemed, the Comtesse did live to the ripe old age of 84, her diet in the last weeks consisting solely of milk and champagne.

● For reasons best known to himself, wealthy English landowner **Sir Thomas Phillips** (1792–1872) refused to allow either cheese or vinegar into his home. He lived at Middle Hill, Gloucestershire, where he set out to have servants and tenants with the same surname as himself. He was a great hoarder of books and professed the desire to own a copy of every book in the world. His collection grew to over 100 000 books and 60 000 manuscripts, a hobby which left him permanently on the verge of bankruptcy. As a result, his three daughters had to make do with just one dress each. Soon the floors of the house began to sag under the weight of paper and Sir Thomas allowed it to fall into a state of disrepair so as to prevent his son-in-law, James Halliwell, an alleged book thief, from inheriting anything of value. Eventually, in 1863, Sir Thomas moved to Thirlestaine House, Cheltenham, to accommo-

date his vast library. There were 103 wagonloads of books to transfer, pulled by 230 horses. The operation required the services of no fewer than 160 men.

● Vita Sackville-West will always be remembered for creating the magnificent gardens at Sissinghurst, Kent, in the first half of the 20th century. Yet her mother, **Lady Sackville**, preferred artificial flowers, notably tin delphiniums, if only because they would not be attacked by slugs. Prior to a visit from her green-fingered daughter, Lady Sackville would attempt to pacify her by racing around the garden and planting up the bare beds with flowers made of velvet, sequins, beads or paper. This was just one of Lady Sackville's eccentricities. She was a great letter-writer but would use any available paper for that purpose, including toilet paper from the ladies' room at Harrods. She also set up curious charities such as the Million Penny Fund, the aim of which was to eliminate the National Debt. Her idea was that famous people should, on their birthday, contribute a penny for each year of their life. Worthy though the scheme was, it met with little interest.

● Thanks to his invention of the reflecting road stud known as the cat's-eye, **Percy Shaw** (1890–1976) became a millionaire. Yet he lived in the same house in Halifax, West Yorkshire, from the age of two right up to his death. Shaw, who never married, owned a Rolls-Royce and had four television sets in the lounge, yet the house possessed neither carpets nor curtains. For he believed that carpets retained unpleasant smells and curtains would deprive him of the opportunity to view his beloved Yorkshire. The factory to produce his new invention was built in the grounds of his own house in 1935. And he ensured that the workmen spared the sycamore tree that he had climbed as a child. The factory still operates today with Percy Shaw's tree poking through its roof.

● The son of one of the richest merchants in Cork, **William Thompson** (1775–1833) was a noted Irish philosopher with a profound dislike for all clergymen and priests. His will forbade 'any priest, Christian, Mohammedan or Hindu' to meddle with his remains and also decreed that his body should be put on display 'to aid in conquering the foolish and frequently most mischievous prejudice against the public examination of corpses'. Unfortunately, the will was read after the funeral which meant that Thompson's body had to be dug up from Drombeg cemetery. Thompson had also instructed that the ribs of his skeleton be 'tipped with silver so that it might present a fashionable appearance'. The will directed that the skeleton should be left to the first co-operative (Thompson was a keen socialist) established in either Great Britain or Ireland. However, a Dr Donovan later claimed that he had been given the job of preparing the corpse and of 'stringing up the bones and sending them as a memento of love to Mrs Wheeler'. Whether Anna Wheeler, an early believer in women's emancipation, ever received the unusual gift is not known.

● Following the deaths of her husband and daughter, California rifle heiress **Sarah Winchester** was informed by a medium that their lives had been taken by spirits and that unless she built a mansion to house the spirits, she too would die. Another stipulation was that the building work must never be completed, and so for the next 38 years, until she eventually died in 1922, Mrs Winchester feverishly added rooms to her house. At the time of her death, the Winchester House, which occupies a six-acre site west of San Francisco, boasted eight storeys, 160 rooms, 2000 doors, 10 000 windows, 47 fireplaces and miles of secret passages and corridors, many of which led nowhere. Mrs Winchester was also obsessed with the number 13. Thus the house had 13 bathrooms, 13 hooks in every cupboard and 13 candles in every chandelier. In the sewing-room, she insisted on there being 13 windows and 13 doors. There were even 13 parts to her will . . . which she signed 13 times.

ECCENTRICS OF THE ARTS

● **James Agate** (1877–1947) was arguably the most flamboyant critic the English theatre has ever known. The wit expressed in his reviews for *The Sunday Times* was supplemented by a passion for golf, cricket, 19th-century French theatre and male brothels. Agate was also an incurable spendthrift and faced a constant battle against bankruptcy. He did not always fight it with great conviction, a favourite ploy being to hire a taxi just to cross the road. He would then keep it waiting until the early hours of the morning while he played bridge at his club. He said he took a masochistic pleasure in the thought of the pounds ticking away on the meter.

● Legendary French actress **Sarah Bernhardt** (1844–1923) had a decidedly unusual travelling companion on tour – a coffin lined with pink silk.

Sarah used to keep it in her bedroom and was said to learn her lines while lying in it. Rumours were also rife that she used the coffin for entertaining a list of lovers, among them Napoleon III, novelist Victor Hugo and the Prince of Wales, the future Edward VII. She joked that the lining regularly had to be changed because of wear and tear. When her young sister Regina was dying of tuberculosis, Sarah willingly gave up her bed and slept in the coffin instead. Among Sarah's other prized possessions was a human skull given to her by Victor Hugo. In 1915, she had her right leg amputated. Dissatisfied with the replacement limb, she heard of an English engineering firm which made sections for bridges. They made a new artificial leg for her with which she was delighted – until she received the bill. Refusing to pay, she received a letter from the manufacturer stating that unless she settled the account, she would have to return the leg. And that is precisely what she did.

● **Clara Bow** (1905–65), the 'It' girl of Hollywood silent movies, had the fur of her two Chow dogs dyed to match the colour of her own flaming red hair. The trio would ride around tinsel town in the actress's sumptuous limousine, also painted red on her orders. The movie industry's transition to sound seriously damaged Miss Bow's popularity. She was terrified of talking pictures and came to view the microphone as her enemy. On at least one occasion, she was seen to seize the microphone and viciously assault it. She ended up a lonely figure, spending her evenings playing poker with her maid and cook.

● London-born **Edmund Kean** (1787–1833) was the greatest actor of his day but also the most wayward. Too drunk to take the stage, he once proceeded to heckle his understudy from the gallery. Another time he dined some ten miles out of London and imbibed so much alcohol that he gave up all thoughts of fulfilling his engagement at Drury Lane that evening. He came up with an ingenious excuse for his absence, claiming that he had dislocated a shoulder when his coach had overturned in a collision with a gaggle of geese. The story was accepted but Kean was obliged to keep up the pretence by playing his next three roles – Richard III, Macbeth and Othello – with his arm in a sling. He was no respecter of audiences. Appearing in *A New Way To Pay Old Debts* at Birmingham, he turned to the audience, saying, with reference to a character's marriage in the play: 'Take her, sir, and the Birmingham audience into the bargain!' If proof were needed that Kean took his drinking every bit as seriously as his acting, it came when he was playing Richard III at Drury Lane. Kean could not bear the thought of abandoning his 'chair' at a drinking club, The Jolly Dogs, which met at the nearby Craven's Head Tavern. The landlord, William Oxberry, bet Kean that he could not get to the Craven's Head after the performance in time to take the chair. Kean's answer was to race through the play at breakneck speed. He positively threw himself into the fight with Richmond, whispering to James Wallack, the actor playing Richmond: 'Kill me quickly tonight. I'm due at The Jolly Dogs!' Wallack complied and Kean, still wearing his royal robes, made it to the tavern just in time.

● **Michel Lotito**, a Frenchman from Grenoble, goes under the stage name of Monsieur Mangetout (M. Eat-All). He was born at midday on 15 June 1950 – half-way through the middle day of the middle month of the middle year of the 20th century – and is convinced that this has given him superhuman powers. In the course of his stage acts, he devours supermarket trolleys, television sets, aluminium skis, bicycles – he says the chain is the tastiest part – plates, razor blades, cutlery, records, coins and even a Cessna 150 light aircraft. He began eating the plane in Caracas, Venezuela, in June 1978 and finished it two years later, taking a few snacks each day. He usually eats around 1 kg (2 lb) of metal a day. Puzzled medical experts discovered that the lining of his stomach and intestines is twice the thickness of the average human being. Consequently, although he can eat metal, glass and other usually indigestible objects, his digestive system is unable to deal with soft foodstuffs such as eggs and bananas.

● Fiery English actor **William Charles Macready** (1792–1873) was often criticized for gesturing too much on stage so, in an effort to curb his natural tendencies, he started rehearsing with his body bound by strings of worsted. When the strings broke, he knew that the particular gesture was essential to the performance. Before playing Shylock in *The Merchant of Venice*, Macready used to warm up in the wings by cursing and pummelling an elderly actor whom he kept on the payroll for precisely that purpose. One day, when the old man failed to appear for his regular beating, Macready was beside himself. It so happened that a fan of Macready's turned up to watch the performance that day but before he could utter a word, he was immediately verbally abused and thrown against a wall by the great actor. His warm-up complete, Macready promptly strode on to stage. Afterwards, Macready expressed a desire to thank the stranger for getting him in the right mood for the play but was informed that he had been taken to hospital. No other actor dared to steal Macready's thunder. Appearing as Hamlet in Norwich, he was furious when the actor playing Claudius, instead of dying upstage when stabbed by Hamlet, expired centre-stage on the very spot which Macready had been reserving for his own demise. 'Get up and die elsewhere, sire!' hissed Macready.

● The son of a doctor, French poet **Gérard de Nerval** (1808–55) was a tortured soul. His real surname was Labrunie but he considered de Nerval to be more splendid. Over the years, his behaviour became increasingly strange and he suffered severe mental disorders for which he was institutionalized on at least eight occasions. He used to be seen walking a lobster at the end of a length of ribbon in the Palais Royal gardens in Paris. In 1855, de Nerval was found hanging from a lamp-post in the city's Rue de la Vieille Lanterne.

● Distinguished English actor **Sir Ralph Richardson** (1902–83) took great delight in his eccentricity, particularly towards the later years of his life. Passionate about motorcycles, he regularly rode one to the theatre even in his seventies, sometimes arriving with his pet parrot, Jose, on his left shoulder. He also kept a ferret called Eddie and, to the horror of his leading ladies, would often secrete a white mouse in his pocket.

● French composer **Erik Satie** (1866–1925) founded his own religious order, a harsh organization by the name of the Metropolitan Art Church of Jesus the Conductor. Satie was the only member. By 1898, he had started calling himself Saint Erik of Arcueil. Satie, who, 11 years earlier had got himself invalided out of the army with bronchitis by standing outside, semi-naked, in the middle of winter, hated warm weather. He described the sun as 'a bore' and 'a bully' and was in his element when it was pouring with rain, a fact borne out by his collection of 200 umbrellas. When he died, six unworn, identical grey velvet suits were discovered in his apartment, along with the umbrellas. He never washed, considering a pumice stone to be more effective and economical than soap, and took to writing letters in a curious medieval script. His musical directions were suitably eccentric – one piece was meant to sound 'like a nightingale with toothache'.

● At the age of 21, German composer **Robert Schumann** (1810–56) invented two imaginary companions, Florestan and Eusebius, who, he said, spoke to him, gave him ideas for literary and musical projects and supported him in times of emotional distress. The twins represented the two sides of Schumann's character – his audacious, manly self was Florestan; his shy, passive self was Eusebius. He wrote about them in an article on Chopin for a Leipzig music journal and the pair were to give direction to his creative work for years to come. He had got the idea from writer Jean Paul Richter whose novel *Die Flegeljahre* (*Adolescent Years*) featured twins Vult and Walt, symbolizing the contrasting sides of a man's character. The schizophrenic Schumann suffered hallucinations and intermittent bouts of mental illness. He attempted suicide, drank excessively and had a long-standing fear of going permanently insane. Finally, he was committed to an asylum where he died.

● 'Carry On' film star **Kenneth Williams** (1926–88) was obsessed with his bowels. He suffered dreadfully from piles and consequently had a deep mistrust of other people's lavatories. Whenever he moved into a theatre for a play, he always had his own personal toilet, for his exclusive use. For the same reason, visitors to his London flat were never allowed to use the lavatory there – Williams insisted that they use the public toilets at nearby Tottenham Court Road tube station. Smoking was also forbidden in his flat which was described by one caller as being like a 'spotless, pristine, monk's cell'.

HERMITS AND RECLUSES

● Renowned for his work on gases, scientist **Henry Cavendish** (1731–1810) was petrified of meeting people. He had the drawing-room of his large house in Clapham, South London, converted into a laboratory so that he would not have to venture outside to pursue his work. In order to avoid talking to his servants, he left notes in letter-boxes scattered around the house. On one occasion, he was so disturbed when bumping into a maid on the staircase that he immediately arranged for the building of another staircase, for his private use. Such was his shyness that even his closest relative, Lord George Cavendish, was only granted an audience of half an hour per year.

● Brothers **Homer and Langley Collyer** were known as the Hermits of Harlem. They lived in a three-storey mansion at 2078 Fifth Avenue along with 136 tonnes of junk, including 14 grand pianos, human medical specimens preserved in glass jars, the chassis of a Model-T Ford, assorted weapons, the roof of a carriage, six US flags and thousands of books. Born in 1881, Homer was the elder brother by four years. Their father was an eminent gynaecologist and Homer became a lawyer while Langley trained as an engineer. Their father died in 1923, followed six years later by their mother, and in the 1930s, Homer went blind. Homer found himself totally dependent on his brother who devised ingenious cures in a bid to restore his sight, putting Homer on a diet of 100 oranges a week plus black bread and peanut butter. Rumour spread throughout the area that a fortune was hidden inside the house and Langley concocted a series of trip wires and booby traps which would bring tons of rubbish crashing down on any burglar. But he took care to carve out a network of tunnels through the mountains of junk

so that he could claw his way to the spot where his brother sat day after day. On 21 March 1947, the police were told that there was a body in the house. They found Homer's corpse but there was no trace of Langley for nearly three weeks. Then, on 8 April, Langley's body was found amidst the piles of rubbish. He had, in fact, died first, having accidentally sprung one of his own traps and suffocated beneath the debris. With nobody to feed him, Homer had starved to death.

● British scientist **Oliver Heaviside** (1850–1925) lived much of his life as a hermit in Devon. Even at the age of 71, when he had finally won recognition for his work (he was to give his name to the Heaviside layer – a band in the upper atmosphere which acts as a huge radio mirror), he was so poor that he was often unable to pay his gas bill. As a result, the gas company cut off his supply and he was forced to spend 15 months without any heat or light in his home, not that gas and Heaviside were suitable companions. Once, after clumsily scalding his face on a gas flame, he answered the door wearing a large blanket over his head, held in place by a rope tied around his neck. He proceeded to peer at his visitor with one eye through a hole in the blanket.

● Billionaire Hollywood film producer **Howard Hughes** (1905–76) had once dated the world's most famous movie stars – including Ava Gardner, Elizabeth Taylor, Lana Turner and Ginger Rogers – but he spent the last 15 years of his life as a recluse. He began to lapse into eccentricity with the marriage to his second wife, actress Jean Peters, in 1957. He insisted that they had separate bedrooms, even separate refrigerators. He became obsessed with health and hygiene, and nobody else, not even his wife, was permitted to touch his food. Not surprisingly, the marriage was short-lived, and after the divorce Hughes retreated to a bungalow in the desert near Las Vegas and hired his 'Mormon Mafia', a group of Mormons whose lot in life was to protect their master from outside contamination. So terrified was he of germs that any visitors were forced to stand in a chalk square drawn outside the house for inspection before being allowed near the front door. His own doctor was only permitted to 'examine' him from the other side of the room. As an added insurance against bugs, Hughes would touch nothing without first wrapping his hand in a paper tissue. Soon even the desert was too public a place for Hughes and he took to living in a series of anonymous hotels. Each move was made in total secrecy, his entire entourage departing via kitchen exits and fire escapes in the dead of night with Hughes strapped to a stretcher. The windows of the hotel room were always darkened and taped and, apart from a bed and a chair, the only item of furniture was film equipment, complete with a screen. He watched *Ice Station Zebra*, starring Rock Hudson, no fewer than 150 times. Hughes became a virtual skeleton. His diet was suitably bizarre – for days he would eat nothing but ice-cream, staying with one flavour until every parlour in the district had run out. His beard hung down to his waist and his hair and nails remained uncut – only twice in ten years did he allow a barber to trim his hair or a manicurist to attend to his nails. Since 1961, he met just three people from the outside world. A keen aviator, Hughes died on a plane taking him from Mexico to his home town of Houston. At his death, his 1.92 m (6 ft 4 in) frame had shrunk by 8 cm (3 in) and he weighed a mere 40 kg (90 lb).

● **Jane Lewson** of Clerkenwell, London, is believed by many to have been the role model for Miss Havisham in Dickens's *Great Expectations*. Mrs Lewson's husband died when she was just 26 and for the remaining years of her life, until her death in 1816, she lived as a total recluse, occupying only one room of her large abode. Wearing clothes which were fashionable when she was married, she always walked with a gold-headed cane. Locals christened her 'Lady Lewson'. She rarely washed in case she caught a chill but instead used to smear her face and neck with hog's lard. The windows were never washed either, in order to maintain an air of perpetual gloom. The house was resplendent with cobwebs and dust although Mrs Lewson did have an ancient retainer who would keep the beds made in all the bedrooms ... in readiness for guests who never ever arrived.

INTELLECTUALS

● Law reformer **Jeremy Bentham** (1748–1832), left his entire estate to London's University College ... on one condition. The stipulation was that he be publicly dissected in front of his friends, then stuffed, dressed in his finest clothes, complete with his favourite walking stick 'Dapple', and mounted in a chair from where he would continue to attend the annual meeting of the university's board of governors. In fact he was not dissected in public nor did he proceed to attend governors' meetings, although his chair-bound figure did make sporadic appearances, including the 150th meeting of the college committee in 1976. He was listed as 'present, but not voting'. His appearances are now confined to the annual Foundation debate. It was not only Bentham's walking stick which was endowed with a grand name. He also knighted his cat and called it 'Sir John Langborn', later extending it to 'The Reverend Doctor Sir John Langborn', presumably as the animal acquired further qualifications.

● British Prime Minister **William Ewart Gladstone** (1809–98) possessed one of the keenest brains of his day. But his verbosity irritated colleagues and acquaintances who strove in vain to find subjects of which the premier had little knowledge. At one gathering, they settled upon ancient Chinese music, only for Gladstone to recall an article he had written on the subject ten years previously.

He once held forth for half an hour on the relative merits of boiled and poached eggs, punctuating his monologue with strange contortions of the body. Lloyd George confessed that he thought Gladstone was more than a little mad. Food was a favourite obsession with Gladstone who believed that the only way of guaranteeing a long, healthy life was to chew each mouthful of food exactly 32 times. At night, he kept warm by sleeping with a stone water-bottle filled with hot tea. Since he rarely slept for over four hours, the tea was still warm when he awoke whereupon he drank it. In his spare time, he took to walking the streets of London searching for fallen women to save. Some were taken home to meet his wife who was herself a shade eccentric. On one occasion, she was seen leaving a supper party in considerable discomfort. It later transpired that she had stuffed several ham sandwiches down the front of her evening dress – and that the sandwiches had been heavily laced with mustard.

● At the tender age of three, **John Burdon Sanderson Haldane** (1892–1965) accidentally cut himself and drew blood. He promptly inquired of his mother: 'Is that oxyhaemoglobin or carboxyhaemoglobin?' Educated at Oxford, Haldane moved to Trinity College, Cambridge, in 1925 to become a Reader in Biochemistry. The archetypal dotty professor, he could be seen riding to university on an old bone-shaker of a bicycle, wearing, even in the depths of winter, an open-necked shirt. In summer, he often swam completely naked in a local pool, puffing on his pipe as he did so. Haldane loved animals and used to train the family cat to sit on top of a door and leap on to the shoulders of unsuspecting visitors. The cobwebs in his study were left undisturbed for years because he did not wish to render any spiders homeless. In 1957, he was offered a post with the Indian Statistical Institute. Asked what the job would mean to him, he instantly replied that it presented him with a wonderful opportunity to stop wearing socks. 'Sixty years of socks is enough', he announced, in a unique fashion statement.

● Irish scholar **Richard Kirwan** (1733–1812) lived in constant fear of catching a cold. As a result, the drawing-room of his house in Dublin's Cavendish Square had a roaring fire burning all the year round. Before going out into the street, Kirwan would stand in front of the fire for several minutes and then open his coat to catch the heat. Having taken in his supply of heat, he was intent on retaining it for as long as possible. He achieved this by hurrying everywhere, thereby posing considerable problems for unfit friends who struggled to keep pace with him. His other obsession was a deep hatred of flies and he paid his servants a small reward for each corpse they produced. Kirwan died in June 1812, aged 79 . . . after catching a cold.

● English social philosopher **Herbert Spencer** (1820–1903) was not one of the world's great travellers. He lived in constant fear of injury and illness. If travelling by horse and carriage, he would often stop the coach and take his own pulse lest the journey might be proving too stressful. If his pulse rate was too high, he would order the driver to return home. Spencer had no qualms about his behaviour causing traffic jams and was wont to bring the carriage to a sudden halt in the middle of London's busy Regent Street. On train journeys, he always took a supply of rugs and cushions as well as a hammock which had to be slung in his private compartment. He reclined in the hammock throughout the journey in order to avoid unhealthy jolts.

ANIMAL LOVERS

● Irish landowner **Adolphus Cooke** was a firm believer in reincarnation. He was convinced that his late father Robert had returned as a turkey on the family estate at Cookesborough and thus instructed his men servants to remove their hats whenever they saw the bird. Women servants

Left When stewed, the humble sea slug was considered a great delicacy by Victorian naturalist Frank Buckland

were obliged to curtsy. Adolphus Cooke owned a large red setter named Gusty who was wont to stray and mix with common dogs. After several misdemeanours, Cooke warned the hound that if he continued with his errant ways, he would be hanged like a criminal. To emphasize the point, the dog was shown a rope and a tree. Shortly afterwards, one evening in 1860, Gusty strayed again and was found near Mullingar. Cooke immediately arranged for the dog's trial to take place the following morning. Labourers were called to give evidence and a special jury found the animal guilty of misbehaviour. Cooke sentenced Gusty to death, saying that the dog was guilty of ingratitude to a fine master who had fed and cared for him since he was a puppy. Nobody was keen to carry out the killing until a local man offered. But when the would-be executioner claimed that the dog had spoken to him in a foreign tongue, Cooke was convinced that the dog too was a reincarnation and his life was spared. Cooke died in 1876 and, in his will, ordered his men to dig deep foxholes since he was certain that he would come back as a fox. Soon after his death, a fox was killed in the kitchen at Cookesborough.

● Naturalist **Frank Buckland** (1826–80), author of the best-selling *Curiosities of Natural History*, delighted in serving guests at his London home with the most bizarre meals. He founded the Society for the Acclimatization of Animals in the United Kingdom to encourage the production of home-grown exotic dishes. At the society's 1862 dinner, the menu featured such delicacies as kangaroo stew, roast parrot and stewed sea slug. One diner described the sea slug as a cross between calf's head jelly and the contents of a glue-pot. Another of Buckland's favourites was mice on buttered toast although he did draw the line at earwigs. He said they tasted too bitter. He also attempted to make elephant's trunk soup but, in spite of being boiled for several days, the trunk was still deemed too tough to eat. The house was suitably chaotic. A mongoose had the run of the place while pet rats scurried over Buckland's desk. He also kept a number of monkeys which were given a glass of beer every night and a drop of port on Sundays. No visitor could ever be sure of what lay around the corner – one lady guest, leaving the dinner-table, stumbled over a dead hippopotamus on the stairs. Frank Buckland clearly acquired his unusual tastes from his father, Dr William Buckland, Dean of Westminster, who confessed to a liking for stewed bluebottles. That was tame in comparison to one of the Dean's other meals. As owner of the embalmed heart of Louis XIV, who had died nearly 150 years earlier, Dr Buckland, who by then was quite mad, ordered the heart to be served to him for dinner one night – and promptly ate it.

● To put it mildly, **Francis Henry Egerton**, eighth Earl of Bridgewater (1756–1829), liked dogs. At the family home of Ashridge House in

Hertfordshire, his dogs dined with him at the table, napkins around their necks, and had their every desire attended to by servants. However, Egerton did not totally indulge them – any hound whose etiquette left something to be desired was immediately banished from the table. Away from Ashridge, the Earl spent much of his time in France and became a familiar sight driving through Paris in his carriage with half-a-dozen dogs inside, each sitting on a silk cushion. The dogs also wore handmade leather shoes which were another of Egerton's passions. He wore a different pair of shoes for each day of the year and every night they were solemnly placed beside those he had worn the previous day until there were rows and rows of them, all in the correct order.

● His Highness **Sir Mahabat Khan Babi Pathan**, Nawab of Junagadh and ruler of the Indian state of Gujarat prior to independence in 1947, owned 800 pedigree dogs, each of which had its own room, complete with electric light and uniformed servant. The bill for their upkeep was estimated at £32 000 a year and that did not include the cost of the state canine weddings and funerals. On the Nawab's orders, these were conducted with tremendous pomp and ceremony, featuring processions of elephants, while the participants were attired in doggy clothes covered with precious jewels.

● **Lionel Walter**, the second Baron Rothschild (1868–1937), took his passion for natural history to unnatural lengths. One of his favourite pastimes was to ride around the Hertfordshire lanes in a trap, drawn by a pony and three zebras. The zebras were added to the menagerie at the family seat at Tring in 1894. Lord Rothschild immedi-

Baron Lionel Rothschild and his team of zebras

ately set about breaking them in but found that they strongly objected to being fitted with harness and bridle. Never one to admit defeat, he persisted and was eventually able to take them to London where he drove his zebra-drawn trap down Piccadilly and into the forecourt of Buckingham Palace. Even he had to admit to some misgivings when Princess Alexandra attempted to pat the leading zebra, with some justification since one of the animals later seriously injured a groom at Tring. Lord Rothschild's mother was obsessed with her son's health and constantly fretted about draughts and damp feet. At 17, the lad developed a 'tiresome cough' and was dispatched to Brighton for six weeks of recuperative sea air. He was accompanied by his pet Australian opossum and his tame dingo and used to walk the latter along the esplanade on a chain. Two years later, the new student arrived at Magdalene College, Cambridge, with somewhat unusual luggage – a flock of several dozen live kiwis. The eccentricities of Lord Rothschild, who went on to create a zoologi-cal museum at Tring, were by no means confined to animals. He once received an unsuspecting visitor to Tring while swinging his stark naked, 140 kg (308 lb) frame in a hammock.

● Naturalist and explorer **Charles Waterton** (1782–1865) loved animals so much that he started to imitate their behaviour. Guests arriving at his home, Walton Hall in West Yorkshire, would often find him lurking in the hallway on all fours. Then, as they hung up their coats, he would growl and nip them in the shin! Even this must have been preferable to his behaviour at one dinner party where he rounded off the meal by dissecting a gorilla on the dining-room table. Following the death of his young wife, Waterton refused to sleep in a bed and, for the next 35 years, spent his nights lying on the floor wrapped in a cloak. A block of wood served as a pillow. Such habits did not have an adverse effect on his health and, even at the age of 80, he was still able to climb trees.

THE MILITARY

● For much of his life, Prussian **Field Marshal Prince Gebhard Leberecht von Blücher** (1742–1819) was haunted by the belief that he was pregnant with an elephant, fathered on him by a French soldier. Blücher, who suffered from fits of senile melancholia, seemed convinced of a French conspiracy. He used to totter around his room on tiptoe because he thought the French had heated the floor to a temperature greater than human flesh could endure. He often imparted his fears to Wellington and, despite his precarious mental state, it was Blücher whose timely intervention sealed Wellington's triumph at Waterloo in 1815.

● Nineteenth-century, US Confederate **General Richard S. Ewell** was prone to bouts of believing that he was a bird and would cock his head to one side, peck at his food and emit curious chirping sounds. The spectacle was made all the more authentic by the fact that he was a bald-headed man with a beaked nose. His regular diet was one of wheat in boiled milk although this was due to an ulcer rather than any flight of fancy.

● Morale in the Greek army fell to an all-time low under **General Hajianestis** who commanded the troops in the 1921 war with Turkey. By no stretch of the imagination could Hajianestis be termed a leader of men. He often refused to get out of bed, claiming that his legs were made of glass or sugar and that they were so brittle they would shatter. On other occasions, he simply pretended to be dead. It therefore came as little surprise when he was relieved of his duties, although his successor, General Tricoupis, only learned of his promotion from a newspaper article shown to him by his Turkish captors.

● A dedicated entomologist, British **Lieutenant Henry Charles Harford** was always on the look-out for rare insects – even in the heat of conflict. When fighting was at its fiercest during the battle of Victory Hill in the Zulu War of 1879, Harford suddenly sank to his knees and let out a loud cry.

His sword and revolver fell to the ground, leading his commanding officer to conclude that he had been shot. In fact, Harford had simply stumbled upon an unusual butterfly and proceeded to examine it in full view of the enemy, blissfully unaware of the bullets which were flying around his head. While he was excitedly reeling off Latin names, his colleagues were diving for cover. Ordered to return to his post before the Zulus inflicted further damage, a reluctant Harford put his prized possession into a tin box and carried on with the battle.

● The famous US Confederate **General Thomas 'Stonewall' Jackson** (1824–63) was a stickler for detail and obeying orders to the letter. As a junior officer, he once wore his army greatcoat throughout a long, hot summer because he had received no orders to change it. At the Virginia Military Institute, he chose to pace up and down outside the superintendent's office in a driving hailstorm rather than deliver his report one minute before the pre-arranged time. Jackson was devoutly religious and considered fighting on a Sunday to be sinful. In 1862, at the height of the Battle of Mechanicsville during the American Civil War, Jackson stood alone praying on a nearby hill, refusing to speak to anyone in the course of the afternoon. In his absence, the Confederates suffered huge casualties. For the battle of Fredericksburg in December of that year, Jackson's

master-plan was for the whole army to strip naked and swim the Rappahannock River in a surprise attack on Union lines. Since it was the middle of winter, the plan was wisely vetoed by General Robert E. Lee.

● Mexican **General Antonio Lopez de Santa Anna** (1814–76) was somewhat accident-prone. Throughout the 1830s, the Mexicans were involved in skirmishes with the Texans. On 20 April 1836, Santa Anna set up camp at the San Jacinto River, overlooking a wood where the Texans were known to be hiding. Given the circumstances, it was perhaps a little unwise to order his troops to take a siesta, for in the middle of their afternoon nap the entire Mexican army was routed by the Texans in just 18 minutes. Santa Anna managed to escape on horseback but was not as fortunate when, fighting the French in December 1838, he lost a leg. For the next four years, Santa Anna kept the leg at his hacienda near Veracruz until, on 26 September 1842, by which time he had virtually become dictator of Mexico, he arranged a special burial service for the detached limb. To the accompaniment of bands and orchestras, his supporters solemnly paraded the leg through the streets of Mexico City before laying it to rest in a national shrine known as the Pantheon of Saint Paula. Two years later, the leg was stolen during riots that marked Santa Anna's fall from power and disappeared without trace.

RELIGIOUS ECCENTRICS

● **Rev. Harold 'Jumbo' Davidson**, rector of Stiffkey in Norfolk, was unfrocked by the Church in 1932, following a series of disagreements regarding his lengthy absences from the parish. It seems that many of these were caused by his unerring eye for pretty girls.

Davidson was incensed by the decision and began protesting his innocence from bizarre platforms, selected to produce the maximum publicity for his cause. He conducted a hunger strike in a barrel and spoke out from the mouth of a stuffed

whale. In 1937, he found an ideal venue for his rantings – a cage at Skegness, Lincolnshire, shared with Freddie the lion. It was to be his last speech. At first, all went well – Freddie was quite placid – but then disaster struck. Either Davidson struck the lion and it turned on him or he accidentally trod on its tail but the result was that the animal reared up and badly mauled the hapless rector who died in hospital. Even his funeral was unconventional, his widow electing to dress all in white, except for black shoes.

Rev. Harold Davidson with daughter Patricia, five years before meeting an untimely end at the paws of Freddie the lion (see p. 25)

● Whereas most men of the cloth love to chat to their parishioners, **Father Denham of Warleggan** in Cornwall positively hated people. He surrounded the rectory with a high, barbed-wire fence and demanded that anyone wishing to see him had to make an appointment. He then waited for his callers, armed with a pocket-watch. Latecomers were turned away. He further alienated his flock by painting the church red and blue. Soon people stopped attending his services altogether so he replaced them with cardboard effigies and continued to preach to those each week. Father Denham led a spartan life. There was no furniture in the rectory and his diet consisted of nothing more than nettles and porridge. His death in 1953 was not greatly mourned.

● Appointed vicar of Morwenstow, Cornwall, in 1835, poet **Robert Hawker** (1803–75) brought a highly individual approach to church matters. Not only did he design the curious chimney-pots of the vicarage (see p. 99) but, instead of a cassock, he chose to wear either a fisherman's jersey and waders or a yellow blanket with a hole for the head, which, he claimed, was similar to a garment worn by early Cornish saints. So dressed, he would tour the parish on a mule, frequently accompanied by his pet pig. For some reason, he usually conducted services wearing red gloves. But his *pièce de résistance* came at weddings where he would reduce the groom to a quivering wreck by merrily tossing the ring in the air before handing it to him.

SPORTING ECCENTRICS

● **Thomas Birch**, a Keeper of books at the British Museum during the reign of Queen Victoria, was a keen angler. To improve his chances of a catch, he devised a costume which concealed him inside an imitation tree-trunk, his arms protruding as branches. With his fishing rod covered by a spray of blossom, he would stand on the river bank, disguised as a tree, for hours on end. He firmly believed that any movements he made would be mistaken by fish 'for the natural effect of a mild breeze'.

● Born into a wealthy Nottinghamshire family, **Sir Julien Cahn** (1882–1944) was a cricket fanatic and, between 1923 and 1941, his team of country-house cricketers played over 600 matches, including tours to Jamaica, North and South America, New Zealand and the Far East. Sir Julien himself had unusually fragile bones and commissioned a pair of inflatable batting pads to protect his legs. Although the pads looked curiously cumbersome, they proved useful run-getters since any ball that pitched off-line was shinned away by him for leg-byes. The only problem was that they were uncomfortable to walk in for any length of time so Sir Julien often resorted to a bath chair to transport him from the pavilion to the wicket and back again.

● Goalkeeper **William 'Fatty' Foulke** (1874–1916) of Sheffield United, Chelsea, Bradford City and England was the heaviest player in the history of professional football. Born at Blackwell, Derbyshire, he stood 1.89 m (6 ft 2½ in) tall and weighed 95 kg (210 lb) at the start of his career. But he expanded steadily to a point where he tipped the scales at a massive 159 kg (350 lb). Foulke was not an adversary to be taken lightly. He could punch the ball from his own goal beyond the half-way line and, as the possessor of a fearsome temper, was capable of inflicting similar damage upon opposing forwards. On one occasion, he picked up a forward around the waist and hurled him into the net. The referee awarded a penalty and did the same during a League game in the 1898–99 season when, playing for Sheffield United, an angry Foulke picked up Liverpool centre-forward George Allan, turned him upside-down and stood him on his head in the mud. He also once stopped a game by snapping the cross-bar. A constant difficulty for Foulke was injury. No stretcher was able to bear his weight and it always needed at least six men to carry him off!

● As the finest cricketer in the land, Gloucestershire and England batsman **William Gilbert 'W.G.' Grace** (1848–1915) considered himself to be above the laws of the game. Consequently, he used to bully umpires and bend the rules to suit his own needs. He told one official who had the audacity to give the great man out: 'They've come to see me bat, not you umpiring'. With that, Grace calmly replaced the bails and continued with his innings. On another occasion, he lofted the ball towards the boundary, only to see a fielder perfectly positioned to take the catch. Before the fielder could do so, Grace declared the innings closed and

forced the umpire to give him not out on the grounds that the ball had been caught after the declaration. He didn't always get his own way. Batting at Bristol, he got a bottom edge and the ball lodged in the top of his pad. Seizing the opportunity to add to his score, he waddled to the boundary with the ball intact and, on crossing the rope, demanded four runs. To Grace's barely-concealed annoyance, the umpire refused. Grace was delightfully unpredictable. In a match in 1893, he shocked his team-mates by suddenly declaring the innings closed with his own score on 93, just seven short of a century. He later explained that 93 was the only score between 0 and 100 that he had yet to make. He was a splendid all-round sportsman. In 1866, having scored 224 for All England versus Surrey at the Oval, he absented himself from the field, nipped down to Crystal Palace and won the 440 yards hurdles at the National Olympian Association's championships. He was regarded with such reverence that when he died on 23 October 1915 of natural causes, the Germans tried to claim him as an air-raid victim.

● Yorkshire slow left-arm bowler **Bobby Peel** (1857–1941), who played for England between 1884 and 1896, was very fond of a drink, all the more so after he had invested his benefit money

Right The figure of goalkeeper William 'Fatty' Foulke (third from left, back row) stood out in Sheffield United's 1902 FA Cup winning team

in the lease of a public house. More than once he drank himself into a condition which the cricketers' bible, *Wisden*, described diplomatically as 'having to go away'. Once his county captain, the austere Lord Hawke, felt obliged to ban him from the team for several days for 'running the wrong way, and bowling at the pavilion in the belief that it was a batsman'. The uneasy relationship between the two men reached a climax during a game with Warwickshire at Edgbaston, Birmingham, in May 1896. Peel had just made his highest score, 210 not out, sharing in an eighth-wicket stand of 262 with Hawke who made 166. The following morning, after a night of celebrations, Peel took the field and relieved himself on the pitch. This was too much for Lord Hawke who promptly decided to banish him from the side for ever.

EXPLORERS

✳ After studying the planets at length, former American army captain **John Cleves Symmes** (1780–1829) concluded that the Earth was hollow and that there was room inside for five other planets. He was also convinced that there were gaping holes at the North and South Poles into which it would be possible to sail. He pointed out that explorers often spoke of mysterious warm air currents melting the ice in polar seas. He maintained that these currents rose from vast cavities at the Poles. Determined to prove his theory, Symmes sought financial backing from the US government for an expedition and distributed 500 pamphlets to influential people from his St Louis trading post, thoughtfully adding a doctor's note stating that he was of sound mind. He planned to tackle the North hole first (which he estimated was 4000 ft (1219 m) in diameter) by setting off from Siberia. In 1823, Congress listened to his demands for scientists, two ships, reindeer and sleighs. Alas, only 25 congressmen supported the mission and Symmes's venture sank without trace. However, his exploits were not entirely in vain – they did inspire Jules Verne to write *Journey to the Centre of the Earth* (published in 1864).

✳ The role model for Jules Verne's Phileas Fogg (*Round the World in 80 Days*, 1873) was American businessman **George Train** (1829–1904) who, in 1870, went around the world in 80 days. It was a highly eventful journey: at Lyons, he was mistaken for a Red revolutionary and was thrown into jail; also in France he became entangled in politics and missed his connecting train; and he outraged the Japanese by jumping into a public bath in the nude. A born traveller (he circled the globe four times in all, the last at the age of 63), Train was the man behind the building of the Union Pacific Railway. He was told: 'If you attempt to build a railway across the desert and over the Rocky Mountains, the world will call you a lunatic'. Such a recommendation immediately made the idea more attractive to Train who later took to calling himself 'The Great American Crank'. The title was not without foundation. He began to adopt curious customs such as shaking hands with himself rather than other people, behaviour which he had observed in China. He also refused to conduct conversations, choosing to communicate via messages scribbled on a pad. That way, he said, he could store up his psychic forces. He invented a new calendar, based solely on the date of his birth, and started consuming peanuts by the bagful, believing that if he ate enough he would live to be 150. In the event, he only made it to 75. Perhaps he needed to eat the shells as well . . .

STYLISH ECCENTRICS

● English high-society dandy **George 'Beau' Brummell** (1778–1840) was so petrified of soiling his shoes on the pavement or of having a strand of hair blown out of place that he would order his sedan chair to be brought inside his London home so that he could board it there. Similarly, he would never raise his hat to a lady for fear of being unable to replace it at precisely the desired angle and, at dinner, he would never turn his head to conduct a conversation lest he creased his cravat. Perhaps Brummell's fastidiousness was understandable – after all, he had, as usual, taken two hours to wash and scrub his entire body with a stiff brush before getting dressed. Brummell died a broken man in Caen Lunatic Asylum in France. He had gambled away his money and had been ousted from the royal court after daring to criticize the clothes and girth of the Prince of Wales.

● **Martin van Butchell**, an 18th-century London dentist, married twice and each spouse was informed that all her clothes must be either black or white. He himself used to ride a white pony daubed with purple spots. The first Mrs van Butchell opted for the black outfits but died young. Tired of the constraints imposed by her husband, she left all her money to a distant relative who was to receive it 'the moment I am dead and buried'. The unscrupulous dentist saw an opportunity to get his grasping hands on her fortune and decided that, although she was dead, she would never be buried. So he arranged to have her body embalmed. He then fitted the corpse with glass eyes, dressed it in Mrs van Butchell's black clothes and displayed it in his drawing-room to the public for four hours a morning, six days a week.

● Farmer **Robert Cook**, who lived at Cappoquin, County Waterford, was known throughout that area of Ireland for his refusal to wear anything but white linen, an eccentricity which earned him the nickname of 'Linen Cook'. An early vegetarian, he would not wear the product of any animal and was thus restricted to linen. And he was obsessed with white, to the point where he would not allow either black cattle or black horses on his farm. When he died in 1726, aged over 80, he was buried appropriately in a linen shroud.

● Brighton beau **Henry Cope** was known as 'The Green Man of Brighton'. Daily, he promenaded along the seafront wearing green pantaloons, a green waistcoat, a green frock coat and a green cravat. His gig, livery, gloves and whip were all green, as were the furnishings at his house – including a green table, green sofa, green chairs, green curtains and even a green bed. Needless to say, the walls were painted green. He also ate only green fruits and vegetables. By 1806, Cope had gone completely mad and hurled himself from the cliff down to the beach below which was golden but with patches of green seaweed. He is believed to have spent his last years in an asylum, bound in a 'straight waistcoat'. It is not known whether it was green.

● **Lord Cornbury**, the third Earl of Clarendon and a cousin of Queen Anne, served as Governor of New York between 1701 and 1708. He took his role as her representative rather too literally and began dressing like her Majesty. He made his entrance at the New York Assembly in 1702, wearing a blue silk gown, a head-dress studded with diamonds and satin shoes. To complete the ensemble, he carried a ladies' fan. A heavily built man, he made a curious sight on the streets of New York at night, dressed in a hooped skirt and powdered wig. He was married but undoubtedly spent more on women's clothes than his wife ever did, although some of his outfits were sent to him by Queen Anne. He would lace himself into 'stays' in a bid to conjure up a figure and once left a reception given in his honour so that he could change his dress.

● Another 18th-century character who liked to

dress as a woman was wealthy Irishman **Ned Eyre** who lived at a house called Linville near Carrick-on-Suir, County Waterford. His cousin, Dorothea Herbert, described him as 'one of the greatest Oddities that Nature or Art ever produced; I say Art, because he studied every possible method to make himself different from Other human beings. He wore clothes which were very bright, his hair like a woman's. He sometimes carried a muff or a fan and was always painted to the Eyes with the deepest Carmine.' Eyre, whose diet consisted of tea, cold water, sweetmeats and pickles, shared his life with two labradors, christened Miss Dapper and Miss Kitsey, and which he treated as his daughters.

● Like many Yorkshiremen of his time, **James Hirst** (1738–1829) of Rawcliffe was an enthusiastic huntsman. The difference was that whereas his colleagues rode horses, Hirst took to the fields on the back of a young bull named Jupiter. The hunt allowed Hirst to join them for his sheer entertainment value, an understandable sentiment considering that he was in the habit of wearing a lambswool hat with a brim 9 ft (2.74 m) in circumference, a red jacket with blue sleeves, a multi-coloured waistcoat produced from his tailor's spare cuts, garish patterned breeches and bright yellow boots. At least the fox would have seen him coming. Hirst later endeavoured to train pigs to act as hounds but their incessant grunting put off both his fellow huntsmen and the fox. His previous experience with swine had included riding the headmaster's pig while at boarding school in Pontefract. In later years, he travelled around in a home-made wickerwork carriage, often pulled by the versatile Jupiter. Hirst also built his own coffin but fitted it with glass doors rather than a lid and, standing it on end, proceeded to employ it as a drinks cabinet. It was finally put to more conventional use when Hirst was 90. His will stipulated that he should be carried to his grave by 12 old maids. Alas only two could be found who were willing to swear that they were still virgins and the numbers had to be made up with local widows.

● **Lady Hester Stanhope** (1777–1839), niece of former British Prime Minister William Pitt the Younger, was once a leading light of London society. But she was devastated when her uncle died in 1810 and, as part of her recuperation, sailed with friends to the Middle East. The journey was a hazardous one and the party were shipwrecked off the Greek island of Rhodes, losing all their possessions. With no European clothes available, they had little option but to don Eastern costume. However, Lady Stanhope flatly refused to wear a veil or indeed any Eastern women's clothes and chose instead to dress in Turkish male attire. The once glamorous figure shaved her head to accommodate a turban and adopted a long robe and bright yellow slippers. She settled in Egypt where, treated like royalty, she continued to dress as a man. Indeed most of the locals thought she was a man.

Towards the end of her life, she moved to the disused hilltop monastery of Mar Elias near Sidon in Lebanon but would not receive any visitors during daylight hours. By the time she died, anything she had accumulated of any value had been stolen by her untrustworthy servants.

● Glasgow Rangers Football Club manager **William Struth** liked to be as smart off the field as his players were on it. Struth, who took over at Ibrox Park in 1920 after his predecessor, William Wilton, had drowned, always used to keep half-a-dozen double-breasted suits hanging in his office. He thought nothing of changing his suit two or three times a day. Despite his eccentricity, there was no doubting Struth's effectiveness as a manager. During his time at the helm, Rangers won the Scottish League title five years in succession between 1927 and 1931.

2

THE HUMAN MIND

CHILD PRODIGIES

● It was shortly before his sixth birthday that **Zerah Colburn** (1804–40) first displayed his remarkable powers of calculation. Born at Cabut, Vermont, the young mathematical genius created such a sensation that he was exhibited throughout the United States before being brought over to England in 1812. There, he was bombarded with questions from experts. He was asked how many times a 12 ft (3.6 m) coach wheel would turn round in 256 miles (412 km). Within two seconds, he had given the correct answer of 112 640. Another interrogator wished to know how many minutes there are in 48 years. Before the question could be written down, master Colburn replied 25 228 800, instantly adding that the number of seconds in the same period was 1 513 728 000. His fame did not last. As he grew older, his powers dwindled and, by the time he was a man, they had disappeared altogether.

● English composer **William Crotch** (1775–1847), the son of a humble Norwich carpenter, was able to play the national anthem on a home-made organ at the age of 2 years 3 months. In 1778, before he was even three, he gave his first public organ recital in his home town and the following year, progressed to giving daily organ recitals in London. His accomplishments at such a youthful age led to his being hailed 'the English Mozart'.

✳ **Andragone DeMello**, born in 1977, became the youngest person to graduate from an American university when, at the age of 11, he gained a degree in mathematics from the University of California at Santa Cruz. At seven weeks old, he had uttered his first word – 'hello'; at two and a half, he was playing chess; at three, he successfully calculated the volume of his bathwater; and at four, he was studying Greek, physics and philosophy.

● Ukrainian **Seriozha Grishin** could talk at four months, walk at eight months and read and play the piano when just over one year old. But his extraordinary talents did not impress his teachers and he was made an outcast at school. His mother Tamara was so distraught that she took him away from school and gave him private tuition. The authorities reacted by committing her to a mental hospital for refusing to let her son attend school. In their eyes, she was clearly not a fit mother. When further evidence came to light, she was released and, in 1987, 12-year-old Seriozha was at last acknowledged as being a boy of exceptional ability and was allowed to sit the entrance exam for Moscow State University. Upon passing, he was immediately accepted into the Faculty of Physics alongside students ten years his senior.

● English poet and writer **Thomas Babington Macaulay** (1800–59) shocked his Presbyterian minister father when, barely a year old, he looked out of the window of his nursery and asked: 'Is the

Seven-year-old Wolfgang Amadeus Mozart seated at the piano, accompanied by father Leopold and 11-year-old sister Marianne

smoke of that chimney coming from Hell?' The eldest of nine children, Macaulay continued in the same precocious vein. By the age of eight, he had written a compendium of universal history as well as 'The Battle of Cheviot', a romantic narrative poem in the style of Sir Walter Scott.

● Born in 1982, **Anthony McQuone** of Weybridge in Surrey could speak Latin and quote Shakespeare at the age of two. He could also identify and repeat the trademark symbols of 200 different models of motor car and was even wont to correct his father's grammar. Anthony told journalists that all the information was passed to him by an invisible grown-up friend called Adam.

● At only three, **Wolfgang Amadeus Mozart** (1756–91) had taught himself to pick out the chords on the keyboard of a harpsichord. At five, he started to compose his own music while his father, Leopold, an adequate violinist, desperately struggled to write down the score for him. At six, young Mozart performed before the Austrian Emperor in Vienna and, with his elder sister, played to Queen Marie Antoinette in Paris. His first compositions were published at seven, by which time he had taught himself to play the violin. At eight, he wrote two symphonies and at 12, he composed his first opera, 'La Finta Semplice'. At 14, he was knighted by the Pope. Yet after such an incredible childhood, Mozart died in poverty at just 35.

DREAMS AND PREMONITIONS

● On 22 May 1979, David Booth, a 23-year-old office manager in Cincinnati, Ohio, telephoned the Federal Aviation Administration at the Greater Cincinnati International Airport and also American Airlines to inform them of an impending disaster. On ten successive nights, he had suffered nightmares about a passenger plane crash. Booth said the plane in his nightmares belonged to American Airlines and his description was that of a DC-10. Three days later, on 25 May, an American Airlines DC-10 crashed at Chicago's O'Hare International Airport, killing 273.

● On the morning of Saturday, 1 June 1974, Mrs Lesley Brennan said she was lying on the sofa at her home in Cleethorpes, Lincolnshire, watching an old movie when the programme was interrupted by a newsflash reporting a huge explosion at the large chemical plant at nearby Flixborough with many casualties. Shortly afterwards, around noon, two friends, Janice and Peter East, called in and Mrs Brennan told them the news. The three forgot all about it until they were watching the early evening news which gave the time of the explosion at around 5 p.m. They laughed at the incompetence of the news team at getting the time wrong. But when Mrs Brennan read in the following morning's newspaper that the accident had happened at 5 p.m. and not lunchtime, she went cold. She bought another paper. It said the same. Her friends were baffled. 'You told us at 12 o'clock', they said. In fact, the plant had blown up at 4.53 p.m., killing 28 people and damaging nearly 2000 factories and shops. It took place five hours after Mrs Brennan had claimed to have heard about it from a newsflash.

● Donald Campbell attempted to break the world water speed record in *Bluebird* on 4 January 1967. But the evening before the attempt, he told a journalist: 'I have the most awful premonition that I'm going to get the chop – I've had the feeling for days.' He decided to consult the cards. Shuffling the pack, he drew two – the Ace and the Queen of Spades. 'These are the same cards that Mary Queen of Scots turned over on the night before her execution', he lamented. 'I think that someone in my family will die soon.' The following morning, as Campbell raced across Coniston Water in the Lake District at nearly 300 mph (482 km/h), *Bluebird* suddenly reared up on her tail, turned a back somersault and plunged to the bottom. Although his teddy bear mascot was found floating on the surface, Campbell's body was never recovered.

● In pre-Revolution France of 1788, writer Jacques Cazotte informed guests at a dinner party of the varying fates which would befall them in the course of the forthcoming uprising. After hearing him predict that the King would be executed, they listened in horror as Cazotte dealt with some of the guests individually. He said playwright Nicolas Chamfort would die some months after cutting his veins with a razor 22 times. He told the Marquis de Condorcet, a noted philosopher/mathematician, that he would die on the floor of a prison cell, having taken poison to cheat the executioner. Turning to playwright and confirmed atheist Jean de la Harpe, Cazotte foresaw that he would become a devout Christian. The predictions were uncannily accurate. Nicolas Chamfort worked for the Revolution at

The Chicago plane crash of 1979, as foreseen by David Booth

first but later criticized its excesses. In 1793, faced with the threat of imprisonment, he tried to take his own life by slashing his wrists. The bid was unsuccessful but he died a few months later. The Marquis de Condorcet was outlawed after opposing the Revolutionaries' Reign of Terror. In 1794, two days after being imprisoned, he was found dead on the floor of his cell. As Cazotte had predicted, he had taken poison rather than face the executioner. Jean de la Harpe was also thrown in prison where, against all likelihood, he became an ardent Catholic. Cazotte's ability to see into the future did not help his own cause, however. For he too was guillotined.

● In 1896, German psychic Madame de Ferriëm had a vision of an impending disaster. She saw bodies being carried out of a coal mine at Dux in Bohemia. She added that doctors were coming from Brüx and that it was extremely cold. A German newspaper published an account of her vision in 1899. The following year, in September 1900, hundreds were killed by an explosion in a coal mine at Dux, near Brüx in Bohemia. A month after the explosion, during an exceptionally cold October, bodies were still being brought out of the mine.

● American Nonconformist minister Arthur Ford seemed to develop a sixth sense during the First World War. Serving as a newly commissioned second lieutenant with the US Army at Camp Grant, Illinois, during the 1918 influenza epidemic, Ford would wake in the morning with a vision of the names of the soldiers who had died at the base hospital in the course of the night.

One of his duties was to collect the list of the deceased from the adjutant's office and, when he did so, he discovered that not only were the names exactly those which he had foreseen but they were also written down in precisely the same order. This experience occurred on three successive mornings but two friends he told remained sceptical. So Ford wrote down the names over a period of seven days and, on each occasion, his list corresponded with the official 'death list' to be issued that day. Then one

morning, he learned that the names he had forseen were no longer those of influenza victims, but of men who had been killed in the fighting in France.

Up to a week after he had dreamed of these names, they would appear in the same order in the newspaper casualty lists.

● In 1935, future British Air Marshal Sir Victor Goddard was still a young RAF officer when he flew over the abandoned airfield at Drem in Scotland. Drem had been allowed to revert to farmland but, as he peered through the clouds and rain, Goddard witnessed a brilliantly lit scene of a bustling airfield in full working order.

On the tarmac stood three biplanes and a monoplane of a design he had never seen before. Emerging through the hangar door was a second monoplane, pushed by two mechanics. The aircraft were painted yellow instead of the then regulation silver and the mechanics wore blue instead of the usual brown dungarees. Returning to base, Goddard described what he had seen to his wing commander who concluded that it was probably a hallucination.

Four years later, at the outbreak of war, Goddard visited Drem and found that it had been rebuilt. Mechanics, dressed in blue, attended to yellow Avro 504s and Magisters. The latter, which were trainer monoplanes, hadn't existed in 1935 but were identical to the ones Goddard had seen on his flight into the future.

● Julia Grant, wife of US General and later President Ulysses S. Grant, described in her memoirs how she awoke on the morning of 14 April 1865 with a strange sense of foreboding. She felt it imperative that she and her husband flee Washington but, because he had been invited to the theatre with President Lincoln that night, General Grant was reluctant to leave. However, his wife was so insistent that he eventually backed down and, making his excuses to the President, left the city. En route to the station, the Grants apparently passed John Wilkes Booth on his way to assassinate Lincoln at the theatre. It was later revealed that Grant had also been on Booth's death list.

> ✳ In 1980, American actor David Janssen, star of *The Fugitive*, had a disturbing dream in which he saw himself being carried out in a coffin. In the dream, he asked what had happened and was told that he had suffered a heart attack. The dream unnerved him to such an extent that he consulted a psychic who advised him to go for a medical check-up. It was too late. Two days later, on 13 February, Janssen died from a massive heart attack.

● Cheshire ploughboy Robert Nixon was a simple soul. His co-workers considered him to be mentally retarded, especially when he began talking to himself. One day in 1485, he was ploughing a field when he suddenly exclaimed: 'Now Dick! Now Harry! Oh, ill done, Dick! Oh, well done, Harry! Harry has gained the day!' His utterances became clear a few days later when it was revealed that at the very moment of Nixon's outburst, Richard III had been killed at the Battle of Bosworth, leaving Henry Tudor to become King. The wily Henry heard of Nixon's exploits and arranged for a record to be made of everything he said. Nixon saw 150 years into the future to forecast the English Civil War as well as foretelling the deaths and abductions of various Kings and predicting that he himself would starve to death in the royal palace. To prevent any chance of starvation, Henry ordered that Nixon should be given as much food as he could eat. This angered the staff of the royal kitchen and when the King had to leave London for a period, the officer placed in charge thought it best to lock Nixon in the King's own closet to protect him from the jealous staff. But then the officer too was called away from the capital and forgot to leave the key to the closet or instructions for Nixon's release. By the time he returned, Nixon had starved to death.

● Mid-way through a meeting to discuss the financial affairs of the papal states, Pius V, who was Pope from 1566 until 1572, suddenly declared: 'Leave all this for now. We must go and give thanks to God. Victory has gone to the Christian fleet.' The efficient treasurer duly made a note of the Pope's announcement in the minutes. It took place, he wrote, shortly before 5 p.m. on 7 October 1571. Two weeks later on 21 October, a messenger from Venice rode into Rome bringing the news that a Christian fleet under Don John of Austria had vanquished the Turkish fleet at Lepanto. The official report of the battle stated that victory had been confirmed just before 5 p.m. on 7 October.

● One of the more impressive sporting predictions was that made by Nashville psychic Spencer Thornton who attempted to name the first three horses home in the 1959 Kentucky Derby. Four days prior to the race, due to be run on 2 May, he wrote down the names on a piece of paper which was then sealed, unread, in an envelope and placed in a vault of the Third National Bank. The vault could be unlocked only by a combination of three keys, kept by two vice-presidents and its custodian. On 4 May, the three men opened the vault and the envelope. Its contents correctly forecast: '*Tomy Lee* in a photo finish; *Sword Dancer*, second; *First Landing*, third.'

● With Napoleon's armies advancing into Russia in 1812, Countess Toutschkoff, the wife of a Russian general, dreamt that she was in a room at an inn, the location being a town with which she was unfamiliar. In the dream, her father entered the room, holding her small son by the hand and told her that her husband had been killed by the French. 'He has fallen', said the father. 'He has fallen at Borodino.' She had the dream on two further occasions and it disturbed her to such an extent that she told her husband. Together, they consulted maps but could find no mention of anywhere called Borodino. On 7 September 1812, the retreating Russian armies turned and attacked the French – at a village called Borodino, 112 km (70 miles) west of Moscow. The Countess and her family stayed at an inn, just a few miles from the battlefront, while her husband commanded the reserve forces. The following morning, her father came into the room, holding her small son by the hand. He relayed the death of her husband with the words: 'He has fallen. He has fallen at Borodino.'

35

● In the late 1850s, young Mark Twain (1835–1910) and his brother Henry worked together on the Mississippi riverboats between St Louis and New Orleans. One night, while staying at his sister's house in St Louis, Mark Twain had a vivid dream in which he saw his brother's corpse lying in a metal coffin which was resting on two chairs in his sister's sitting room. A bouquet with a single crimson flower at its centre had been placed on Henry's chest. A few weeks later, Twain and his brother journeyed back separately from New Orleans to St Louis. Henry travelled on the *Pennsylvania* whose boilers exploded near Memphis, causing many fatalities. Henry was badly injured and died a few days later. Most victims of the disaster were buried in wooden coffins but a group of Memphis women, touched by young Henry's plight, raised money to provide a metal coffin. So when Mark Twain went to pay his last respects, he found the body in a metal coffin on two chairs in his sister's house. The only thing missing was the bouquet. But as Twain stood beside the body, a woman entered the room and placed on Henry's chest a bouquet of white flowers. At its centre was a single red rose.

✳ King William I of Württemberg completed the building of Rosenstein Castle near Stuttgart in 1829 but didn't live there for another 35 years because a gypsy had prophesied that the King would die in the building. In 1864, when he was 83, the King finally moved into the castle. Five days later he died.

● In May 1812, Cornish innkeeper John Williams had a disconcerting dream on three successive nights. It was of the House of Commons and involved the shooting of a prominent politician. Living so far from London, Williams had no clue as to the identity of the figure in his dream but when he told a relative, who did frequent the capital, he was stunned to hear that his description matched that of the Prime Minister, Spencer Perceval. Several days later, news reached Cornwall that Perceval had been murdered in the lobby of the House of Commons.

MIRACLE HEALING

● Three-year-old Frances Burnes was given just weeks to live in the 1970s after surgeons had diagnosed malignant cancer. As a last resort, her mother, Deirdre, flew her to the shrine of Lourdes in south-west France. There Frances bathed in the waters and a few days later, returned to her home in Glasgow where she amazed doctors by beginning to make a remarkable recovery. Within three weeks, the doctors could find no trace of the carcinoma which had riddled her with pain. A month later, she was back at playschool. One specialist admitted: 'In medical terms, we can only call it a miracle.'

✳ Eighty-four-year-old Ellen Head had been 90 per cent blind for three years when her flat at Newcastle, New South Wales, Australia, was shaken by an earthquake for five seconds in December 1989. As a result of the tremor, she regained her sight.

● In 1977, teenage English psychic Matthew Manning, who had already made his name by reproducing precisely Picasso's painting style (he claimed that Picasso's spirit was guiding his brush from beyond the grave), turned his attention to healing. To disprove the doubters, he agreed to submit to a series of strict tests at the Mind Science Foundation in San Antonio, Texas, USA. The tests showed that simply by touch and concentrating his mind, Manning was able to alter the electrical resistance of the human skin and to speed up the death of certain types of cancer cells. On a tour of West Germany in 1981, doctors who examined Manning's patients before and after his healing sessions reported an immediate 95 per cent improvement. In Freiburg, Manning met the wife of independent consultant Dr Otto Ripprich. Frau Ripprich had been unable to straighten her right arm for several months after she had sustained crippling nerve and muscle damage in an accident. To the astonishment of her husband, she was able to straighten her arm fully after just five minutes' treatment from Manning.

● Devastating injuries sustained in the First World War left Liverpudlian Jack Traynor with a total-disability pension. He had received two bullet wounds, one of which made a hole in his skull, the other rendered his right arm paralysed. His health deteriorated further when, in 1923, he began to suffer from epilepsy and was unable to walk. That year, he was taken on a pilgrimage to Lourdes where he was lowered painstakingly into the communal bath. Four days later, he jumped out of bed, washed and shaved himself and walked out of the hospice unaided. Returning to England, he landed a job as a coal merchant, got married, fathered two children and led a perfectly normal life until he died from pneumonia in 1943. Throughout, the Ministry of Pensions continued to pay him the full disability pension since they refused to accept that someone who had been decreed totally disabled could become totally cured.

OUT-OF-BODY EXPERIENCES

● Catholic friar St Anthony of Padua (1195–1231) travelled widely as a preacher through France and Northern Italy, but never in such spectacular fashion as on one day in 1226 when, according to numerous witnesses and official Church records, he preached two sermons in two different places at the same time. While preaching at a church in the French town of Limoges, he suddenly halted in the middle of his prayers, pulled the cowl of his robes over his head and knelt silently for several minutes. The congregation waited patiently until he finally rose to his feet once more and resumed his address. But later that day it emerged that while the figure of St Anthony had been kneeling in full view of the congregation at Limoges, he had simultaneously appeared before the congregation of another church several kilometres away and proceeded to read the lesson. He then vanished from the pulpit as mysteriously as he had arrived.

● Confined to his bed with serious food poisoning, Dr Auckland Geddes recounted his strange experiences in a 1937 paper to the Royal Medical Society of Edinburgh, Scotland. 'I suddenly realized that my consciousness was separating from another consciousness which was also "me". Gradually, I realized that I could see not only my body and the bed in which it was, but everything in the whole house and garden, and then I realized that I was seeing not only things at home, but in London as well, in fact wherever my attention was directed. I was free in a time dimension of space.' He then recalled how his spirit had re-entered his body. 'I saw my doctor leave his own patients at his surgery and hurry over to my house and I heard him say: "He is nearly gone". I heard him quite clearly speaking to me on the bed, but I was not in touch with my own body and I could not answer him.'

● While serving as a volunteer ambulanceman in Italy during the First World War, American author Ernest Hemingway (1898–1961) was wounded by a burst of shrapnel. As he lay injured and semi-conscious, waiting for medical assistance, he underwent a weird experience. He later described it as: '. . . my soul, or something, coming right out of my body, like you'd pull a silk handkerchief out of a pocket by one corner. It flew around and then came back and went in again, and I wasn't dead any more.'

PHOBIAS

✳ Queen Christina of Sweden, who ruled from 1632 to 1654, had a phobia about fleas. She was so terrified of them that she ordered the construction of a tiny cannon just 10 cm (4 in) long, so that she could spend hours firing miniature cannonballs at the fleas which infested the royal bedchamber.

✳ Sigmund Freud (1856–1939), the father of psychoanalysis, suffered from siderodromophobia, a fear of train travel.

✳ Actress Katharine Hepburn had a phobia about dirty hair. When she was at Twentieth Century Fox, she apparently used to tour the set sniffing people's hair to make sure that it had been washed.

✳ German physicist Professor Philipp Lenard (1862–1947) suffered from onomatophobia, the fear of certain names. The name which drove him to despair was that of Sir Isaac Newton, a curious state of affairs since Newton died 135 years before Lenard was born. The professor's phobia originated from a confirmed hatred of all British scientists whom he accused of stealing German ideas. Consequently, he couldn't bear to speak Newton's name or even to see or hear it. At the Universities of Heidelberg and Kiel, where he lectured, Lenard would always turn his back on the students if Newton's name had to be mentioned. A member of the class would then write the offending name on the blackboard but it had to be rubbed out again before Lenard would continue with the lecture.

✳ The German composer Robert Schumann (1810–56) had a phobia about all metal objects (metallophobia), particularly keys. This was thought to be a reaction against physician Dr Carl Helbig who resorted to hypnosis in an attempt to cure Schumann's mental fatigue. He used magnets and keys to put Schumann into a trance and the composer, associating them thereafter with that unwelcome experience, developed a wholesale fear of them.

✳ American actress Natalie Wood (1938–81) suffered from hydrophobia – a fear of water. She died by drowning.

UNUSUAL PHOBIAS
Clinophobia – fear of going to bed
Ecclesiaphobia – fear of churches
Eisoptrophobia – fear of mirrors
Genuphobia – fear of knees
Ichthyophobia – fear of fish
Levophobia – fear of the left side
Linonophobia – fear of string
Nephophobia – fear of clouds
Pediophobia – fear of dolls
Pogonophobia – fear of beards

SUPERSTITIONS

● **King Edward VII** (1841–1910) was extremely superstitious and frequently consulted the noted palmist Cheiro who told him that the numbers six and nine would guide his life. The King's names, Albert and Edward, each had six letters and he had been born on the ninth day of the month. He married in 1863 (a number which, when split into pairs, makes 9 + 9) and his bride's name, Alexandra, had nine letters, as did that of her father – Christian IX. On becoming King in 1901, Edward was stricken with appendicitis and feared that he would die, but Cheiro said that could not happen until six and nine came together. Reassured, he asked Cheiro to select a date for the coronation. The palmist chose 9 August. Cheiro was as good as his word and Edward reigned for nine years before dying at the age of 69.

● Beatle **John Lennon** also believed that the number nine affected everything in his life. He and son Sean shared a birthday of 9 October. Future manager Brian Epstein first attended a Beatles concert at the Cavern in Liverpool on 9 November 1961 and clinched a record contract with EMI on 9 May 1962. The group's first record, 'Love Me Do', was on Parlophone 4949. Lennon met Yoko Ono on 9 November 1966 and thought it significant that their New York apartment was on West 72nd Street and their Dakota home was no. 72 (7 + 2 = 9). Similarly, he placed great store by the fact that, as a student, he had taken the no. 72 bus from his home to Liverpool Art College. This fixation sometimes manifested itself in his songs which included titles such as 'Number 9 Dream', 'Revolution 9' and 'One After 909', written at his mother's house – 9 Newcastle Road, Wavertree. Lennon was shot dead by Mark Chapman late on the evening of 8 December 1980 in New York but the five-hour time difference meant that it was 9 December in Liverpool. His body was taken to the Roosevelt Hospital on Ninth Avenue.

✳ When Princess Margaret was born at Glamis Castle, Scotland, in 1930, the registration of her birth, which had taken place on 21 August, was delayed so that her number on the register would not be the unlucky 13.

● Theatre producer **Lawrence Wright** was so superstitious that when his 13th production, *On with the Show*, opened at the North Pier, Blackpool, in the summer of 1938, he announced that it was his 14th. He had good cause for alarm. First, the theatre burned down and all of the props were destroyed. A smaller venue was found where top-of-the-bill Tessie O'Shea sprained her wrist, preventing her from playing the ukelele. Then Harry, of The Five Sherry Brothers, was taken ill with gastric trouble, as was pianist Peggy Desmond, the latter being unable to play for a week. There was more. Robert Naylor lost his voice while

Frank Randle had to have all his teeth taken out and Dorrane, of 'Alexis and Dorrane Speciality Dancers', was ordered to take a complete rest. Meanwhile, two members of the 'Health and Beauty Chorus' sprained their ankles and one of the dancing 'Viennese Romancers' injured her leg on the stairs. To cap it all, the theatre manager collapsed and the wardrobe mistress fell and sprained her arm. Only then was it discovered that there were 13 people in the cast, 13 musicians in the band and 13 songs in the show.

● A late 19th-century cure for whooping cough in Yorkshire was to drink a soup containing nine frogs. But it only worked provided the patient had no prior knowledge as to the contents of the broth. An additional remedy for whooping cough was to feed the sufferer with milk which had previously been partly lapped by a ferret.

● It was once believed that if a wealthy woman married a man with debts, the creditors would be unable to reclaim their money from her as long as she was married naked. Such a wedding took place in 1797 at St Philip's Church in Birmingham. The local newspaper reported the big day thus: 'The moment she understood the priest was ready at the altar, she threw off a large cloak, and in the exact state of Eve in Paradise, walked deliberately to the spot, and remained in that state till the ceremony was ended.'

● In medieval Britain, the cure for convulsions was to take parings from the nails, hair clipped from the eyebrows and the crown of the head, and to tie them all up in a cloth. The bundle, with a halfpenny added for good measure, was then left at a crossroads and whoever picked it up was said to take on the disease. For this reason, people were somewhat reluctant to pick up strange-looking parcels at crossroads.

The world's largest hat? No, John Evans demonstrating another balancing feat to the folk of Heanor, Derbyshire (see p. 53)

3

ENDEAVOUR

CURIOUS EVENTS

THE AMERICAS

● **Armadillo racing** takes place annually at Fort Worth, Texas, over a flat course. Teams of grandfathers and grandsons work together racing the animals along the course. The armadillos, sensing danger, curl up into a ball and are thus able to be propelled across flat, open spaces, apparently by lung-power.

● One of the highlights of the Vancouver Sea Festival, held each July, is the Nanaimo to Vancouver **Bathtub Race**, across the choppy waters of the Strait of Georgia. Competitors take to the sea in a variety of tubs to tackle the 55 km (43 mile) course.

● A **clam shell pitching tournament** takes place in September on the beach at Cape May, New Jersey. Competitors come from as far afield as Europe and Canada to demonstrate their skill at skimming a quahog clamshell into a hole dug into the sand.

● A familiar sport throughout rural areas of the United States is that of **cow-pat tossing**, the aim being to hurl a dried cow-pat or 'chip' as far as possible. Local rules vary. Some events used to allow the pats to be moulded into a spherical, more aerodynamic shape but under the non-sphericalization and 100 per cent organic rule (introduced in 1970), Steve Urner tossed one 266 ft (81.1 m) at the Mountain Festival, Tehachapi, California, on 14 August 1981.

● In Mexico, 2 November is known as the **Day of the Dead** when, according to Indian folklore, the deceased return to life. It is marked by macabre graveside picnics where families offer marigolds, tequila and foodstuffs to the dead and then embark on a feast of their own. Sitting in cemeteries, they tuck into such delights as chocolate hearses and coffins, sugar skeletons and wreaths and fancy breads adorned with skulls and crossbones.

● In 1978, as an antithesis to the glittering Rose Parade, held each year in Pasadena, California, on New Year's Day, a group of local dissidents decided to organize their own spoof parade. They christened it the **Doo Dah Parade** and it has gone on to become the byword in tackiness with floats deliberately decorated in the worst possible taste, inept drill teams and a routine where businessmen in suits perform precision drills with their briefcases. Yet it has become so popular that the authorities had to plead with the organizers not to arrange it for New Year's Day lest it upstaged the Rose Parade itself. So now the Doo Dah Parade takes place on Thanksgiving.

● Calaveras County, California, is home to the annual **Jumping Frog contest** each May, an event inspired by the Mark Twain story 'The Notorious Jumping Frog of Calaveras County'. Handlers watch anxiously to see whether months of intense training has enabled their frog to jump the furthest.

● In the second week of July, the town of Talkeetna, Alaska, is the setting for the **Annual Moose Dropping Festival**. The festival, which raises money for the local museum, features drinking and dancing plus stalls selling moose-dropping jewellery. Little brown balls, heavily coated with varnish, can be purchased for use as earrings and necklaces. But pride of place goes to the moose-dropping throwing competition. Contestants stand in a large circle and toss gold-painted moose droppings into a target area, the winner being the one who gets closest to the centre target.

● Outhouses on wheels race over a 1½ mile (2.4 km) course through the streets of Dawson City, Yukon, each September in the **Great Klondike Outhouse Race**. Contestants unable to bring their own outhouse can rent one for the day.

● Just about the most spectacular race in South America is the rarajipari or **kickball race** in which two teams of Tarahumara Indians try to outpace each other at kicking a wooden ball across inhospitable, mountain countryside. The race can last several days and cover distances up to 200 miles (322 km). In order to stay awake, the competitors have to wear rattles on their bodies.

● A gentle alternative to Spain's Running of the Bulls is the annual **Running of the Sheep** at Reedpoint, Montana. Each September hundreds of sheep charge down Main Street for six blocks. Contests are held for the ugliest sheep and the prettiest ewe while shepherds assemble to recite poetry.

● St Anthony is considered in Mexico to be a healer of animals and so on **St Anthony's Day**, 17 January, people take their pets to church. The dogs and cats, many of them decorated with flowers and ribbons for the occasion, sit side by side with bags of insects and worms, brought to be blessed in the hope that this will prevent the creatures from damaging crops.

● The **World's Shortest St Patrick's Day Parade** is held on 17 March down Buchanan Street in Maryville, Missouri. The parade route is less than half a block and is shortened each year. The 1993 route was just 98½ ft (30 m) long.

● In Sanborn, Minnesota, in mid-July, they celebrate **Watermelon Day** to pay homage to the nation's favourite fruit. The main attraction is a melon-seed spitting contest at which the considerable distance of 45 ft (13.7 m) was attained by one spitter in 1973. A similar event is the Calico Annual Tobacco Chewing and Spitting Championships, held north of Barstow, California. At the 1982 contest, Randy Ober of Bentonville, Arkansas, spat a tobacco wad a mighty 47 ft 7 in (14.5 m).

ASIA

● **Bean throwing night** or setsubun is celebrated on 3 February each year in Japan to mark the end of winter and the start of spring. That night, shouting 'Good luck in! Evil spirits out!', Japanese families scatter beans around their homes with each person throwing one bean for every year of his life. The beans are thought to possess magical powers and also to be a symbol of fertility.

● Annually, in December, the Meghauli airstrip in Nepal is closed down and transformed into the venue for the annual **World Elephant-Polo Championships**, a slower but more physical version of the game on horseback.

● An equally robust event is the annual **Gotmaar Festival** in Pandhura, India, held on the day following the September full moon. The town's 45 000 inhabitants divide themselves into two groups and start hurling rocks at each other until sunset when the fighting ends. The festivities can get out of hand. In 1989, there were 616 casualties, including four deaths.

● Each year in early May, **kite fights** take place in Japan. Competing teams tie razor blades and broken glass to the edges of their kites and fly them against one another, the object of the exercise being to rip the opposing kite to shreds. The winning team is the one whose kite is still airborne.

● In Tokyo on 7 July the **Tanabata Matsuri** is held. This festival celebrates the only day of the year when, according to legend, the Weaver Princess (Vega) and her lover the cowherder (Altair) can cross the Milky Way to meet. People write their wishes on pieces of coloured paper, hang them on to bamboo branches and then float them down a river the following day.

AUSTRALASIA

● Each June, the waters off Mindil Beach at Darwin in the Northern Territory, see the start of the **Beer Can Regatta**, a race between craft built from beer and soft drinks cans. Tens of thousands of cans are lovingly assembled over a period of months to make a variety of vessels ranging from skiffs and simple rafts to intricate model galleons.

● An international **brick-throwing contest** is held each July at Stroud, New South Wales, between teams representing the Australian, English, American and Canadian towns named Stroud. So that the ladies don't feel left out, there is also a rolling-pin throwing contest.

● A delightful alternative to England's famous regatta at Henley-on-Thames is staged each October at Alice Springs in Australia's Northern Territory. It is the **Henley-on-Todd Regatta**, the difference between the Thames and the Todd being that the Todd River is invariably dry. But this does not prevent a series of races for canoes, including such standard events as pairs, eights and coxless fours, because all the boats taking part are bottomless. The crews' legs protrude through the holes and they simply run down along the river bed course.

● With a summit just 43 m (140 ft) above the surrounding plains, Mount Wycheproof in Victoria is registered as the lowest mountain in the world. So the **King of the Mountain Festival**, held annually in October, is not as grand as it sounds although the foot race up the mountain is given added spice by the fact that the contestants must each carry a sack of wheat weighing 140 lb (63.5 kg).

● The **National Penny-Farthing Championships** are staged in February at Evandale, Tasmania. Riders come from mainland Australia and foreign lands to climb aboard penny-farthing bicycles and race through the village streets.

● A curious sport in Polynesia is that of **race walking underwater**. In the shallow waters around the Pacific islands, a 70 yd (64 m) long course is marked out on the sea-bed using wooden pegs. The walkers, who have no breathing apparatus, carry a heavy stone to keep them under water and are not allowed to swim. The clear water allows the race to be watched from the surface by spectators in boats.

UK AND IRELAND

● In the 19th century, Yorkshire folk bound for a seaside holiday in Blackpool, used to stop off at the Corner Pin public house at Ramsbottom, near Manchester, for refreshment. They would feel so refreshed that they started fighting the locals. One day, the inn's landlord, a man named Higginbottom, saw a group of youngsters throwing stones at the Yorkshire puddings which had been left to cool down on the ledges of the pub roof prior to lunch. He decided to turn it into a Battle of the Roses, between Yorkshire and Lancashire, with Lancashire black puddings replacing stones. Thus since 1837, competitors have hurled black puddings on to the roof of the Corner Pin, aiming to dislodge the Yorkshire puddings nestling there. The contest has now acquired the title of the **World Black Pudding Knocking Championships** and is held on the first weekend in September, attracting some 150 entrants from as far afield as the United States, Australia, Canada and Germany. It starts at noon and ends at 4 p.m., each contestant being allowed three lobs. A ladder is in constant use to replace fallen Yorkshire puddings. The first prize is the winner's height in beer.

● **Blessing the Fields** is a religious ceremony with a difference. Held on the fifth Sunday after Easter, it takes place on board the Welshpool and Llanfair Light Railway which runs between Welshpool and Llanfair Caereinion in Powys, Wales. The service is conducted by the Reverend of St Mary's Church, Castle Caereinion, and prayers are taken each time the train stops at one of the six stations along the 8 mile (12.9 km) route.

● Also in Powys, Llanwrtyd Wells is the venue for the annual **World Bog Snorkelling Championships**, held each May. Entrants, who have to pay £4 for the privilege, must swim 60 yd (54.8 m) in their snorkels through a murky, weed-infested peat bog in as fast a time as possible. There is rarely any great rush to congratulate the winner.

● Since 1771, villagers at Hallaton in Leicestershire have taken part in an Easter Monday ritual known as **Bottle Kicking and Hare Pie Scrambling**. The day begins quietly enough with a church service at which a hare pie is blessed. In the afternoon, villagers gather at the church gates where the rector distributes half of the pie for consumption. The throng then parades through the village to the Butter Cross in the market where red, white and blue ribbons are attached to three small wooden casks known as 'bottles'. At a nearby spot called Hare Pie Bank, the remnants of the pie are thrown about or 'scrambled for'. Then it is the turn of the 'bottle kicking' contest between the villages of Hallaton and Medbourne. Two of the three 'bottles' are filled with beer and to win one of the teams must carry, kick or push two 'bottles' over their opponents' line. The respective goal-lines are two streams a mile apart. It is said that the ceremony dates back to an occasion when two ladies from Hallaton, returning home across the fields, were confronted by a raging bull. As the beast bore down on them, a hare ran across its path, thus distracting it and allowing the ladies to escape. To show their gratitude, they instituted the custom of giving out hare pie once a year.

● In early August, the streets of South Queensferry in the West Lothian region of Scotland come alive for **Burry Man's Day**. Dressed in white flannels covered from head to foot with the burrs of the burdock plant, the Burry Man, who is always a native of Queensferry, parades 7 miles (11.3 km) through the town. His arms are held outright and he is supported by two attendants and staves decor-ated with garlands of flowers. Throughout the journey, he does not say a word but is liberally supplied with whisky which he is obliged to take through a straw. The origins of the Burry Man are shrouded in mystery but one theory is that, centuries ago, a man shipwrecked on the nearby coast, dressed himself in burrs in the absence of clothes.

● **Cheese-rolling** has taken place on the 1 in 2 slopes of Cooper's Hill near Birdlip in Gloucestershire since the 15th century. The custom, which originally exercised the villagers' rights to graze sheep on the hill, is enacted on Spring Bank Holiday Monday. At 6 p.m., local youths line up at the top of the hill, alongside 7 lb (3.2 kg) circular Double Gloucester cheeses. The starter slowly counts to four. At the count of three, he sends the cheeses rolling down the hill and at four, the competitors follow. Anyone lucky enough to catch a cheese before it reaches the bottom gets to keep it. This is not an event for the faint-hearted. In 1992, eight people were injured, including one competitor who sustained a broken hip and head injuries. During food rationing in the Second World War, wooden dummy 'cheeses' were used with a small piece of the real thing inside.

● **The Dunmow Flitch** is an intriguing Whitsun ceremony whereby a flitch of bacon is awarded to any couple who can prove before the specially assembled jury of six bachelors and six spinsters that they have neither quarrelled nor regretted their marriage for a year and a day. Held at Great Dunmow in Essex, it dates back to at least the 14th century, having been referred to by Chaucer in his prologue to *The Wife of Bath's Tale*. It is considerably more light-hearted than in days of old with learned counsel appearing for both the claimants and the bacon.

● **Egg-throwing** takes place annually on the village green of Aldbourne in Wiltshire. Each competitor gathers six raw eggs, not more than two days old, and hurls them on to the village green. The winner is the one who can pitch his egg the furthest without it breaking. Distances of over 87 m (285 ft) have been recorded.

● The **World Flounder Tramping Championships** were first staged in 1976 to settle a wager as to who could catch the biggest flounder in Scotland's Urr estuary. The flounder, a flat-fish, lies on the bottom of the shallow estuary in Dumfries and Galloway and buries itself in the mud when the tide goes out. Rods, lines and nets are conspicuous by their absence as, each summer, some 200 competitors wade chest-high into the water with bare feet. Praying for a shortage of crabs, they step slowly through the mud until they feel the tell-tale wriggling of the flounder beneath their toes. The fish can then be captured either with a three-pronged spear called a leister or by manual dexterity. The flounder must be alive at the weigh-in.

● The annual **Egremont Crab Fair** attracts visitors to Cumbria from all over the world – just for the privilege of witnessing the World Gurning Championships. To gurn means to 'snarl like a dog, look savage, distort the countenance' and the winner of the contest is the one adjudged to have pulled the most grotesque face through a horse collar called a braffin. The Crab Fair was first held in 1267 but the origins of gurning are more obscure. Some say it all started with the mockery of the village idiot. The townsfolk would throw a horse's collar over him and make him pull funny faces in exchange for a few pints of ale. Another theory is that a drunken farmer arrived home, to be confronted by an irate wife. As he shouted, 'Stop gurning, woman!', he thrust a horse collar over her head, at which her facial expression became even more manic. In the 19th century the event was called Grinning for 'bacca (the chewing of tobacco being an aid to facial contortion) but assumed the title of the World Gurning Championships in the 1950s. The Crab Fair, which also features such contests as the fastest clay-pipe smoker, plays host to some 40 gurners each September. Among recent star performers was the appropriately named Ron Looney, a local gurner who was crowned world champion for six successive years between 1978 and 1983.

Eamonn Andrews (second from right) with Spike Milligan and a troupe of gurners, 1969 vintage

● The **Haxey Hood Game** is played in the Humberside village of Haxey on the Twelfth Day of Christmas. It is a boisterous form of rugby conceived following an incident involving the first Lady de Mowbray in the late 13th century. The story goes that while she was out riding, her hood blew away and a dozen gallant farmworkers set off to retrieve it. Her ladyship was so impressed that in her will she left a piece of land called the 'Hoodlands' to the village on condition that they re-enacted the event each year. The central participants in the game are the Fool (whose face is blackened and smeared with red ochre and who wears trousers of sackcloth with coloured patches and a red shirt), 12 Boggins (or farmboys) and one King Boggin. The 'hood' is a thick piece of rope, about 3 ft (0.9 m) long and covered with leather. The game starts at the top of Haxey Hill when the Fool throws the 'hood' into the air. There ensues a huge scrum, often lasting several hours, as hundreds of villagers converge and try to outwit the Boggins by smuggling the 'hood' into a local public house. As soon as the landlord can reach out and touch it, the game ends, free drinks are served and the 'hood' is kept on the premises until the following year.

● The Monday and Tuesday after Low Sunday (the second Sunday after Easter) are known as **Hocktide**. In England, this was traditionally a time for collecting private rents and donations for the church but the only surviving ceremony is at Hungerford, Berkshire. It was in 1364 that John of Gaunt awarded the town fishing rights in the River Kennett and grazing rights in the adjoining meadows and, every Hocktide since then, two elected tutti men (tutti = tithing) tour the 100 houses with common rights to collect the requisite tithe – a penny from every man and a kiss from every woman. The tutti men wear morning coats and top hats and bear a stave with a cluster of oranges on the top. In exchange for paying the tithe, each commoner takes one orange. The fruit is then replaced on the stave by an official orange scrambler who accompanies the tutti men. Following the ceremony, a civic luncheon is held, at which John of Gaunt is toasted.

● The game of **hurling** is still played at two venues in Cornwall on Shrove Tuesday. At St Columb Major, some 500 participants scramble for a small ball made of applewood, covered with silver leaf. The game is between two teams, the Townsmen and the Countrymen, whose respective goals are two miles apart. The Town goal is a stone trough at Cross Putty, a mile south-west of the market square, and the Country goal is a trough on the Wadebridge road, a mile to the north of the village. If either of these goals proves unreachable, a goal can be scored by taking the ball outside the parish boundary. The game starts in the market square and ends with the first goal. The ball can be hurled or carried but never kicked. At the finish, the ball is transported around the village public houses and dipped in jugs of beer. An early description of the game was given by Richard Carew in his survey of Cornwall in 1602. 'The ball in this game may be compared to an infernal spirit; for whosoever catcheth it fareth straightaways like a mad man, struggling and fighting those that go about to hold him; and no sooner is the ball gone from him, but he respiteth the fury to the next receiver and himself becometh peaceable as before.' A similar game takes place on Shrove Tuesday on the beach at St Ives. At 10.30 a.m., the Mayor throws the ball from the wall of the parish church and whoever holds the ball at the stroke of noon is declared the winner.

● The annual **Knaresborough Bed Race** in North Yorkshire takes place over a 2 mile 63 yd (3.28 km) course which crosses the River Nidd. The fastest bed pushers to date were the Vibroplant team who covered the course in 12 min 9 sec on 9 June 1990.

● A most unusual game of bowls is the **Knighthood of the Old Green**, played at Southampton. The Southampton Town Bowling Association was formed in 1299 and its green is reputed to be the oldest in the world. This competition dates back to 1776. Players go under the title of 'gentlemen commoners' and are supervised by 'knights of the green' who dress for the occasion in top hats and tails. The first man to win seven ends is acclaimed a knight of the green but this can take several days since there may be any number of players and each has to bowl two woods. The distance from the nearest wood to the jack is carefully measured and recorded and the woods are then removed for the next contestant.

● A sport which has yet to acquire Olympic status is **naked racing** which was a popular pastime in 19th-century Lancashire. An onlooker at a race in 1824 at the village of Whitworth, near Rochdale, wrote: 'The runners were six in number, stark naked, the distance being seven miles, or seven times round the moor. There were hundreds, perhaps thousands, of spectators, men and women, and it did not appear to shock them as being anything out of the ordinary course of things.'

● Back in the 15th century, a housewife at Olney in Buckinghamshire was said to be making pancakes when she suddenly heard the bells summoning her to church. Accordingly, she dashed along the road with frying pan still in hand. To commemorate this event, a **pancake race** takes place at Olney just before noon on Shrove Tuesday. All the housewives in the race must wear apron and headscarf and must toss their pancakes three times along the course which measures slightly over 400 yd (366 m). Since 1949, a similar pancake race has been run at Liberal in Kansas.

● Once confined to school playgrounds, the noble art of **peashooting** has its own world championships, staged each summer at Witcham in Cambridgeshire. The event began simply to raise funds for the village hall but proved so popular that it has become part of the local calendar. For the first round, competitors fire five peas at a circular target, the 16 highest scorers progressing to the knock-out phase. Some experts favour putting all five peas in the mouth at the same time and then, by deft use of the tongue, firing them off in machine-gun fashion. However, in the knock-out section, competitors fire alternately and so must reload. In order to improve their aim, some have even been known to employ expensive rifle sights.

● The **Race against the Train** is held each August over a 14 mile (22.5 km) course between Tywyn and Abergwynolwyn in Gwynedd, North Wales. Around 700 runners try to out-speed a 8 mph (13 km/h) steam locomotive on the Tal-y-llyn Railway. Spectators watch the race either from the train itself or from another which follows on behind.

● The annual free-for-all known as **Shrovetide football** dates back hundreds of years. Sedgefield in County Durham claims to have played it in 1027 but the earliest written record belongs to Chester (1533). Puritan Philip Stubbes was not a fan. In his 1583 diatribe *The Anatomie of Abuses*, he wrote: 'For as concerning football playing, I protest unto you that it may rather be called a friendly kind of fight than a play or recreation . . . And hereof groweth envy, malice, rancour, choler, hatred, displeasure, enmity, and what not else; and sometimes fighting, brawling, contention, quarrel picking, murder, homicide and great effusion of blood.' The most famous game, first recorded in 1682, takes place at Ashbourne in Derbyshire between the 'Up'ards' (those born north of the Henmore stream) and the 'Down'ards' (those born to the south). The two goals are the mills at Clifton and Sturston, three miles apart. The ball, which is slightly larger than a conventional football, is filled with cork and dust to discourage long kicking. For a goal to be scored, the ball has to be struck against the mill-wheel. The first goal wins the game and the successful player, who immediately acquires hero status, gets to keep the ball for a year. The ball may be kicked, carried or thrown but usually makes painfully slow progress in a series of rugby-like 'hugs', invisible to spectators. Much of the action occurs in the Henmore stream which separates the two goals. The game starts at 2 p.m. and often continues until well after dark. If no goal has been scored, proceedings are called to a halt at 10 p.m. The raucous nature of Shrovetide football upset the authorities and, in 1891, the police made a conscious effort to prevent the Ashbourne event taking place, only for the ball to be smuggled in under a lady's skirt. However by 1928, it had acquired such respectability that the then Prince

It may not yet have acquired Olympic status but the sport of cow-pat tossing is taken very seriously in Canada and the US (see p. 41)

of Wales was invited to Ashbourne to start the game.

● First held in 1973, the United Kingdom **Snuff-Taking Championships** at Feniton in Devon test the powers of nasal restraint to the full. For a sneeze or a cough means instant disqualification. Twenty-five official servers are seated along a line of tables, each with two spoons containing different brands of snuff. Competitors must move along the line in as fast a time as possible, inhaling a pinch of all 50 brands from the back of their hand whilst exercising care not to spill any, a mistake which incurs a time penalty.

● New Year's Eve at Stonehaven, Grampian, witnesses a spectacle known as **Swinging the Fireballs**. People march through the town swinging great balls of fire made from wire netting and filled with driftwood, pine cones, twigs and oil-soaked rags. The balls are then thrown into the harbour to mark the start of the New Year. The ceremony is believed to hark back to the superstitions of the early Middle Ages when the town's ancestors tried to charm the sun from the heavens during the cold winter months.

● The climax to Bonfire Night celebrations at Ottery St Mary in Devon is a colourful custom called **tar-barrel rolling**. Eight or nine large barrels, the insides of which have been coated in bitumen and primed with paraffin, are lit in turn and carried through the streets on the shoulders of strong men whose arms are swathed in protective sacking soaked in water. When the men can stand the heat no longer, the barrel is passed to another. The parade begins at 8 p.m. and the last barrel is rolled into the village square around midnight. To the sounds of cheering and singing, the tar-barrellers then tear off their protective cladding and toss it into the flames. Tar-barrel rolling is thought to have been introduced to celebrate the landing of William III at Torbay on 5 November 1688.

● A sport with unknown origins is that of **toe-wrestling**, a popular pastime at Ye Olde Royal Oak Inn at Wetton, Derbyshire. The wrestlers are seated opposite one another barefoot and enter into combat using only the big toe of their chosen foot. Rules state that the non-participating foot has to be raised from the floor. The aim, as in traditional wrestling, is to pin down one's opponent.

● Also known as 'bullets', **Ulster Road Bowls** sees an iron ball (a cannon ball was used originally) tossed along a winding country road to discover who can cover a distance of 2 miles (3.2 km) in the lowest number of throws. Bowls of ½ mile (0.8 km) are not unusual. The sport, which is particularly popular in County Armagh, attracts keen betting.

● In 1770, the will of Richard Clay from Bourne, Lincolnshire, provided for an annual gift of bread to the poor people of Eastgate Ward, the cost of which was to be met by the rent of a piece of meadowland. The land, now known as White Bread Meadow, has subsequently been let each year at Easter by an auction in which the bidding is only valid while two boys are running up and down a length of road some 200 yd (183 m) long. The length of time the boys – known as the **White Bread Runners** – have to keep on the move depends upon the keenness of the bidding. If a bid is made while the boys are running, they have to race off again. The auction is concluded only when no higher bid has been received during their double run. The successful bidder becomes the lessee of the meadow for a period of 12 months.

● At 6 p.m. on 1 March, the bells of the parish church at Lanark, Scotland, ring to herald the start of a race called **Whuppity Stourie** (or Scoorie). Deriving from an ancient pagan ritual designed to keep evil spirits away, the race involves local children racing anti-clockwise three times around the church, armed with paper balls attached to pieces of string. In the course of the race, they hit each other with these lightweight weapons. The whole thing used to end in an undignified scramble for money thrown to the ground by town officials but nowadays the winner is simply presented with a small prize. Whuppity Stourie was actually banned by magistrates in the 19th century because it was too violent. In those days, the runners were youths rather than children and they would round off the festivities by marching en masse to fight their counterparts in nearby New Lanark.

● The first **World Worm-Charming Championships** were held at Willaston, Cheshire, on 5 July 1980. The inaugural winner, 20-year-old Tom Shufflebotham, a farmer's son, charmed 511 worms out of his three-metre square plot in the allotted time of 30 minutes. The worms are coaxed to the surface by vibrating garden forks and other implements in the soil. Many competitors use water too but are now required to test it by sample drinking before use. This follows a spate of unsavoury incidents where the water had been laced with washing-up liquid, a banned stimulant which irritates the worm's skin and drives the poor creature to the surface. Such practices were not deemed to be within the spirit of the contest.

EUROPE

● Each year on Shrove Tuesday, the townsfolk of Binche in Belgium don huge ostrich feather hats and dress as Incas to commemorate the Spanish conquest of Peru. The celebration was first ordered back in 1549 when Binche was under Spanish rule and, for some curious reason, is still faithfully carried out today even though the Spaniards have long gone. As the Gilles (the dancers in the rites of renewal) parade through town in their white top hats with flowing ostrich plumes, they pelt passers-by with oranges which are said to symbolize the gold of the Incas. Any young men who are not Gilles arm themselves with short broomsticks (or ramons) and strike anyone foolish enough to venture into town without wearing a fancy hat or a red nose.

● On 17 February 1530, the citizens of Florence played a football match in defiance of the Spanish King Charles V whose troops were besieging the city. To commemorate that historic encounter, each June Florence's Piazza della Signoria comes alive for the **Calcio**, a game of football in which all of the players wear 16th-century costume. Four teams of 27 players take part – White, Blue, Red and Green – named after the four leading quarters of the city. Teams use any method, including sheer brutality, to force the ball into the opponents' net, the proceedings being overseen by the Major General Sergeant who rides around in a suit of armour on a white charger. The winning team receives the traditional prize of a white heifer.

● Among customs designed to kill off winter is one held in Arles-sur-Tech in the French Pyrenees on Candlemas, 2 February. A man dresses up as a bear, resplendent in furry coat and mask, and is chased by villagers armed with guns and sticks. They catch him, tie him up, allow him to escape, chase him again and finally pretend to shoot him. Then everyone in the village dances around the dead bear of winter and welcomes the coming of spring.

● On Easter Sunday night throughout Germany,

giant oak wheels, 7 ft (2.1 m) in diameter and weighing around 800 lb (363 kg), are tightly stuffed with straw, set on fire and rolled down hillsides into the valleys below, watched from neighbouring hilltops by thousands of spectators gathered around bonfires. The omens are said to be good if the wheels are still burning when they reach the valley.

● The most predictable sporting result in the world is that of the statue race which takes place during the **Festival of Candles** at Gubbio in Northern Italy. Since the 12th century, the people of Gubbio have staged the race to commemorate St Ubaldo who is said to have saved the town from invasion. Every May, statues of St Ubaldo, St George and St Anthony are paraded in that order through the town on the top of 9 m (30 ft) poles before being raced up the nearby 820 m (2690 ft) high Monte Ingino to the Church of St Ubaldo. The track up the mountain is too narrow for overtaking and so the result of the race hasn't varied since its inception. The statues always reach the church in the same order – St Ubaldo, St George and finally St Anthony.

● The world's first **Festival for Grandmothers** was held in July 1992 at Bodo in Norway. Grannies were invited to ride motorcycles, racehorses, skydive and scuba dive in the freezing waters of the North Sea, 80 km (50 miles) above the Arctic Circle. The star of the show was 79-year-old Elida Anderson who became the world's oldest bungee-jumper.

● The annual **Flying Cat Ceremony** at Verviers in Belgium consists of the launch of a toy cat attached to a small balloon from the tower of the old Church of St Remacle. The foundation for this bizarre event is said to be based on fact. Apparently in 1641, a Verviers apothecary conducted his own experiment in aerodynamics by launching a live cat attached to inflated pigs' bladders from the same church tower. According to accounts of the time, the cat landed on its paws and ran off unharmed.

● The Spanish town of Buñol stages an annual event called **La Tomatina**, a mass fight with 68 000 kg (150 000 lb) of ripe tomatoes. The event dates back to 1944 when the local fair was marred by hooligans throwing tomatoes at the procession. Now the fair is nothing more than a sideshow to the 90-minute long tomato fight, at the end of which the participants are only too pleased to be hosed down.

● The inaugural **European Lawn Mower Championships** took place in October 1989 on the Saint-Pardoux racetrack near the French town of Limoges. The sport was created in the United Kingdom in 1975 by former rally driver Jim Garin. The machines are fitted with car engines and can attain speeds of over 90 km/h (55 mph). They are usually ridden by seated contestants.

● Horse racing at breakneck speed around Siena's Il Piazza del Campo, the **Palio** is the present-day equivalent of *Ben Hur* – but without the chariots. The most famous horse race in Italy dates back to 1238 and has remained largely unchanged ever since. Ten horses, each representing different districts of Siena, hurtle round three laps of the fan-shaped town square – a distance of around 1100 m (1200 yd). The race takes just 90 seconds but the preliminaries last much longer. Each horse is taken to the church of the district it is representing in order to be blessed before the altar. And the pre-race procession goes on for two hours.

For the race itself, some 35 000 spectators cram together in the centre of the square to watch the horses thunder past, while a further 5000 hang precariously from windows and balconies.

Despite certain precautions – a bank of thick mattresses is erected to protect the animals from the walls of the Cafe Barbero at a turn known as the 'corner of death' – it remains a dangerous race. Three horses had to be destroyed in 1993. It is tough on the jockeys too, as witnessed by the fact that the rules of the Palio state that it is the first horse to cross the line, with or without a human on its back, which is declared the winner. This rule also counters any hint of skulduggery among the riders.

Human palio races were also staged in medieval

Italy, principally to shame the enemy. During a siege, a race would often be arranged by the besiegers under the castle walls as a challenge, indicating that the runners were not afraid. The soldiers of Lucca organized one such race beneath the walls of Florence in 1325 and followed it with an event for local prostitutes.

In Arezzo, after ten years of occupation by the soldiers of Perugia, a race was held in which the girls ran topless. This proved such an attraction that the Pisans staged a similar event in Florence in 1363.

● The **Shepherds' Race** takes place on St Bartholomew's Day, 24 August, at Markgröninegen, Germany. The event dates back to at least 1443 and was originally held to show that the shepherds could run faster than any of their errant sheep. There are races for shepherd boys and shepherdesses, all barefoot, on a field near the town. The winners are crowned and presented with the ultimate trophy, a garlanded sheep, which they later lead back into the centre of Markgröninegen at the head of a festival procession.

● Every February, St Moritz in Switzerland stages a decidedly unusual horse race meeting. For it takes place on a frozen lake covered with six inches of snow. The horses, which compete in flat and hurdle races, wear special shoes with two studs at the back and a toe grip at the front. The jockeys also have added protection and face the occupational hazard of being blinded by a blizzard whenever the competing horse in front kicks up snow.

● In some villages in the Nordmark region of Germany, a wooden goat – a symbol of fertility – is carried with musical accompaniment to a house where the occupant is soon to be married or to the home of a shy bachelor who is thought to need encouragement in such matters. The animal is welcomed inside and 'fed' and 'watered'. In the Weserbergland district of Germany, wedding parties last two or three days, starting at 9 a.m. Male guests who arrive unshaved or late are promptly plastered with a paint brush full of

whipped cream and shaved with a huge wooden knife while being forced to drink a large glass of vermouth on an empty stomach. Meanwhile in the Lower Rhine region, it is by no means uncommon for a hedgehog to be placed in the wedding bed.

Belgium's famous Wedding of the Giants

● The **Wedding of the Giants** takes place on the last Sunday in August at Ath in Belgium. Each year, on the eve of the town festival, eight colourful 3.6 m (12 ft) tall reed-built giants parade through the streets for the 3 p.m. wedding of Gouyasse, the patron of crossbowmen, and his bride at the 18th-century St Julien Church. Given the scale of the proceedings, kissing the bride is an art form.

ODD FEATS

● Lotan Baba, a 37-year-old Indian mystic, subjects himself to various ordeals in the hope of bringing peace to the world. Accordingly, he once stood still for seven years and, in 1993, completed an epic 2500 mile (4023 km) roll across India. On 11 August 1994, he brought his talents to Britain and, wearing T-shirt and shorts plus protective bandages on his elbows and knees, set off on a 3 mile (4.8 km) roll through the wet streets of London from Westminster to the peace pagoda in Battersea Park. Lotan's exploits have made him a national hero in India.

Lotan Baba rolls across Battersea Bridge during his roll for peace in August 1994

● A $100 000 bet struck at London's National Sporting Club in 1907 sent 31-year-old playboy Harry Bensley off on an attempt to walk round the world without once showing his face. The rules stipulated that Bensley must push a pram, wear an iron mask at all times and set out with only £1, a collection of postcards and a change of underwear. He had to travel through a specified number of British towns plus 125 towns in 18 other countries, in the course of which he somehow had to find himself a wife – an onerous task since she too was not permitted to see his face. To finance himself, he had to sell the postcards. He left Trafalgar Square on 1 January 1908, wearing a 2 kg (4½ lb) iron helmet and pushing a 90 kg (200 lb) pram. At Newmarket races, he met King Edward VII and sold him a postcard but was soon arrested by an over-zealous policeman at Bexleyheath in Kent for selling postcards without a licence. The magistrate ordered Bensley to remove the mask in court but when the situation was explained to him, the official relented and Bensley escaped with a 2s 6d (12½p) fine and his mask intact. Over the next six years, Bensley pushed his pram across 12 countries, passing through New York, Montreal and Sydney. He received 200 offers of marriage but rejected them all. In August 1914, he arrived in Genoa, Italy, with just six more countries to visit. However, the First World War had broken out and the patriotic Bensley wanted to do his bit for king and country. So the bet was cancelled and the gallant Bensley was given a consolation prize of $4000 which he donated to charity. He died in 1956 at Brighton, Sussex.

● On 8 May 1958, Australian Ben Carlin arrived back in Montreal, Canada, having circumnavigated the world in an amphibious jeep. He had completed the last leg of the Atlantic crossing (the English Channel) back on 24 August 1951 and in total his journey consisted of 62 765 km (39 000 miles) over land and 15 450 km (9600 miles) by sea and river.

● Over a period of 15 months, ending on 9 March 1985, 32-year-old Jagdish Chander crawled 1400 km (870 miles) from Aligarh to Jamma, India, to propitiate Mata, his revered Hindu goddess.

● Between 26 July and 13 August 1930, Charles Creighton and James Hargis of Maplewood, Missouri, drove their Model A Ford 1929 roadster in reverse from New York to Los Angeles without once stopping the engine. The distance covered was 5375 km (3340 miles). They arrived back in New York in reverse on 5 September, thus completing 11 555 km (7180 miles) in 42 days.

● Welsh builder John Evans, who lives at Heanor in Derbyshire, likes to balance things on his head. To date, his different loads have included 77 milk crates, 63 bricks, a 68 litre (15 gallon) barrel of beer, a 109 kg (240 lb) Welsh dresser and two women weighing around 95 kg (210 lb).

● In 1975, Rev. Geoffrey Howard, a parish priest from Manchester, England, pushed an ancient Chinese sailing wheelbarrow across the Sahara Desert from Beni Abbes in Algeria to Kano in Nigeria, a distance of 3220 km (2000 miles). He covered it in 93 days, thanks partly to the sailing wheelbarrow which caught the trade winds that blow across the Sahara and which also proved invaluable for storing water, food, camping equipment and medical supplies. He was supported on his trek by a two-man British Army team in a Land Rover but they were only permitted to give him fresh food and water at pre-arranged locations.

● Johann Hurlinger from Austria walked 1400 km (870 miles) on his hands in 55 daily ten-hour stints from Vienna to Paris in 1900, averaging 2.54 km/h (1.58 mph).

● Over a period of 37 days between 1 August and 6 September 1984, Brian 'Cub' Keene and James 'Wilbur' Wright drove their Chevrolet Blazer 14 531 km (9031 miles) in reverse through 15 US states and Canada. Although the vehicle bore a prominent sign 'Stuck in Reverse', it did not impress law enforcement officers in Oklahoma who insisted that the pair drive forwards out of the state.

● Having survived a train crash, a typhoon and a robbery, 50-year-old French journalist Claude Mosse, endeavouring to emulate Jules Verne's journey around the world in 80 days, arrived back at London's Reform Club on 7 September 1977 with five hours in hand. Alas he was refused entry because the club had blackballed him in his absence, claiming that his trip was nothing more than a publicity stunt.

● On 24 May 1989, Bengt Norberg of Appelbo, Sweden, drove a Mitsubishi Colt GTi-16V on two side wheels non-stop for 310.333 km (192.873 miles) in a time of 7 h 15 min 50 s at Sweden's Rattvik Horse Track.

● Arvind Pandya of India ran backwards across the United States from Los Angeles to New York in 107 days between 18 August and 3 December 1984. He repeated the feat over the 1512 km (940 miles) between John O'Groats, Scotland, and Land's End, Cornwall, in 26 days 7 h between 6 April and 2 May 1990.

● Known as 'The Human Fly', George Gibson Polley scaled 2000 buildings in the United States without ever slipping or falling. His climbing career started in 1910 when his family moved to Chicago. Admiring an expensive suit in a shop window, young George told the store owner: 'I'd stand on my head on top of this building for a suit like that'. The owner accepted the challenge, George got his suit and a mountain of publicity. As his fame spread, he was often hired for store openings. In Boston, Massachusetts, he climbed 150 m (500 ft) up the Custom House; at Hartford, Massachusetts, he scaled three buildings in one day; and in Providence, Rhode Island, he shinned up a flagpole blindfold. When Polley was climbing the 57-storey Woolworth Building in New York, which in the 1920s had the distinction of being the tallest in the world, a policeman stuck his head out of a window on the 30th floor and arrested him for climbing a building without an official permit. After surviving all these daredevil escapades, George Polley died from a brain tumour at the age of 29.

● On 19 May 1990, Peter Rosendahl of Las Vegas, Nevada, rode his 24 in (61 cm) wheel unicycle backwards for a distance of 75.1 km (46.7 miles) in a time of 9 h 25 min.

● The leading light in the art of backwards walking was Plennie L. Wingo of Abilene, Texas. On 24 October 1932, 36-year-old Wingo arrived in Istanbul, Turkey, at the end of a 8000 mile (12 875 km) transcontinental reverse marathon. He had set out from Santa Monica, California, on 15 April 1931.

SPORT

ATHLETICS

● Officials at the 1952 Olympics in Helsinki, Finland, were taken by surprise when the 1500 metres was won by Josef Bartel from Luxembourg. Nobody had anticipated a Luxembourg athlete winning a medal and so when it came to the victory ceremony, there was no trace anywhere of the score to the Luxembourg national anthem. An embarrassing delay ensued before the musicians struck up a hastily improvised version.

● The least competitive athletic event in history was probably the over-89 age group in the 1989 World Veterans' Championships staged at Eugene, Oregon. It was dominated by 94-year-old Wang Ching Chang from Taiwan who captured gold in the 100 metres, 200 metres, shot putt and javelin. But in each of these events, Chang faced just one opponent, the comparatively youthful but perennial runner-up, 90-year-old Herbert Kirk from Montana.

● Following a superb run in the 1938 Natal provincial marathon, South African athlete Johannes Coleman stormed across the finishing line at Alexander Park, Pietermaritzburg, confident that he had shattered the world record. At the time it stood at 2 h 26 min 42 s and on entering the park, Coleman's own watch had shown 2 h 23 min. He eagerly sought out the timekeeper for confirmation, only to find the trusty official drinking tea in the refreshment room. The timekeeper meekly apologized for his absence, saying that nobody had expected any of the runners to arrive back so soon. As a result, Coleman's record was unable to be ratified.

● At the end of the marathon in the 1954 European Championships in Berne, Switzerland, Russian athlete Ivan Filin strode into the stadium clear of Finland's Veikko Karvonen. But once inside the stadium, the Soviet runner took a wrong turn and lost over 100 metres before he realized his mistake. By the time he had got back on course, the best he could manage was third place.

● Canadian Hilda Strike lost the women's 100 metres final at the 1932 Olympic Games in Los Angeles by a matter of centimetres to Polish-born American Stella Walsh whose name had been westernized from the less pronounceable Stanislava Walasiewiczowna. When Walsh died in 1980, caught in the crossfire during an armed robbery in Cleveland, Ohio, the autopsy revealed that she was a man.

● Travelling to the 1896 Olympic Games, the United States team arrived in Athens several days late, having forgotten that the Greeks still used the Julien calendar and were thus 11 days in advance.

● Trailing home nearly 39 minutes behind the previous finisher in the marathon at the 1979 Pan

Right Athlete Stella Walsh, winner of the women's 100 metres at the 1932 Olympics, was later found to be a man

American Games at San Juan, Puerto Rico, Wallace Williams of the Virgin Islands was horrified to find the stadium locked. Everybody had forgotten about him and gone home.

BOXING

● Preparing for his bout in the New York Golden Gloves championships in January 1992, Daniel Caruso was psyching himself up by pounding his gloves into his face prior to the introductions.

Unfortunately he overdid it and scored a direct hit with one punch, breaking and bloodying his own nose. Doctors examined him and declared that he was unfit to box.

● Sierra Leone lightweight John Coker was disqualified before the 1966 Empire and Commonwealth Games in Kingston, Jamaica, because he couldn't find any gloves to fit him. Coker, who was also an Oxford rugby blue, scoured Kingston but nowhere catered for his huge hands and particularly his exceptionally long thumbs. Consequently, he was disqualified prior to the competition for failing to be properly equipped.

Jack 'Nonpareil' Dempsey and Johnny Reagan found themselves fighting the rising tide as well as each other. When the contest was resumed at a drier venue, Dempsey won after 45 rounds

● The world middleweight title fight between Jack 'Nonpareil' Dempsey and Johnny Reagan on 18 December 1887 on the sea front at Long Island, New York, had to be abandoned after eight rounds when the tide came in and flooded the ring. Another spot was found 25 miles away and the contest resumed later that day with Dempsey retaining his crown.

● Unknown to all but himself, American world middleweight champion Harry Greb (1894–1926) successfully defended his title several times while blind in one eye. Greb's handicap was only revealed when he died following an eye operation two months after losing the crown to Tiger Flowers. Nicknamed 'The Human Windmill', Greb held the world title for three years, defending it nine times.

● One of the briefest excursions into the ring was that by Ralph Walton against Al Couture at Lewiston, Maine, on 23 September 1946. Walton was still adjusting his gum shield in his corner when Couture knocked him out. The fight officially ended after 10½ seconds – and that included the 10-second count.

● In the course of a world lightweight title fight at Vernon, California, on 14 July 1912, the champion, American Adolph Wolgast, and challenger Joe Rivers connected with simultaneous blows in the 13th round, causing both men to slump to the canvas. Neither appeared capable of getting to their feet until referee Jack Welch stepped in. He raised Wolgast to a semi-standing position and propped him up while counting out the unfortunate Rivers.

CRICKET

● At Old Trafford, Manchester, in July 1863, a team of one-legged cricketers competed against a team of one-armed players. The one-legged team struck the ball well but were slow in the field and at running between wickets; the one-armed players were agile in the field but their batting and catching ability was limited. All the players were pensioners including one man, Letford, who had no legs at all but still managed to make 10 in each innings, the second time being not out. In the end, the one-legged team won by 21 runs.

● When Grantchester Meadows near Cambridge flooded and froze over in December 1878, the University immediately challenged Cambridge Town CC to a Gown v Town game of cricket. A three-day game on ice followed, the only change to the rules being a ban on fast bowling. It ended in a draw, Town being dismissed for 328 and Gown replying with 274-4.

● Sussex batsman H.J. Heygate was given out in the match against Somerset at Taunton on 22 May 1919 because he failed to reach the crease within two minutes of the fall of the previous wicket. Poor Heygate was crippled with rheumatism and couldn't make it to the middle in time when the ninth Sussex wicket fell in their second innings. He was shown on the score-card as 'absent'. A less enigmatic score-card was used in the final of the 1958–59 Qaid-I-Azam Trophy in Karachi. Abdul Aziz was injured in the first innings and the scorecard thus read: 'Abdul Aziz retired hurt . . . 0'. The injury proved to be fatal and the scorer, not wishing to leave any room for doubt, wrote for the second innings: 'Abdul Aziz did not bat, dead . . . 0'.

● When a no-ball came his way during the match with Kent at the Oval in 1938, Surrey opening batsman Laurie Fishlock advanced boldly down the wicket and launched himself into a full-blooded drive. In his eagerness to exploit the situation, he overdid the aggression for as he swung at the ball, his bat snapped in two. Consequently, he barely made contact with the ball and it carried through to the wicket-keeper who, thinking quickly, caught the ball and broke the wicket. A batsman cannot be out caught or stumped from a no-ball but Fishlock, with no bat to ground, had to return to the pavilion, adjudged run out.

● Batting at Kalgoorlie, Australia, in the 1970s, Stan Dawson was struck by a speedy delivery that ignited a box of matches which he had secreted in his hip pocket. To add to his woe, Dawson was run out as he tried to beat down the flames.

● The day after achieving an honourable draw in the Lord's Test Match with England, the West Indies travelled to Sion Mills, Londonderry, to play Ireland in a one-day match in July 1969. It was expected to be a formality for the mighty West Indies whose side included six of those on Test duty. Yet they were bowled out for just 25, which was itself something of a recovery since at one stage they had been 12–9. Ireland duly completed a historic victory by nine wickets.

● An unusual game of cricket takes place on a sand-bar called Bramble Bank in the middle of the Solent, the stretch of water between Hampshire and the Isle of Wight. Bramble Bank only surfaces twice a year for about an hour at a time when the water is at its lowest at the spring and autumn equinox. The result is a sandbank measuring some two acres, liberally dotted with pools of water. It was first used as a cricketing venue in the early part of the century but when yachtsman Uffa Fox organized a game there in 1954, it was the first such encounter since 1922. Employing oars as bats, Fox's men scored 29, thus defeating a team from Parkhurst Prison (principally officers) by seven runs. Parkhurst was somewhat handicapped by the fact that only seven of its team were able to land. A more recent match took place in 1984 when the Royal Southern Yacht Club from Hamble challenged the Island Sailing Club from Cowes. The players waited eagerly in a flotilla of boats for the moment when the island emerged from beneath the sea. They then took the field wearing Wellington boots and whites. Island Sailing Club lost by eight wickets, the winning hit being a six and lost ball.

● The First Test between Young Sri Lanka and Young England, 3–6 February 1987, was briefly halted when a large iguana crept sinisterly across the square at the Columbo Cricket Club ground.

GOLF

● Playing in the qualifying round of the Shawnee Invitational for Ladies at Shawnee-on-Delaware, Pennsylvania, around 1912, Maud McInnis succeeded in taking 166 strokes for the 130 yd (119 m) 16th hole. Her problems began when she drove her tee shot into the Binniekill River and the ball floated downstream. Not to be denied, she clambered into a boat with her husband manning the oars and set off in pursuit of her ball. Eventually 2½ km (1½ miles) down the river, her spouse dutifully keeping score, she managed to beach the ball on terra firma. Unfortunately, the journey back to the 16th green from such an unusual approach necessitated playing through a wood. This did little for her score and it was 165 shots and nearly two hours after driving off that she finally holed out. It is not known whether she qualified for the later stages of the tournament.

● In 1913 at Wellington, Shropshire, a curious game of golf took place between a golfer and a fisherman. While the golfer, Rupert May, struck a conventional ball with conventional clubs, the angler, J.J.D. Mackinlay, cast a 71 g (2½ oz) weight. Mackinlay, excelled at the long game – his longest cast, 96 m (105 yd), being within 11 m (12 yd) of the world record at the time – but short casts proved more troublesome. However, he was spared the ordeal of trying to land the weight in the hole. When within a rod's length of the cup, he ran the weight to the rod end and dropped into the hole. On five occasions, his line broke but he was allowed another shot without penalty. The gallant Mackinlay managed to complete the course in 102, 15 strokes more than his opponent.

● Rufus Stewart, the professional at Kooyonga Golf Club, South Australia, and a former Australian Open champion, played 18 holes in total darkness at the Kooyonga course in 1931 without losing a single ball. He went round in a highly creditable 77. In August 1970, a night-time golf competition, teeing off at midnight, was staged at the Summit Golf and Country Club, Ontario. Special rules included a one-stroke penalty (instead of two) for a lost ball and the enforced retirement of any competitor who lost 12 balls. Seven players took part, the winner being Lief Pettersen with a round of 84.

● On 18 November 1929 at Belmont Springs Country Club, Massachusetts, James Cash Jr got a hole in one at the 16th. The ball actually stopped on the rim of the cup but was helped in by an earth tremor. Playing at the Bay of Quinte Club, Belleville, Ontario, in 1934, Jack Ackerman was dismayed to see his tee shot come to rest on the lip of the hole. But then a butterfly landed on the ball, causing it to drop in for a hole in one.

● London stockbroker Richard Sutton was challenged to a bet that he couldn't play golf through the heart of the city, from the south side of Tower Bridge to White's Club in St James's Street off Piccadilly, a distance of around 3½ miles (5½ km), in under 200 strokes. On 23 April 1939, using only a putter, with which he crossed the Thames at Southwark Bridge, Sutton completed the course in 142. The secret of his success was that he kept out of trouble by only hitting the ball short distances, so avoiding the ignominy of a wayward iron shot landing in the middle of a bunch of bananas outside a greengrocer's.

● A cross-country golf competition was organized as part of Ireland's three-week national festival of An Tostal in 1953. A total of 150 golfers drove from the first tee at the Kildare Club, the aim being to hole out on the 18th green of the Curragh course, some 8 km (5 miles) away. Among the natural hazards en route were the main Dublin to Cork railway line and highway, the Curragh Racecourse, a maze of army tank tracks and around 150 telephone lines. The winner was Irish international and British Walker Cup player Joe Carr with a score of 52.

● Two Californian teenagers, Bob Aube (17) and Phil Marrone (18) went on a golfing safari in 1974 from San Francisco to Los Angeles, a distance of over 800 km (500 miles). It took them 16 days and they used over 1000 balls.

● Ernest Smith, the professional at Davyhulme Golf Club, Manchester, was bet £100 that, on one day, he could not play five rounds of golf in five different countries, scoring under 80 each time. On 12 June 1939, Smith and Sidney Gleave, a racing motorcyclist, set off on their epic journey. Travelling by plane, they achieved the following timetable: 3.40 a.m., Prestwick St Nicholas (Scotland); Smith's score 70; duration 1 h 35 min. 7.15 a.m., Bangor (Northern Ireland); score 76; duration 1 h 30 min. 10.15 a.m., Castletown (Isle of Man); score 76; duration 1 h 40 min. 1.30 p.m., Blackpool, Stanley Park (England); score 72; duration 1 h 55 min. 6 p.m., Hawarden (Wales); score 68; duration 2 h 15 min.

● American professional Harry Gonder decided that achieving a hole in one was merely a matter of perseverance. So one day in 1940, armed with two witnesses and a supply of caddies to tee up and retrieve balls, he embarked on an endurance test to see how long it would take him to get an 'ace' on a 160 yd (146 m) hole. Ball after ball he hit towards the flag. His 86th attempt finished just 15 in (38 cm) short but, generally, he was having difficulty finding his range. As the hours ticked by, Gonder started to feel hungry and after 941 balls he stopped for refreshment in the hope that it would improve his fortunes. The ploy nearly worked for his 996th shot hit the pin and bounced 3 in (8 cm) away. At 8.10 p.m., his 1162nd stopped 6 in (15 cm) short and, beginning to get into his stride at last, his 1184th missed by 3 in (8 cm). It was a false dawn. As the church bells struck midnight, Gonder struck his 1600th ball. Like most of its predecessors, it finished nowhere near the target. By now fatigue was beginning to set in and a nasty blister appeared on his hand. Still he battled on and was nearly rewarded twice in the space of a few minutes. His 1750th shot hit the pin as did the 1756th which ended up no more than 1 in (2.5 cm) from the hole. That seemed to convince him that it was just not his day. So at 2.40 a.m., 16 h 25 min after first teeing off, Gonder's 1817th shot finished 10 ft (3 m) from the pin – and he gave up.

● Playing at Rickmansworth Golf Club, Hertfordshire, over Easter 1960, Mrs Paddy Martin achieved three holes in one – on Good Friday, Saturday and Easter Monday. All three came at the 1125 yd (114 m) 3rd hole with the same eight iron and the same ball.

● On 2 September 1964, Norman L. Manley got two successive holes in one at par-4 holes – 'double albatrosses'. His feat took place at the Del Valle Country Club, Saugus, California, on the 330 yd (302 m) 7th and the 290 yd (265 m) 8th, both slightly downhill, dog-leg holes. The two 'aces' enabled Manley to return a course record 10-under-par, 61.

● On 5 February 1971, Captain Alan Shepard, commander of the *Apollo 14* spacecraft, became the first person to play golf on the moon. Using a one-handed swing, he hit two balls with an iron head attached to a makeshift shaft. He claimed that his first effort, helped by the reduced force of gravity on the moon, travelled 200 yd (183 m). His second was a miserable shank.

● The highest golf shot on Earth was played on 22 January 1989 by American Gerald Williams from the summit of Mt Aconcagua, Argentina, 6960 m (22 834 ft) above sea-level.

● The annual Elfego Baca tournament consists of just one hole. The tee is set on the top of Socorro Peak, New Mexico, 2208 m (7243 ft) above sea-level. The hole, a patch of dirt 18 m (60 ft) in diameter, is 4 km (2½ miles) away and 750 m (2500 ft) below. The competition was first staged in 1969 and the course record stands at 11, held by Mike Stanley.

● P.C. Chase and John North finished all square in their regular weekly match at Woking Golf Club in Surrey on 30 October 1972 without halving a single hole. The odds against that happening are 1 413 398 to 1.

● In 1975, missionary Dave Freeman founded the least hospitable golf course in the world – the High Country Club, set on the frozen waters of the Beaufort Sea in Northern Canada, 645 km (400 miles) inside the Arctic Circle where temperatures drop to below −40 degrees Fahrenheit. The nine-hole course, which has the comfort of sand greens, is staked out each winter by Bill Josh, the base manager of the local airline at Victoria Island. It is surely the only course in the world where polar bears are a natural hazard.

HORSE RACING

● The 1949 Midland St Leger trial at Birmingham attracted just two runners, *Ridge Wood* (ridden by Gordon Richards) and *Courier* (ridden by Tommy Lowrey), and goes down in history as probably the slowest race ever run. Both jockeys were under strict instructions not to make the pace under any circumstances, so when the tape rose both froze to the spot. *Courier* actually turned to face the opposite direction before the starter, losing patience, sent his assistant to crack the whip. At this, the horses broke into a slow canter, covering the first furlong in nearly 1½ min. To a chorus of jeers, it was *Ridge Wood* who eventually passed the finishing post first, covering the one mile, five furlongs (2.6 km) in 5 min 14 s, more than twice the standard time. The race clearly took little out of the winner for *Ridge Wood* went on to win the St Leger itself that year.

● The most famous ending to a Grand National was the 1956 race, run at Aintree on 24 March, when the Queen Mother's *Devon Loch*, ridden by

Dick Francis, was well clear on the run-in and being urged home by a roar of approval in anticipation of a royal victory. But less than 45 m (50 yd) from the winning post, *Devon Loch* inexplicably spreadeagled on the flat. It appeared that he had lifted his forelegs as if to jump a non-existent obstacle before realizing his error. While the crowd watched aghast, the well-beaten *E.S.B.* passed the stricken *Devon Loch* to claim the prize. The mystery surrounding *Devon Loch's* capitulation fired Dick Francis's imagination and set him on course to becoming a highly successful thriller writer.

● Amateur rider Mr Stuart Kittow and his mount *Tango Shandy* were the only partnership left intact as they approached the final fence of a novice chase at Newton Abbot, Devon, on 28 August 1984. But, with victory seemingly a formality, the horse's saddle slipped. They somehow blundered over the last but then Mr Kittow also lost his irons. Determined to make it to the winning-post, he hung on grimly around the horse's neck until, just a few yards from the finish and with no saddle at all now, he slipped and hit the ground. Still Mr Kittow would not be denied and he desperately clung to the reins as he was dragged across the finishing line. Since he still had some form of contact, albeit tenuous, with his horse at the finish, Mr Kittow thought he had won but the stewards took a different view and disqualified horse and rider. Instead the spoils went to *Legal Session* who, after falling, had been remounted to finish a distant second. Mr Kittow had the satisfaction of being heartily cheered to the unsaddling enclosure (a superfluous requirement in his case) by an appreciative crowd.

● The Waterloo Hurdle at Haydock Park, Lancashire, on 9 December 1992 had to be restarted after the entire field took the wrong course. As they set off, the jockeys found the second hurdle blocked off by marker dolls and so they bypassed it. Convinced that they should have jumped it, the jockeys pulled up their mounts at the end of the first circuit and the race was restarted to include the second hurdle. The stewards held an inquiry into the fiasco and discovered that it had been caused by a groundsman inadvertantly turning over two pages in his racecard. Thinking the race was a steeplechase, he had blocked off the wrong obstacle.

● *Esha Ness* has gone down in history as the horse which won the Grand National that never was. At Aintree on 3 April 1993, following one false start, the tape again failed to rise properly and all but nine of the 39 runners set off despite the starter's frantic attempts to recall them. Several others were pulled up half-way but a few kept going.

First past the post at the end of two circuits and over 4 miles (6.4 km) was 50–1 outsider *Esha Ness* ridden by John White, blissfully unaware that anything was amiss. His joy was short-lived as the race was declared void.

MOTOR SPORT

● A single crash at the 1927 Le Mans 24-Hour Race in France destroyed the chances of the entire three-car Bentley team. The prelude to this catastrophe was the spinning of a Schneider car at the White House corner. It half-blocked the road, forcing Callingham's 4-litre Bentley to roll into the ditch where it was followed moments later by Duller's 3-litre Bentley, at the time a full two laps adrift of its more powerful team-mate. Close behind, Sammy Davis in the third Bentley managed to avoid the ditch but still sustained extensive damage. It took him half an hour to get going again by which time his chance had gone.

● Charismatic French racing driver Jean Behra (1921–59) wore a plastic right ear after the original had been severed in a crash during the 1955 Tourist Trophy race at Dundrod, Northern Ireland. In case history repeated itself, Behra always kept a spare plastic ear in his pocket.

● The schedule set by the organizers of the 1972

Bandama Rally held in West Africa was so severe that there were no finishers. The last two drivers left in the event, Tony Fall and Shekhar Mehta, simply ran out of time.

RUGBY

● Playing for Kukris against Panaga in a match in Brunei, Dick Dover broke from a scrum and ran 70 yd (68 m) to touch down unchallenged. His team-mates were more puzzled than pleased for, disorientated by the wheeling of the scrum, Dover had run the 75 yards to 'score' near his own posts.

● Selected to play for France against Scotland in 1911, Gaston Vareilles jumped off the team train to buy a sandwich. Delayed by a queue, he returned to the platform to see the train and his team-mates disappearing into the distance. He missed the match and was never picked to play for his country again.

Another Frenchman with unhappy memories of playing Scotland was Jean-Pierre Salut who, about to take the field for the 1969 international in Paris, broke his ankle while running up the stairs from the dressing-room to the pitch. He was thus carried off before even making it on to the pitch.

● In 1966, Colwyn Bay RFC set off on their 80 km (50 mile) journey to play Welsh rivals Portmadoc. Once there, they got changed, the referee ran out on to the pitch and both teams were lined up ready for the kick-off when it was suddenly realized that something was missing – there was no ball. So the match was abandoned.

● Jamie Kahakura, 26-year-old stand-off, had played two games for New Zealand Rugby League club Whakaki in the 1989 Gisborne East Coast Competition when his career came to an abrupt halt. He was banned from playing for being a woman.

SOCCER

● The least competitive football league in the world is on the Isles of Scilly. There are only two teams on the islands – the Gunners and the Wanderers – and they play each other every week in the league, the only break being when they meet in the Cup.

● Welsh referee Clive Thomas once added 45 minutes in stoppage time at the end of a match. It was a boys' club game staged on a pitch on top of a mountain at Blaengwynfi, West Glamorgan, and every time the ball went out of play, it rolled down the mountainside.

● Russian international goalkeeper Lev Yashin (1929–90), who played 78 times for his country, always took two caps to a match. He wore one and put the other behind him in the net for luck.

● The highlight of the opening day of the 1894–95 season was a remarkable 'game of three halves' between Sunderland and Derby County. The appointed referee, a Mr Kirkham, was late arriving and in his absence, John Conqueror of Southwick officiated. After 45 minutes' play, Mr Kirkham arrived and asked Derby, who were losing 3–0, if they wanted to start again. Naturally they accepted this unusual offer and so the teams played a further 90 minutes. There was no happy ending for Derby. They lost 8–0 . . . and that was not counting the three goals they had conceded under Mr Conqueror.

● The gathering gloom forced Crewe referee Aaron Scragg to abandon the First Division match between Sheffield Wednesday and Aston Villa in November 1898 with just nine minutes remaining. Although Wednesday were leading 3–1 and the result seemed a foregone conclusion, the two teams were ordered to play the remaining nine minutes at a later date. This they did, 15 weeks later in March 1899. Wednesday scored again to win 4–1 but the result did not prevent them being relegated or Villa being crowned League champions.

● At a village near Birkenhead in 1910, a game was arranged between a team who had their arms strapped to their sides and their boots and stockings removed, and a team perched on 2 m (6 ft) high stilts. Those on stilts found it difficult to make contact with the ball while their opponents, with no arms for balance, kept falling over. In the end, the tied-arm team won.

● Pressing hard for promotion to Division One in 1938–39, Sheffield United's cause was being hampered by indifferent home form. For although they were playing well away, they were drawing too many games at their Bramall Lane ground. So it was decided to treat the last three home games as away fixtures. Each match-day morning, the players were driven by bus from Sheffield to Derbyshire where they had lunch before returning to the ground. The psychology worked. United won two and drew one of those vital games to secure promotion.

● Arriving at Middlesbrough railway station in the late 1940s, the Bolton Wanderers entourage were horrified to discover that the players' shin-guards were missing. The Bolton trainer, Bill Ridding, went out and bought 22 paperback romantic novels as temporary replacements. Ridding went on to manage the club from 1951 to 1968.

● Dave Mycock's benefit game for Halifax Town in 1952 really was a game of two halves. Town played Halifax Rugby League Club and in the first half, they played soccer, in the second rugger. The soccer score was 1–1, the rugger score 17–17. The Rugby League side were awarded a penalty on the stroke of half-time to allow them to equalize and the generosity was reciprocated near the end of the second half when Town were given a penalty kick in front of the posts which enabled them to draw level.

● Referee Henning Erikstrup was about to blow for full-time with Norager leading Ebeltoft 4–3 in a Danish league match in April 1960 when his dentures suddenly fell out. As he scrambled around on the pitch in an effort to recover them, Ebeltoft equalized. Despite vehement protests from Ebeltoft, Mr Erikstrup disallowed the goal, replaced his false teeth and promptly blew the final whistle.

● With just a few minutes left, a South American (Libertadores) Cup tie between Argentinian champions Boca Juniors and Sporting Cristal from Peru, played at the Bombonera Stadium, Buenos Aires, on 17 March 1971, exploded into a mass brawl. Referee Alejandro Otero called in the police and the 19 players who had committed sending-off offences – three had managed to steer clear of the trouble – were all arrested. Three were taken to hospital, the other 16 to the local police station. They were given 30 days in jail although the sentences were later suspended. Similar indiscipline prevailed in May 1993 at a Paraguayan league match between Sportivo Ameliano and General Caballero. Trouble flared after two Sportivo players were sent off and a ten-minute fight ensued, at the end of which referee William Weiler was forced to dismiss a further 18 players, including the remainder of the Sportivo team. Understandably, the match was abandoned.

● When a woman named Rosemary Mello threw a flare on to the pitch during a 1990 World Cup qualifier between Chile and Brazil, it had unexpected repercussions. Chile were banned from the next World Cup; their goalkeeper, Rojas, overacted so much during the incident that he was banned for life; and Ms Mello went on to appear nude in *Playboy* magazine.

● On 27 February 1993, HFS Loans League team Congleton were forced to call off a minute's silence to mourn the death of the club's oldest fan . . . when he walked into the ground. As 85-year-old Fred Cope arrived at the ground for the Cheshire club's match with Rossendale, he assumed the flag flying at half-mast was in tribute to former England captain Bobby Moore who had died that week. But when he picked up the programme and read his own obituary, he thought he had better notify someone of his well-being.

4
ARTS AND ENTERTAINMENT

ART

● Sarah Biffin (1784–1850) from Liverpool became a celebrated painter even though she was born without arms or legs. She used to hold her pen, pencil or brush in her mouth.

French artist Pierre-Auguste Renoir (1841–1919) was so severely stricken by rheumatism towards the end of his life that by 1910, he was unable to walk. Although his fingers were no longer supple, he continued to paint – by strapping the brush to his hand.

● West of Amarillo, Texas, on Interstate Highway 40 (the famous Route 66) can be found The Cadillac Ranch, a work of art consisting of ten Cadillacs nose down in the ground in an orderly row. All of the cars have recently been painted red by unknown artists. The idea was conceived by Stanley Marsh III, an Amarillo rancher and artist on whose land the vehicles are buried.

● Congo, a chimpanzee at London Zoo in the late 1950s, was such a talented artist that Picasso bought one of his paintings.

Left Christo has 'wrapped' three Florida islands in pink plastic tutus (see p. 66)

● The aim of Dadaism, a movement born in Zurich in 1916, was to contradict established beliefs, particularly through art and sculpture. Dadaism rapidly spread to New York where its leader in the early 1920s was painter Marcel Duchamp. His 'anti-art' campaign included a version of the Mona Lisa with a moustache but his *pièce de résistance* was an abstract composed of wire, varnish, dust and paint, held together between sheets of glass. En route to an exhibition in Brooklyn in 1923, the glass smashed. Undeterred, Duchamp tried to turn the mishap to his advantage by triumphantly unveiling it as 'The Last Refinement'. The irony of his work is that although it was intended to be a rejection of art it now fetches huge prices.

✳ The youngest exhibitor at the Royal Academy of Art's Annual Summer Exhibition was Lewis Melville 'Gino' Lyons. Born on 30 April 1962, his 'Trees and Monkeys' was painted on 4 June 1965 and exhibited on 29 April 1967.

● Author of *The Stendhal Syndrome*, Dr Graziella Magherini has studied case histories of over 100 tourists in Florence, Italy, who have suddenly been taken ill when faced with great works of art. She named the disorder after the 19th-century French novelist who became overwhelmed by the frescoes in Florence's Santa Croce Church. Dr Magherini revealed that the main sufferers are infrequent travellers who, possibly suffering from jet lag, are overcome when confronted with something from the past. Symptoms include stomach pains, dizziness and heart palpitations. The syndrome is said to be caused partly by the shock of an overwhelming sense of the past — when confronted by a historic work of art. Among the most unhealthy works of art are Michelangelo's statue of David and Caravaggio's painting of Bacchus.

● In 1961, the Museum of Modern Art in New York displayed 'Le Bateau' (The Boat), a painting by the French artist Henri Matisse (1869–1954). It measured 142 × 112 cm (56 × 44 in) and for 47 days nobody noticed that it had been hung upside down.

● The 'No Art' movement sprang up in 1950s America as a form of social and political protest. The leading lights — Michelle and Stanley Fisher, Sam Goodman and Boris Lurie — exhibited their work at the March and Gertrude Stein galleries in New York between 1959 and 1964. They created paintings and sculptures which consisted of chaotic assemblages of rubbish, bloody dismembered toys, excrement and sexual fetishes, and had titles such as 'Doom', 'Vulgar Show' and simply 'No'. They were designed to shock and disturb the viewer. The 'No artists' claimed that they were saying 'no' in their art to issues such as exploitation, pollution, poverty and the arms race.

● Plans for the Church of St Ignazio in Rome included the biggest dome in the city apart from St Peter's. But, in 1691, with only the dome still to be built, the money ran out. Then someone had a brainwave. If they could not afford a real dome, they would have the next best thing – a painting of one. Italian artist Andrea Pozzo (1642–1709), a master of perspective and famous for his illusionist work, was summoned to paint a dome on the church's flat ceiling. Viewed from the entrance and nave, it looked remarkably realistic and, although it was intended purely as a temporary measure until sufficient money could be raised for a proper dome, Pozzo's creation has remained ever since.

● The world's first underwater artist is Belgian scuba diver Jamy Verheylewegen. He started his unusual pursuit after crushing a nerve in his back, an injury which left him crippled for 18 months. Since 1983, he has produced over 400 paintings. He uses oil paints on a synthetic fibre and his paintings are mounted on an easel weighed down with 6 kg (13 lb) of lead. He has worked at depths of up to 37 m (120 ft). The end products are often exhibited underwater with lead weights attached, anyone wishing to view them having to be taken down by bathyscaphe.

SCULPTURE

● The world's only underwater statue of Christ can be seen in the John Pennecamp State Park at Key Largo, Florida. The 2.8 m (9 ft) bronze replica of 'Christ of the Abyss' was created by sculptor Guido Galletti for placement in the Mediterranean. But in 1961 it was given to the Underwater Society of America by industrialist Egidi Cressi. The statue stands in 6 m (20 ft) of water. The base rests on the sandy floor and the top is viewed from the surface by visitors in glass-bottomed boats.

● Bulgarian sculptor and environmental artist Javacheff Christo, born in 1935, has a style all of his own. He has a mania for huge outdoor sculptures, most of them wrapped in paper, plastic or fabric. He started wrapping in a small way in Paris in the 1950s, choosing manageable objects such as bottles, chairs, bicycles and cars. By the 1960s, he had moved on to bigger things. In 1962, he built a 4 m (13.1 ft) high, 3.2 m (10½ ft) wide wall of oil drums in the Rue Visconti, Paris.

A total of 90 drums were used. In New York in 1964, he wrapped his first store front, but the real breakthrough came in 1968 when Christo wrapped his first buildings.

His outstanding achievement was the packing of the 2500 sq m (27 000 sq ft) Kunsthalle in Berne, Switzerland, to celebrate the museum's 50th anniversary. In the same year, he wrapped two buildings at Spoleto in Italy, skyscrapers in Lower Manhattan and New York's Museum of Modern Art. The following year he took his talents to Australia and wrapped 1.6 km (1 mile) of coastline, 15 km (9.5 miles) south of Sydney, in polypropylene sheeting. It took three weeks to complete.

His works became ever more ambitious with Valley Curtain (1972), a 400 m (1312 ft) wide, 91 m (300 ft) high drape across a mountain valley at Rifle, Colorado, and, in 1976, 'Running Fence', a 40 km (24.5 mile) long curtain in Northern California. 'Running Fence' was the culmination of three years' work and represented an outlay of over $2 000 000. The fence started near Petaluma, Sonoma County, and finished at the cliffs overlooking Bodega Bay on the Pacific coast. For its construction, 2050 panels of nylon fabric were hung from 5.5 m (18 ft) high steel poles. Christo said: '"Running Fence" can be described very simply: 40 kilometres of diaphanous white fabric running over the hills, emerging from the sea and disappearing into the sea again.'

Christo was by no means finished and, in September 1985, shrouded Paris's Pont Neuf in 33 450 sq m (40 000 sq yd) of canvas. In 1991, he erected 1760 yellow umbrellas along the Tejon Pass in Southern California and 1340 blue umbrellas in Ibaraki Prefecture, north of Tokyo. Each umbrella weighed 221 kg (488 lb). Sadly on 26 October, 33-year-old insurance agent Lori Jean Keevil-Mathews, who had gone to view Christo's Californian work, was killed when a gust of wind tore one of the umbrellas loose from its steel anchors and the umbrella crushed her against a boulder. Christo immediately ordered the dismantling of the umbrellas in both countries. Sadly, four days later there was a further tragedy when 57-year-old crane operator Wasaaki Nakamura was electrocuted by a power line as he prepared to take down one of the Japanese umbrellas.

> ✳ The equestrian statue of the Roman emperor Marcus Aurelius – the largest bronze Roman sculpture in existence – was once used as a gibbet. Pope John XIII employed it for such an unlikely purpose in AD 965 to hang an unruly city prefect by his hair.

The remarkable Cadillac Ranch, 12 km (8 miles) west of Amarillo, Texas, on Route 66 (see p. 65)

✴ When Louis François Roubillac (*c.* 1695–1762) started work on his sculpture of composer George Frederick Handel in 1737, he decided he didn't like Handel's own ears. So for the statue, which now stands in Westminster Abbey, he modelled the ears on those of a London lady instead.

● Brazilian sculptor Antonio Lisboa (1738–1814) managed to continue working even after he had lost the use of his hands. In his mid thirties, he fell victim to a mysterious crippling disease and thereafter was forced to work with hammer and chisel strapped to his arms, earning him the nickname of 'Aleijadhino' meaning 'Little Cripple'. His creative flair did not appear to suffer, however, and he was over 60 when, between 1800 and 1805, he produced his *pièce de résistance* – 12 large stone figures known as The Prophets which stand in the Brazilian town of Congonhas do Campo.

● Among the unfinished works of Italian sculptor and artist Leonardo da Vinci (1452–1519) was a statue of Francesco Sforza, the father of Leonardo's patron, Ludovico Sforza. Leonardo never completed the bronze casting of the statue and when French soldiers invaded Milan at the end of the 15th century, their bowmen used the unfinished model for archery practice and destroyed it.

● Creative Salvage was a term coined by British designer Tom Dixon in the mid 1980s to describe items of furniture which he made from junk. The idea also found favour with jewellery designer Simon Cox, who made odd pieces from scrap metal and from small bones of dead birds and fish, and Robin Cooke who created a cocktail cabinet from the front of a Mercedes car. The Creative Salvage Ideal Home Exhibition was held at the Cuts Gallery and One Off, London, in August 1985.

The previous year in London, Robin Cooke had founded, along with Joe Rush and Joshua Bowler, the Mutoid Waste Co. as a creative response to unemployment and inner-city decay. None of the company founders had received formal art training but this did not prevent them from constructing bizarre sculptures from broken machines, wrecked cars and motorcycles and other assorted junk. The group lived in the vehicles they built and led a nomadic existence, touring waste sites for inspiration.

● One of the world's most bizarre sculptures is Arman's 'Long Term Parking' at Jouy-en-Josas, south of Paris. In 1982, he embedded 58 wrecked cars in an upright concrete rectangle over 60 m (200 ft) high. To keep the car sculpture in pristine condition, the vehicles are polished daily.

A multi-storey car park with a difference – Arman's 'Long Term Parking' sculpture

● Until it was blown up by Irish Republicans in 1929, the statue of King William of Orange on horseback stood on College Green, Dublin. After its destruction, the statue, minus its head, was dumped in a scrapyard and forgotten. Then during the Second World War, Dublin's water supply was threatened by the fact that thousands of gallons were being lost each day as a result of leaky old pipes. Lead for repairs was in constant demand so when an engineer chanced upon the remains of the statue and noticed that the private parts of King William's horse were made of solid lead, weighing 9.5 kg (21 lb), he had no hesitation in carrying out emergency surgery. Although the problem of the leaky pipes was solved, council officials were so embarrassed that they kept the matter under wraps for years.

MUSEUMS

✳ The **Museum of The Mousetrap** at Newport, Gwent, contains some 150 mouse and rat traps, including a 5000-year-old Egyptian trap and a French trap in the shape of a guillotine.

✳ **Potter's Museum of Curiosity** at the Jamaica Inn, Cornwall, is the work of taxidermist Walter Potter. The centrepiece of the museum, which Potter founded in 1861, are intricate tableaux featuring stuffed animals supplied to Potter by local breeders and farmers. 'The Rabbits' School' has 20 genuine stuffed rabbits sitting on benches, reading books and doing their sums. There is also a kittens' tea and croquet party with 37 ginger-and-white stuffed kittens – the ladies decked with jewels, the men wearing cravats – all sitting at a long table eating baked mouse tart.

✳ Amsterdam's **Piggy Bank Museum** displays some 12 000 piggy banks in assorted styles and sizes. There are gold ones, silver ones and even piggy banks in the shape of the Taj Mahal and Winston Churchill. Some are mechanical, including a magician who makes the money disappear under his hat.

The kittens' tea party at Potter's Museum of Curiosity, Cornwall (© Stefan Richter)

69

✳ **Berlin's Escape Museum** houses some of the bizarre devices used by those who succeeded in crossing the Berlin Wall from East to West Germany. They include a Czech student's home-made plane in which everything except the engine, the gas tank and the wheels was either constructed by hand or from recycled materials. The propeller was carved from wood. Another exhibit is Johan Gerich's Mini. He smuggled out his fiancée in a hollowed-out passenger seat.

✳ The **Mütter Museum** in Philadelphia houses a collection of 3000 objects which people have either swallowed or inhaled. Among the exhibits are a small metal battleship, ammunition and a pair of opera glasses. Other highly personal items include bladder stones removed from US Chief Justice John Marshall, a piece of John Wilkes Booth's thorax and the cancerous tumour that was removed from the upper left jaw of President Grover Cleveland.

✳ The **Tragedy in US History Museum** at St Augustine, Florida, features such macabre exhibits as the car in which actress Jayne Mansfield was decapitated on 29 June 1967 and the ambulance in which President Kennedy's assassin, Lee Harvey Oswald, was taken to hospital after being shot by Jack Ruby. There is even the stretcher which bore Oswald's body.

LITERATURE

● In a 1631 version of the Bible, printed in London by the King's printers, Robert Barker and Martin Lucas, the word 'not' was omitted from the Seventh Commandment, thus encouraging its readers to commit adultery. On learning of the error, King Charles I called all 1000 copies back and fined his printers £3000.

● Today hailed as a master of the English language for books such as *Lord Jim* and *Nostromo*, novelist Joseph Conrad (1857–1924) could not speak a word of English until he was 19. Born in Poland under the name of Teodor Jozef Konrad Walecz Korzeniowski, he built up a knowledge of English after becoming a mariner on British merchant ships in the 1870s. Conrad's first novel, *Almayer's Folly*, was published in 1895 by which time he was 38.

● British novelist John Creasey (1908–73) could have been forgiven for abandoning all hopes of becoming an author. For he received 743 rejection slips under his own name and 25 *noms de plume* before finally getting his first book published in 1932.

Between then and his death, he had another 563 books published, totalling over 40 000 000 words.

● One night in February 1862, London-born poet and pre-Raphaelite painter Gabriel Charles Dante Rossetti (1828–82) arrived home to discover his beloved wife Lizzie dying from an overdose of laudanum. He blamed himself for her death, bitterly regretting being away working on a set of lyrical poems when he might have been able to save her. As a mark of respect and to erase them from his memory, he placed the only manuscript of the poems in her coffin. Seven years after his wife's death, Rossetti claimed that her spirit came to visit him in the form of a chaffinch and told him to retrieve his poems. On the night of 4 October 1869, he had her remains dug up and he reclaimed the manuscript from the coffin. *The Poems*, as they were called, were published in 1870. The first edition sold out within two weeks and by the end of the year, six further editions had appeared in print.

● A book in German on the Archbishop of Bremen, published in 1609, was borrowed from Sidney Sussex College, Cambridge, by Colonel Robert Walpole in 1667–68. It disappeared from the shelves for 288 years until it was found by Professor Sir John Plumb in the library of the then Marquess of Cholmondeley at Houghton Hall,

Norfolk, and returned to its rightful home. No fine was demanded.

Another seriously overdue library book was, ironically, *The Book of Fines*, borrowed by the Bishop of Winchester in 1650 from Somerset County Records office. The tome, a register of property transactions in Taunton between 1641 and 1648, remained with the Bishop's office for some 200 years and then with the Church commissioners for another century. When it was finally returned to Somerset County Library in 1985, it had built up a fine of around £3000.

A copy of Dr J. Currie's *Febrile Diseases* was taken out of the University of Cincinnati Medical Library in 1823 by a Mr M. Dodd. It was returned on 7 December 1968 by his great-grandson, having accumulated a fine of about $2646.

● In May 1966, *The Times* of London heard from a Fijian woman that she had just completed their crossword no. 673 from the issue of 4 April 1932.

The woman was stationed in Fiji as the wife of a civil servant and the crossword had been in an edition of the newspaper which had been used for wrapping. Consequently, it had lain uncompleted for 34 years before being discovered.

> ✱ In 1939, Ernest Vincent Wright published a novel called *Gadsby*. Although there were over 50 000 words in it, none contained the letter 'e'. The only 'e's in the entire book were those in the author's name.

● The smallest printed book was an edition of the children's story *Old King Cole* measuring 1 mm × 1 mm. Eighty-five copies of it were published in March 1985 by Gleniffer Press of Paisley, Strathclyde. The pages could be turned only by using a needle.

LANGUAGE

✱ *The Guinness Book of Records* states that the world's most succinct word is the Fuegian (southernmost Argentina and Chile) word *mamihlapinatapai*, meaning 'looking at each other hoping that either will offer to do something which both parties desire but are unwilling to do'. The Scottish *tartle* is almost as admirable. It means 'to hesitate in recognizing a person or thing, as happens when you are introduced to someone whose name you cannot recall'.

✱ The longest abbreviation is SKOMKHPKJCDPWB, the initials of the Syarikat Kerjasama Orangorang Melayu Kerajaan Hilir Perak Kerana Jimat Cermat Dan Pinjam-meminjam Wang Berhad. It is the Malay name for the Cooperative Company of the Lower State of Perak Government's Malay People for Money Savings and Loans Ltd, in Teluk Anson, Perak, West Malaysia. The abbreviation for this abbreviation is Skomk.

✱ The longest place-name in the world is Taumatawhakatangihangakoauauotamateaturipukakapikimaungahoronukupokaiwhenuakitanatahu, the 85-letter Maori name for a hill 305 m (1002 ft) above sea-level in the Southern Hawke's Bay district of New Zealand's North Island. It means: 'The place where Tamatea, the man with the big knees, who slid, climbed and swallowed mountains, known as landeater, played his flute to his loved one'.

MUSIC

● New York band Kid Creole and The Coconuts notched up a remarkable seven UK hits between 1981 and 1983, including three in the Top Ten, but never once entered the US Top 100. Their UK Top Ten hits were 'I'm A Wonderful Thing, Baby', 'Stool Pigeon', and 'Annie I'm Not Your Daddy'.

● The shortest album is by Gadfly whose six-track instrumental recording lasts a total of just

32 s. The artist told *Record Mirror*: 'It would have been shorter but I got carried away with the solo!' The 1974 single 'The Mistake' by Dickie Goodman on Rainy Wednesday Records is less than one second long and is a short extract from the record's B-side, 'Energy Crisis '74'.

● Italian-born composer Jean Baptiste Lully (1632–87), the director of music at the court of Louis XIV, had the misfortune to die from an injury sustained while conducting. In 1687, he was directing a Te Deum (a Latin hymn of thanksgiving to God) in Paris when he inadvertently struck himself on the foot with the heavy, long staff which he was beating on the floor to indicate the tempo. Soon an abscess developed, swiftly followed by the onset of gangrene and Lully died from blood poisoning, aged 54.

● Romanian folk singer Joan Melu attracted an audience of nil for her August 1980 concert at the 2200-seater Capitol Theatre in Melbourne. Undeterred by the lack of audience response, she proceeded to fulfil her obligation to give a two-hour performance, complete with an interval and encores.

UNUSUAL INSTRUMENTS

✳ Brazilian composer Gilberto Ambrosio Garcis Mendes specializes in choosing unconventional instruments for his pieces. In his line-up for 'Cidade cité city' (1964), he listed 'a dust catcher, floor polisher and a television set'. Eight years later, he demanded an electric fan and an electric shaver for his musical 'O objeto' and coffee cups, spoons and a medicine dropper in 'Pausa e menopausa'. His most unusual request was in 'Son et Lumiere' (1968) where he called for a piano, tapes, photographic flashes and 'a very beautiful woman pianist who walks like a mannequin'.

Mendes is by no means the only composer with unusual musical tastes. At the Hoffnung Music Festival in London in 1956, vacuum cleaners were solemnly cued in and out during Malcolm Arnold's 'A grand grand overture' while Ferde Grofé requested a typewriter for his piece 'Tabloid' and a bicycle pump for 'Free Air'.

Other composers issued odd instructions. Richard Orton's 12 brass players in 'Brass Phase' (1978) are to sit on revolving stools but this pales into insignificance beside German composer Karlheinz Stockhausen's instructions to performers who choose to play his 'Goldstaub' ('Gold dust'). He told them to: 'Close your eyes, just listen. Live completely alone for four days without food, in complete silence, without much movement, sleep as little as necessary, think as little as possible. After four days, late at night, without conversation beforehand, play single sounds. *Without thinking* what you are playing close your eyes, just listen.'

● In 1984, Hubert Molard, a Strasbourg carpenter, created the Lilliput organ, measuring just 2.8 cm (1.1 in) wide. It had a keyboard of 23 keys, a pedal board of 12 pedals, a memory of 96 notes and a programme for eight pieces of music. The only way to play it was with a toothpick.

● On 29 August 1969, Robert Moran involved the entire population of San Francisco in a motor-musical extravaganza entitled '30 Minutes for 39 Autos'. Car horns and lights, a Moog synthesizer, tape recorders and broadcasting facilities, both radio and television, were all 'conducted' by Moran. Even home and office lights were turned on and off by the audience acting on broadcast cues.

● The longest rendering of the national anthem took place on the platform of Rathenau railway station, Brandenburg, Germany, on the morning of 9 February 1909. 'God Save the King' was played non-stop 16 or 17 times by a German military band, waiting for King Edward VII to emerge. The reason for the King's delay was that inside the train he was having difficulty dressing in the uniform of a German field-marshal.

● The largest musical instrument ever constructed is the Auditorium Organ in Atlantic City, New Jersey, USA. Completed in 1930 but now only partially functional, it boasted two consoles (one with seven manuals and another movable one with five), 1477 stop controls and 33 112 pipes. It had the volume of 25 brass bands, with a range of seven octaves.

The largest known brass instrument is a contra-bass tuba standing 7½ ft (2.28 m) tall, with 39 ft (11.9 m) of tubing and a bell 3 ft 4 in (1 m) across. It was constructed for a world tour by the band of American composer John Philip Sousa (1854–1932) c. 1896–98. It is now owned by a circus promoter in South Africa.

✳ Such was the vanity of Italian violinist Niccolò Paganini (1782–1840) that he deliberately chose to play on frayed strings in the hope that one of them would break, thus affording him the opportunity to display his virtuosity on the remaining strings.

● The most monotonous piece of music must surely be 'Vexations' composed by Frenchman Erik Satie. It is a 52-beat sequence played 840 times with as little variation as possible and with the indication *très lent* (very slow). Its first performance, in New York in 1963, took a group of ten pianists working in relay 18 h 12 min. In the course of the second performance in 1966, which took 18 h 40 min, one of the pianists, Charlotte Moorman, attempted to liven up proceedings by appearing naked from the waist up. The first solo performance of 'Vexations' was given by Richard Toop in London on 10–11 October 1967. He was sustained during his ordeal by cucumber sandwiches, black bread and chocolate. The following year, Toop tackled the piece again, taking 29 h.

● Two records featuring the 'singing voices' of dogs have reached the UK charts. In 1955, a group of Danish dogs called the Singing Dogs reached

number 13 with a medley of 'Pat-a-Cake', 'Three Blind Mice', 'Oh Susanna' and 'Jingle Bells'. In August 1982, a team of British dogs called the Wonder Dogs attained the dizzy heights of number 31 with 'Ruff Mix'. Not to be outdone, in December of the same year the Singing Sheep reached number 42 in the UK charts with a collection of computerized sheep sounds to the tune of 'Baa Baa Black Sheep'.

● That most patriotic of national anthems, the American 'Star Spangled Banner', was actually written by an Englishman. In 1814, America was at war with Britain. The British were shelling Fort McHenry near Baltimore when a young American, Francis Scott Key (1779–1843), went to the fort to ask for the release of a friend who had been taken prisoner. The commander agreed but kept both Key and his friend in custody for the night of 13 September 1814 until the bombardment was over. During his enforced detention, Key wrote a poem about the Stars and Stripes flag that had been flying throughout the attack. But the tune he had in mind to accompany the poem had been written years earlier by an Englishman, John Stafford Smith. In 1931, the song became the official anthem of the United States.

● In 1877, Russian composer Peter Ilyich Tchaikovsky (1840–93) received a letter from a wealthy middle-aged widow, Nadezhda von Meck, telling him how much she admired his music and offering to pay him a generous annual allowance on one condition – that they must never meet. The reasoning behind this curious stipulation was that the widow was convinced that if she were to meet her idol in the flesh, she would be bitterly disappointed. It so happened that the arrangement suited Tchaikovsky perfectly. For although he was married, he was generally uncomfortable in female company. For the next 14 years, the couple conducted a relationship by correspondence only. Occasionally they attended the same concerts in Moscow where they would observe one another from a distance. Once they did come face to face and Tchaikovsky politely doffed his hat to his benefactor. She blushed and was rendered speechless, at which Tchaikovsky became equally flustered and they both hurried off in opposite directions.

● The only song to appear in the UK Top 20 in four different versions simultaneously is 'Unchained Melody'. It happened in the week of 17 June 1955 when Al Hibbler, Jimmy Young, Les Baxter and Liberace all had hits with the song. Young's version reached number one, Hibbler made number two, Baxter's peaked at number 10 and Liberace's got to number 20.

Then in 1990, there were two versions of 'Unchained Melody' together in the US Top 20 – both by the Righteous Brothers, one recorded in 1965, the other in 1990.

● Such was the arrogance of German composer Richard Wagner (1813–83) that he would only conduct the music of Mendelssohn provided he could wear gloves. This was because Mendelssohn was a Jew. At the end of the performance, Wagner would remove the gloves and toss them to the floor, leaving them to be disposed of by the cleaners. It was Wagner's anti-Semitic attitude which later led to his music and ideals being adopted by the Nazis.

CINEMA

FILMS

● The story of a farm cat and its adventures with other animals, Kon Ichikawa's film *The Adventures of Chatran* (Japan 87) had a cast of cats, dogs and assorted farm animals – with not a human in sight. The film became Japan's box office hit of the year. *Jonathan Livingston Seagull* (US 73) also had no credited human performers although the opening sequence did show some fishermen in a boat. The cast was composed solely of seagulls.

● The first film to come complete with appropriate smells was *Behind the Great Wall* (US 59), a wide-screen travelogue about China. Featuring the new wonder phenomenon of 'Aromarama', a process devised by Charles Weiss which involved circulating the various scents through the cinema's ventilating system, the film was premièred at the DeMille Theater, New York, on 2 December 1959. It was accompanied by a range of 72 smells including oranges, spices, incense, smoke, burning pitch and a barnyard of geese. The following year, Michael Todd Jr came up with an American thriller, *Scent of Mystery* (US 60), made in 'Smell-O-Vision'. It was premièred at the Cinestage, Chicago, on 12 January 1960, the scents used (they included pipe tobacco, garlic, oil paint, wine, boot polish, ocean ozone and wood shavings) being piped to individual seats on cue from the film's 'smell track'.

● In Samuel Fuller's war film, *Big Red One* (US 80), all of the Nazi concentration camp guards were played by Jews. Equally strange casting occurred in *The Writing on the Wall* (France/Belgium 82), a tale of the Northern Ireland troubles in which all of the Protestants were played by Catholics and the Catholics by Protestants.

● The 1968 Czech film *Happy End* runs backwards. All of the characters walk backwards, food emerges from mouths and in the opening shot, a guillotined body joins the head. The dialogue is forwards as far as the structure of the words is concerned and therefore intelligible, but the responses come before the questions they answer.

● The première of *The Incredible Mr Limpet* (US 64) was held underwater. The story of a man who was transformed into a fish, it was shown by Warner Bros on the ocean floor with the help of a submerged screen at Weeki Wachi, Florida. An invited audience of 250 sat in a glass tank 6 m (20 ft) below the surface.

CENSORSHIP

✱ In the 1920s the British Board of Film Censors, once described as a collection of 'ex Colonels, and maiden aunts in long flowered frocks', banned any form of screen relationship between coloured men and white women, but not between white men and coloured women. The commonly held view at the time was that black men were better endowed than their white counterparts. So in the minds of the BBFC, any screen relationship between a coloured man and a white woman was deemed particularly unsavoury, bringing as it did strong sexual connotations.

✱ In 1964 the Peking Cinema Institute banned an educational film entitled 'Elementary Safety in Swimming in Rivers, Lakes and Seas'. The safety element was considered a bourgeois trait, calculated to undermine revolutionary daring.

✱ Josef Goebbels was Chief Censor for the Third Reich and, in his 12 years of command, he personally viewed every one of the 1363 films produced before they were passed for public screening.

This was an extremely liberal period for the German film industry – with one exception. For Hitler had ordered that any woman character in a film who broke up a marriage must die before the end credits.

✱ In 1928, Benito Mussolini banned all foreign war films from Italian screens because he deemed that they singularly failed to acknowledge Italy's contribution to the First World War.

✱ In the 1920s, 243 800 m (800 000 ft) of kissing scenes were cut from US films in Japan since Tokyo's Prefect of Police considered kissing to be 'unclean, indecorous and likely to spread disease'.

In 1932, Japan cut a scene of Sylvia Sidney being embraced by Cary Grant in *Madame Butterfly* (US 32) as her elbow was exposed. Even today, Singapore has strict rules about 'suggestive prolonged kissing' and will not permit it in Malayan-language movies.

✱ When the 1915 film *The Hypocrites* (US) depicted a nude girl, the Mayor of Boston, Massachusetts, demanded that clothes be painted on to the woman's body frame by frame.

In early Clarabelle Cow cartoons, the cow's udder was always discreetly draped by an apron for fear of upsetting the guardians of morality.

In the 1920s, over-exposed legs and shoulders were forbidden on screen in most US states. Chicago cut a scene of a family man drawing the curtains of his house lest the idea should be conveyed that he was intending to kiss his own wife or attempt something even more daring. Pennsylvania would not even permit scenes of women knitting baby garments.

By 1934, censorship in the United States was so strict that British producer Herbert Wilcox found that he could only get *Nell Gwynn* (GB 34) released in the US by shooting a special scene, solely for America, in which Charles II married the orange girl!

● The most belated film première took place at the Cinématheque Française, Paris, in April 1984 when the completed version of André Antoine's 64-year-old film about canal life, *L'Hirondelle et la Mésange* (Belgium 20), was presented for the first time.

The film had originally been shelved because distributor Charles Pathé disapproved of the rushes and refused to release it. Many years later, six hours of the unedited rushes were discovered in the State Film Archive and edited by Henri Colpi in a manner faithful to Antoine's style. The audience was totally captivated.

● The last Nazi epic film, *Kolberg*, was released in January 1945 when only a handful of cinemas were still operating in Berlin. Consequently, fewer people saw the film than actually appeared in it! The cast of 187 000 included entire army divisions diverted from the front on the orders of Goebbels.

● The only full-length feature film to be made without a camera was Barcelona artist Jose Antonio Sistiaga's 75-minute animation story *Scope, Colour, Muda*. Sistiaga was the only person working on the film which he made between October 1968 and February 1970 by painting each frame direct on to the film stock.

● For the first Tarzan film, *Tarzan of the Apes* (US 18), starring Elmo Lincoln, all of the apes were played by football players from the New Orleans Athletic Club dressed in ape costumes. But the lion in the film was real and, despite being sedated, it suddenly pounced on Lincoln. Seizing a knife from a spectator, he stabbed his feline co-star to death.

● Many films have misleading titles, among them the 1927 Rin Tin Tin vehicle, *Tracked by the Police*. The title was chosen by Warner before the script was even written. As it turned out on screen, Rin Tin Tin was the tracker with never a policeman in sight. *Thirteen Women* (US 32), the story of a half-caste girl who avenges her childhood racial abuse by murdering each of her now adult tormentors, has only ten women in it. Similarly, *Her Twelve Men* (US 54) saw Greer Garson as a schoolteacher at the head of a class of 13 pupils. *Roundup Time in Texas* (US 37) is about roundup time on the South African veldt; *Big Hand for a Little Lady* (US 66) was released in Britain as *Big Deal at Dodge City* yet was actually set in Laredo; and *Krakatoa, East of Java* (US 68) was a geographical howler. Krakatoa was 322 km (200 miles) west of Java.

● Blake Edwards's 1982 movie *The Trail of the Pink Panther* (GB) has the distinction of being the only film on which production began after the death of the star. It was assembled mainly from clips and out-takes from five earlier Pink Panther movies starring Peter Sellers (1925–80) as the hapless Inspector Clouseau. These were linked together by shots featuring an uncredited Sellers lookalike filmed from a distance or heavily disguised, and flashbacks to Clouseau's youth, using child actors. Sellers's widow Lynne Frederick was so horrified by the end result that she sought and won a multi-million dollar settlement for infringement of her late husband's contractual rights.

✳ Since dogs are colour blind, in Samuel Fuller's movie *White Dog* (US 84), the story of a dog trained to attack black people, all of the shots seen through the eyes of the dog were filmed in black and white.

FILM-MAKERS

● To ensure the accuracy of his 1934 epic, *Cleopatra* (US), **Cecil B. DeMille** (1881–1959) dispatched a team led by art director William Cameron Menzies to Egypt to study the colour of the Pyramids. The trip cost $100 000. Menzies visited a total of 92 pyramids and reported back to DeMille that the pyramids were indeed the colour expected – sandy brown. What made the expedition all the more pointless was that the film was to be in black and white.

● American newspaper magnate **William Randolph Hearst** (1863–1951) was smitten with chorus girl Marion Davies. They first met in 1914 when she was appearing in *The Movie Queen* at New York's Globe Theater. At the time he was 50 and she was just 14. She was to become his protégée as well as his mistress and he ordered that every Hearst newspaper was to mention her name at least once in every issue. This instruction was faithfully carried out for the next 30 years, long after Miss Davies had retired from the screen, but was rescinded within 24 hours of Hearst's death.

● After seeing a preview of the first Mickey Mouse movie in 1928, MGM boss **Louis B. Mayer** (1885–1957) flatly refused to put aspiring cartoonmaker Walt Disney under contract because he was convinced that pregnant women would be petrified by the sight of a 3 m (10 ft) high rodent on screen. Mayer doubtless took some comfort from the fact that in 1935 Romania banned Mickey Mouse because the character was said to be frightening children.

● When Austrian director **Erich von Stroheim** (1885–1957) made *The Merry-Go-Round* (US 23),

he had the guardsman extras dressed in pure silk underclothes monogrammed with the emblem of Austria's Imperial Guard. Although the garments were not visible, von Stroheim maintained that they helped the actors to feel part of the Hapsburg dynasty.

PERFORMERS

● **Lauren Bacall**'s voice had to be dubbed for the singing scenes in *To Have and Have Not* (US 44) but because she has such a deep speaking voice, no suitable female singer could be found. The problem was solved by using a male singer instead. So the voice heard coming from Lauren Bacall's lips is really that of Andy Williams!

✳ Mel Blanc (1908–89), who provided the voice for Bugs Bunny, was allergic to carrots.

● American actress **Marguerite Clark** (1881–1940) was not permitted to kiss on screen – an order given by her husband, Harry Palmerson-Williams, whom she married in 1918. At the time, Clark was Mary Pickford's principal rival as 'America's Sweetheart' but, although she made another dozen films, her career was severely damaged by the no-kissing clause and she retired in 1921. Another who was not allowed to be kissed on screen was actress **Evelyn Venable**. Her father had a clause to that effect inserted in her 1933 contract with Paramount. **Clara Bow** (1905–65) had it written into her contract with Paramount that none of the workmen or technicians was to use profane language in her presence. In return, Paramount insisted that she remain single and in 1926 offered her a $500 000 bonus on condition that she kept herself free of scandal during the tenure of the contract. She failed to collect. Cross-eyed **Ben Turpin** (1874–1940) was insured to the tune of $100 000 against the possibility of his eyes ever becoming normal again. In the early 1930s, RKO insured **Roscoe Ates** (1892–1962) against losing his trademark nervous stutter and in the same period, **Jimmy 'Schnozzle' Durante** (1893–1980) insured his famous nose for $100 000. In

1931, a Warner's contract ordered boxing fan **Vivienne Segal** not to yell at prize fights in case she strained her voice while **Maurice Chevalier**'s contract with Paramount, signed as talkies were being introduced, was rendered invalid if he ever lost his French accent!

● French leading lady **Claudette Colbert** insisted that sets be built around her so that she could make all her entrances with the right side of her face shielded from the camera. This was

Lauren Bacall's singing voice had to be dubbed by Andy Williams for the 1944 film *To Have and Have Not*

because her right side was apple-cheeked and the lights brought that out even more. She stipulated that any shots of her right profile must be long shots, never close-ups.

● American comedian **W.C. Fields** (1879–1946) was so worried about losing his cash that when-

ever he found himself with any loose change, he immediately opened a bank account. Among the pseudonyms he used were Figley E. Whitesides, Aristotle Hoop, Ludovic Fishpond and Cholmondley Frampton-Blythe. Fields never made any note of these accounts, a number of which are still believed to be open in the United States.

BIG BREAKS

✻ **Judy Garland** (1922–69) landed a contract at MGM by mistake. Louis B. Mayer saw 14-year-old Judy and 15-year-old Deanna Durbin in a 1936 short called *Every Sunday* and instructed an aide to 'Sign up that singer – the flat one.' He was referring to Durbin, who, on occasions could sound a trifle flat, but the aide misheard, thinking Mayer had said 'the fat one' and signed dumpy little Judy Garland.

✻ **Clark Gable** (1901–60) got his big break when, working as a telephone repair man, he came to mend the phone of drama coach Josephine Dillon. Gable broke off his engagement to another girl and married her. She took him under her wing and won him his first screen roles in films such as *The Merry Widow*, *The Plastic Age* and *North Star*.

✻ **Roscoe 'Fatty' Arbuckle** (1887–1933) got his first break due to a blocked drain. A plumber's mate, he was summoned to unblock producer Mack Sennett's pipes one day in 1913 and Sennett immediately offered the 120.6 kg (266 lb) Arbuckle a job in his Keystone Kops comedies

By 1919, Arbuckle was Hollywood's highest-paid star with a $1m contract, but within two years his career had been wrecked when he was charged with the manslaughter of 'good time girl' Virginia Rappe.

Arbuckle was acquitted but the adverse publicity hit him hard and in 1922 he became the first screen star to be banned by the newly established Motion Picture Producers and Distributors of America.

● **Joyce Grenfell** (1910–79), who specialized in the archetypal eccentric English spinster, was American on both sides of her family. Her mother was Nancy Astor's sister. Similarly, **Leslie Howard** (1890–1943), who personified the English gentleman in films, had Hungarian parents and was brought up speaking only German.

● The mother of child actor **Allen Clayton Hoskins** dressed him up as a girl to audition for the role of Farina in the Our Gang comedy films. The deception fooled producer Hal Roach, enabling Master Hoskins to appear in drag for two films in the series, *Boys Will Be Joys* and *Seeing Things*, both made in 1925. During that 12-month period, Hoskins also had to convince Roach of his femininity off-screen.

● At less than 1.75 m (5 ft 9 in) tall, American screen hero **Alan Ladd** (1913–64) presented a problem to the Hollywood studios. If his leading lady was tall, the studio countered the height difference either by ordering a trench to be dug for her to stand in during romantic scenes or by building a small platform for Ladd.

● Daredevil American silent film star **Harold Lloyd** (1893–1971) took to wearing gloves on screen after losing part of his hand, including thumb and forefinger, in a publicity stunt that went wrong. While shooting the 1920 movie *Haunted Spooks*, Lloyd posed for a publicity photograph with what he assumed to be a fake prop bomb when it suddenly proved to be only too real.

● The sexy bottom wiggle which became the trademark of **Marilyn Monroe** (1926–62) was caused by the fact that she had weak ankles and bandy legs. Turning these potential problems to her advantage, she further accentuated her walk by sawing a quarter of an inch (6 mm) off the right heel of all her shoes.

● Mexican romantic lead **Ramon Novarro** (1899–1968) ordered his house guests to wear nothing but black, white or silver to match the black fur and silver decor of his Frank Lloyd Wright-designed mansion.

● In the early 1950s, American dancer/comedian **Donald O'Connor** made six films with Francis the Talking Mule but handed over his leading role to Mickey Rooney when he learned that the mule was receiving more fan mail than him.

✳ Canine movie star **Rin Tin Tin** had a valet, a personal chef, a limousine and a chauffeur for his own exclusive use. He also had his own five-room dressing-room complex on the studio lot.

● **Lupe Velez** (1908–44), star of the Mexican Spitfire series of the early 1940s, possessed the ability to rotate her left breast while the other remained motionless. She could also counter-rotate it, a feat which her Australian co-star Leon Errol described as 'so supple and beautiful you couldn't believe your eyes'.

THE STAGE

● The shortest theatrical performance on record was Lord Lytton's play, *The Lady of Lyons*. Its first and last night took place at London's Shaftesbury Theatre on 26 December 1888. After waiting for an hour, the audience were sent home because nobody was able to raise the safety curtain. Barely more successful was *The Intimate Revue*, which opened (and closed) at London's Duchess Theatre on 11 March 1930. It was a calamity of errors from start to finish and with each scene change taking as long as 20 minutes, the management scrapped seven scenes in order to get the finale on before midnight. The run was described as 'half a performance'. In December 1983, the comedy *Bag* opened at Grantham, Lincolnshire, to an audience of nil, and in the same year, at the Edinburgh Festival Fringe, a production of *Ubu Roi* by the Freie Theateranstalt company from West Berlin closed after just 15 minutes of its sole performance. The show's director and star, Hermann van Harten, had intended the cast to include a pig as well as a number of parrots and cockatoos but had forgotten about the quarantine restrictions. The pig in particular was a key character since it played Ubu Roi's wife so an understudy porker was hastily acquired from the nearby East Lothian city farm.

Alas, its 'acting' left a lot to be desired and after a quarter of an hour, van Harten decided to abandon the rest of the show and give the audience their money back.

● At the Edinburgh Festival Fringe in 1981, the Bogan Club performed *2001* in the back of a Hillman Avenger car at venues around the city. The maximum audience for each performance was four. An even smaller theatre was that which seated an audience of just two – and that was only achieved by one perching on the other's lap. It was designed by Marcel Steiner in 1972 and built on a 650-cc Russian-made Neval motorcycle. Steiner once performed *The Tempest* in the car park of the Royal Shakespeare Theatre, Stratford-upon-Avon while the RSC was doing the same play inside. With some justification, it was called 'The Smallest Theatre in the World'.

✳ Spanish playwright Lope de Vega Carpio (1562–1635) claimed to have written 100 of his plays in less than a day each. In total, he wrote nearly 2000 plays plus 1500 lyric poems. Over the years, his daily output amounted to an average of 20 pages.

● *Hamlet* was performed without Hamlet at London's Richmond Theatre in 1787 when an inexperienced actor by the name of Cubit was too overcome to take the stage on the second night of the run. Among the audience was Scottish novelist Sir Walter Scott who concluded that his fellow spectators believed the play to be much improved without its central character.

● The curse of *Macbeth* is supposed to date from its first performance, 7 August 1606, when Hal Berridge, the boy actor who was to play Lady Macbeth, was stricken with fever only an hour before the performance was due to commence and died in the tiring-room in the middle of the play. Since then, it has been deemed bad luck to mention the play by name. It must always be referred to as 'The Scottish Play'. Also actors must never quote from *Macbeth* in the theatre dressing-room, the only antidote being to go outside, turn around three times, spit, knock on the door three times and beg admittance. There have been many examples of misfortune associated with *Macbeth*. In 1934, four different actors played the title role in the space of a week at the Old Vic – Malcolm Keen lost his voice; Alastair Sim went down with a bad chill; Marius Goring was sacked by director Lilian Baylis; and finally John Laurie took over. In 1954, on a tour of the play in Dublin, there was an attempted suicide, the company manager broke both legs and an electrician electrocuted himself. And in Cape Town, a stage-hand happened to mention the name of the play to a passing stranger. No sooner had he done so than a spear, poised high in the air on a crane, fell on to the stranger's head, killing him instantly.

● The writer of over 70 dramas, pantomimes, comic operas and farces, John O'Keefe (1747–1833) was blind from his late twenties and so on first nights his son would take him to the theatre pass-door in order that he could listen to the audience response. If hisses were heard, he would put his hands over his ears and would stay like that until his son tugged at his sleeve and said, 'Now father, listen again', an indication of a marked improvement in the audience reaction.

● Legendary American actor/director Orson Welles (1915–85) always wore a false nose on stage because he detested his own. During a production of *Moby Dick* at London's Duke of York's Theatre in July 1955, in which Welles played Captain Ahab, the nose began to fall apart during a major speech. 'Tell him his nose is falling off', hissed Kenneth Williams, who was playing Elijah, to Gordon Jackson (Ishmael). It was too late. By then, the nose was hanging over Welles's mouth. As he screamed: 'Get that white whale, men!', the nose dropped off completely and landed at his feet, a swift kick dispatching it into the stalls.

TELEVISION AND RADIO

● After breaking his ankle in a fall, actor Conrad Phillips who played the Swiss folk hero William Tell in the 1958 swashbuckler *The Adventures of William Tell*, had to play an entire episode from a wheelchair.

● The highest number of 'takes' for a television commercial is 28 by British *comediénne* Pat Coombs while endeavouring to promote a breakfast cereal in 1973. 'Every time we came to the punchline, I just could not remember the name of the product', she said five years later, still unable to recall the name. 'It was some sort of muesli but the name was practically unpronounceable.' The commercial was never finished. Pat Coombs might have derived some consolation from the knowledge that Marilyn Monroe did 59 'takes' of a scene from the 1959 film, *Some Like It Hot*. Her only line in the scene was, 'Where's the Bourbon?'

● In an episode of the comedy series *Dad's Army* (1968–77), Captain Mainwaring (played by Arthur Lowe) was supposed to have a bomb put down his trousers and Private Fraser (John Laurie) was meant to fish for it. Lowe strongly objected and told writer Jimmy Perry: 'I don't have bombs down my trousers and I'm certainly not having John Laurie's arm down my trousers.' The scene was rewritten with the bomb down Corporal Jones's trousers instead. After that, Lowe had a clause added to his contract which stated that he would not remove his trousers nor would he allow bombs to be put down them.

● The 1978 Yorkshire Television situation comedy, *Life Begins at Forty*, starring Derek Nimmo and Rosemary Leach, was sold to East Germany – not as comedy, but as part of their adult education programme to encourage people to have more babies.

● In September 1994, it was reported that plans to sell children's favourite Postman Pat to Japan had run into trouble because Pat only has three fingers on each hand. And the missing little finger is the sign of Japan's Mafia – the Yakuza – who have the finger amputated to show that they have strength of character and can be trusted. While negotiations were taking place to discuss whether Pat should acquire another finger before being translated into Japanese, a spokesman for the Japanese Embassy in London said: 'The amputated finger is an image which is very strongly linked with the Yakuza and I can imagine that a children's book dealer would be concerned'. But Max Rutherson, Japanese specialist at the auctioneers Sotheby's, countered: 'It is true the Yakuza do cut off their fingers, but Postman Pat hardly looks like a gangster. He doesn't even look as though he's amputated a finger. He just happens to have three.'

● An incompetent hairdresser on the 1970 detective series *Randall and Hopkirk (Deceased)* led to actor Kenneth Cope, who played the ghost of Marty Hopkirk, wearing his wig the wrong way round. It was the third episode before anyone spotted the error.

● In 1985 when the last episode of Jackie Collins's mini-series *Hollywood Wives* was inadvertantly transmitted in Britain with 15 crucial minutes missing, the absence of complaints to television company switchboards led observers to conclude that none of the 10 million viewers had noticed.

● A few minutes after 8 p.m. on Sunday 30 October 1938, a sombre voice interrupted an American radio broadcast to warn: 'Ladies and gentlemen, I have a grave announcement to make'. The voice went on to say that Martians had landed in New Jersey and were sweeping all before them. Little did the American public know that the announcement was part of a CBS radio production of H.G. Wells's *War of the Worlds*, presented by Orson Welles and his Mercury Theatre of the Air, and nothing more than a hoax designed to boost ratings. Although people were warned not to, they immediately panicked, particularly when hearing fake witnesses, many played by actor Joseph Cotten, recounting how thousands had been killed by Martians' death-rays. The programme ended with an announcer shouting hysterically from the top of the CBS building that Manhattan was being overrun. His commentary tailed off in a strangled scream. By now, the roads of New Jersey were jammed with cars heading for the hills. Many fled from their homes with wet towels on their heads in the belief that this might protect them from the nauseous space gases they had heard about. Restaurants emptied in New York and in the Deep South, women prayed in the streets. Marines were recalled to their ships in New York harbour, ready to defend the nation against the Martian invaders. When the hoax was revealed, Welles was not a popular man. Dozens of people filed lawsuits against CBS but all were subsequently withdrawn.

The closest British counterpart, an altogether more harmless ruse, was carried out on an edition of the high-brow current affairs programme *Panorama* on 1 April 1957. Viewers saw presenter Richard Dimbleby reporting on a bumper spaghetti harvest in southern Switzerland, walking between spaghetti-laden trees as farmworkers loaded the crops into baskets. Hundreds of people rang the BBC, wanting to know where they could obtain spaghetti plants. Producer Michael Peacock informed them that listeners should plant a small tin of spaghetti in tomato sauce.

5

BUILDINGS AND STRUCTURES

CASTLES, PALACES AND STATELY HOMES

● Prince Michael Alexievich Golitsyn had infuriated Anna Ivanovna, Empress of All the Russians, by marrying an Italian Roman Catholic. The girl died soon after the wedding and, as punishment, the Empress ordered the Prince to marry again – this time to an ugly serving wench. In a further act of spite, the Empress ordered an ice palace to be built for their wedding night in St Petersburg. In the winter of 1740, architect Peter Eropkin designed a vast ice palace, 24.4 m (80 ft) long, 10 m (33 ft) high, 7 m (23 ft) deep, complete with towers, a ballroom and a bedroom. Inside the bedroom was a four-poster bed with mattress, a quilt and two pillows, all carved out of ice. In the grounds, ice birds, painted in their natural colours, perched in sculpted ice trees and the figure of an ice-man in Persian costume sat on top of a full-size ice elephant. A 7.3 m (24 ft) spout of water jetted from the elephant's trunk during the day. At night, it was replaced by petroleum so that the elephant spouted flame. There were also six ice cannons. The ice used in the various constructions was selected for its transparency and each block was carefully measured before being cut

and lifted into position. The only thing not made of ice was the wooden fence around the palace. After the wedding, the Prince and his unlikely bride suffered the humiliation of being publicly bedded down in the frozen bed chamber. When spring came, the ice palace melted. The Empress died later that year. Ironically the odd couple stayed married.

● The most unusual police station in Britain is at 15th-century **Kirby Muxloe Castle** in Leicestershire. Lord Hastings began work on the castle in 1480 but his execution three years later on the orders of King Richard III ensured that the building would never be completed. Over 500 years later, PC Charles Staniforth of Leicestershire Constabulary suggested to English Heritage that the old custodians' office, which was originally intended to be the porter's room, would make an ideal beat office. It would also allow him to keep an eye on the castle in case of vandalism. So on 6 September 1994, PC Staniforth officially took up residence at Kirby Muxloe.

● Known as the Dream King, Ludwig II of Bavaria lived in a fairytale world of myths and legends (see p. 8). At the age of 18, Ludwig first

Left The House in the Clouds at Thorpeness (see p. 91)

heard the music of Richard Wagner and set himself up as Wagner's patron. Ludwig decided to build a castle to stage Wagner's then little-known operas, taking the theme for the building from the operas and the German legends which inspired them. The result was **Neuschwanstein Castle**, designed by a Munich scene painter and perched high on a crag in the Bavarian Alps. Completed in 1881, it took 17 years to build, although some areas, including the throne room, were never finished. With its magical towers, turrets and lofty spires, Neuschwanstein was a natural role model for Walt Disney to copy when he created Disney World.

● Ferdinand Cheval, a French postman, drew the inspiration for his miniature **Palais Idéal** at Hautrives from a chance encounter with a stone. One day he stubbed his toe on a stone and nearly fell. 'The offending stone was of such an unusual shape,' he said, 'that I picked it up and took it with me. Seeing that nature displays itself as a sculpture, I said to myself, I shall become a mason and an architect.' His palace of pebbles stands 25.9 m (85 ft) wide, 7.9 m (26 ft) deep and 10 m (33 ft) high and took him 33 years to build between 1879 and 1912.

● William John Cavendish Bentinck Scott, the Fifth Duke of Portland, was so horrified by daylight that from 1860 he built 25 km (15 miles) of tunnel under **Welbeck Abbey** in Nottinghamshire.

He built a vast complex of underground rooms, including what was then, at 53 m (174 ft) long, the biggest ballroom in the country, a 75 m (250 ft) library, a billiard room large enough to accommodate 12 tables, and a glass-roofed riding school known as Tan Gallop which measured 117 m × 34 m (385 ft × 112 ft) and was 16 m (52 ft) high (this has now been demolished). One tunnel, measuring 2 km (1.25 miles) long, extended from the Duke's coach-house to the town of Worksop, thus enabling him to come and go in secrecy whenever he wanted to catch the train to London. The tunnel was wide enough to take two carriages and was illuminated at night by hundreds of gas jets.

The Duke, who died in 1879, never invited anyone to his home. Only his valet was allowed near him. In the event of illness, the doctor had to wait outside while the valet took the Duke's pulse. The doors of each room in the house had double letter-boxes, one for incoming and one for outgoing notes.

CHURCHES AND CATHEDRALS

● Fleeing from persecution, Christians in the Cappadocia region of Turkey hollowed out volcanic rocks to make tiny churches and monasteries. Over 350 churches have been carved out of volcanic tufa in the Goreme Valley, ranging in date from the 7th century to the late 13th century. Some have been carved from rock cones 50 m (164 ft) high and most have elaborate architectural features, decorated with geometric or pictorial frescoes.

● The 14th-century twisted spire of the **Parish Church of Our Lady and All Saints** at Chesterfield in Derbyshire has warped from the perpendicular as a result of its lead and timber covering. When last measured, the 228 ft (69.5 m) high spire had a lean of 8 ft 7¾ in (2.63 m) to the south, 9 ft

5⅜ in (2.87 m) to the south-west and 3 ft 9½ in (1.2 m) to the west. The problems arose when the church was being built. At the time the Black Death was raging and many skilled craftsmen died. The survivors were inept at seasoning wood and for the spire used green timbers which over the years have distorted under the pressure of the heavy lead covering. The 13th-century church at Ermington in Devon also boasts a twisted spire but the corkscrew effect is by no means as pronounced.

● Built in 1962, the **United States Air Force Academy Chapel** at Colorado Springs, Colorado, is made up of 17 aluminium spires pointing to the sky. The spires consist of 100 tetrahedrons, each 75 ft (22.8 m) long, and the spaces between the spires are filled with stained-glass strips in 24 colours. The chapel was designed by Walter Netsche. From the front, it resembles hands in prayer; from the side, it looks like an army parade ground, the regiment in perfect step.

● The $20 million **Crystal Cathedral** near Los Angeles, California, is made entirely from glass except for white steel trusses and wooden fittings. It was built in 1980 at the behest of American TV evangelist Robert Schuller whose preaching career had begun 25 years earlier in a disused drive-in cinema. The cathedral, which is made from over 10 000 panes of glass, is designed in the shape of a four-cornered star and creates an impressive backdrop for the weekly cable television programme delivered from its pulpit.

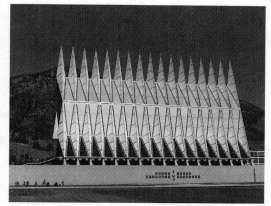

A regiment in perfect step – the US Air Force Academy Chapel at Colorado Springs, USA

● Nestling in a hollow at Daymer Bay, North Cornwall, 13th-century **St Enodoc Church** was once almost completely submerged in sand. During the early 19th century, strong winds off the sea whipped inland and buried the church up to its roof. Locals called it the 'sinkininny church', in the belief that the church was sinking. The only method of entry was through the north transept roof, a feat performed by the vicar every Christmas to keep his stipend (ecclesiastical law stated that a vicar had to enter his church at least once

a year). The church was eventually dug out from the sands in 1863.

● The **Floating Church of the Redeemer for Seamen** was built in New York in 1851 and could only be reached by boat. Floating on the twin hulls of two clipper ships off the coast at Philadelphia, its wooden exterior was painted to resemble brown stone while the interior was large enough to accommodate a bishop's throne.

Today a 32.9 m (108 ft) long boat, the *Cristo Rey*, serves as a church on the Rio Parana in Argentina. The **Church of San Fedelino** on the Mera River at Novata Mezzola in Italy is built on land but is also accessible only by boat. Its island site was selected in the 3rd century as a safeguard against persecution by the legions of Roman Emperor Maximianus.

● Designed by P.V. Jensen-Klint, the facade of **Grundtvig Church** in Copenhagen, Denmark, is built to resemble mighty organ-pipes which rise to 30 m (98 ft) high. Viewed from the front, the church, which was built from 6000 yellow bricks, has tiny portals and a sheer brick wall, topped by organ-pipe-like climbing gables. Building began in 1921 and was eventually finished in 1940 by Klint's son Kaare following his father's death.

● The 750-year-old **Church of St George** in the Ethiopian village of Lalibela is built vertically downwards. It has been cut out of the rock in the shape of a cross and is surrounded by a trench. The top of the church is flush with ground level as if it had been dropped into a hole. There are 11 other curious churches in the area, either sunk into the ground or tunnelled into hillsides. It is said that King Lalibela, after whom the village is named, spent all his wealth on the creation of these places of worship.

● Swiss architect Charles-Edouard Jeanneret, better known as Le Corbusier (1887–1965), was principally noted for his box-like designs. But his **Chapel of Notre-Dame-du-Haut** at Ronchamp in France was a great departure of style, as much a sculpture as a building. Built between 1950 and 1954, the chapel has a roof shaped in the bold curve of a ship's bow. It was designed as a pilgrimage church but the interior is so small (seating only 50 people) that any sizeable group of pilgrims must remain outside. To accommodate them, a pulpit and altar were built on an outside wall.

● In the 14th century, the adjoining villages of Reepham, Whitwell and Hackford in Norfolk were each determined to have their own church. So three parish churches were built – all in the same churchyard. Only two stand today, **All Saints, Hackford,** having been virtually destroyed by fire in 1543. The damaged tower was demolished in 1790, leaving just a ruined arch. The other two, **St Mary's, Reepham,** and **St Michael's Whitwell,** are joined by a common vestry. The former now serves the three parishes and although St Michael's remains consecrated, it is chiefly used as a village hall.

Another English village with two churches in one churchyard is **Swaffham Prior** in Cambridgeshire. Swaffham Prior was once divided between the Prior of Ely and a group of knights from Brittany. Ely staked first claim and in the 12th century had the Church of St Mary's built there. Around 1250, the French decided to build a second church, SS Cyriac and Julietta. By 1667, it was realized that the presence of two churches was unnecessary so the nave of St Cyriac's was demolished, leaving just the bell tower. Then, in 1767, St Mary's was struck by lightning and, rather than carry out expensive repairs, a plain Georgian church was built on to the old St Cyriac's tower. However, this did not prove a success and St Mary's was restored after all.

● In 1883, Spanish architect Antonio Gaudi (1852–1926) assumed responsibility for the design of a large church in Barcelona – **La Sagrada Familia** (Church of the Holy Family). It had already been started as a conventional neo-Gothic building but Gaudi promptly abandoned these plans and came up with a fantastic design of his own, a startling mix of Gothic and Art Nouveau. Around the church were to be 18 pointed towers 115 m (375 ft) high with, at the centre, a great tower 170 m (557 ft) high. Gaudi intended the towers to symbolize the 12 apostles, the four evangelists, the Virgin Mary and, the tallest of all, Christ himself. He saw the church's three facades as representing the birth, death and resurrection of Christ. He also envisaged three sets of bell towers topped by stone statues of cherubim with wings that moved in the wind. To provide the intricate decoration he desired, Gaudi employed sculptor Lorenzo Matamala to create a series of ornate carvings in the huge concavities below the gables of the towers. All of the sculptures are connected by curved surfaces so that the overall effect is one of cladding. Many of the sculptures depict plants and animals, others convey the childhood of Christ. All are based on life models, the inhabitants of Barcelona being picked to match their biblical counterparts. A Roman soldier featured in a tableau depicting the Massacre of the Innocents was modelled on a local waiter. Even the birds Gaudi chose were killed and then arranged into position for the sculptor to copy. But Gaudi's ideas were too ambitious and, as yet, his masterpiece remains unfinished. There are those who doubt that it ever will be.

● The world's smallest church is the chapel of **Santa Isabel de Hungria** in Colomares, a monument to Christopher Columbus at Benalmadena, Malaga, Spain. It is an irregular shape and has a total floor area of just 1.95 sq m (21⅛ sq ft). St Gobban's Church in Port Braddan, County Antrim, Northern Ireland is also on the small side, measuring 3.66 m × 1.98 m (12 ft 1½ in × 6 ft 6 in).

● The **Temppeliaukio** or Taivallahti Church in Helsinki, Finland, is sunk into a rock crater. It was designed by brothers Timo and Tuomo Suomalainen for an architectural competition in 1969. Also known as the Underground Church, its interior walls were blasted from bedrock and it has a dome 13.1 m (43 ft) high. This is the only part of the church visible from outside. The dome is made from 22 km (13.7 miles) of copper woven into a ribbon-like pattern. The church's setting gives it superb acoustics and makes it a popular venue for concerts.

COMMERCIAL BUILDINGS

● James Wines's disaster-based designs for the exteriors of **BEST stores** changed the face of supermarket shopping in the United States. In 1977, Wines and his colleagues at SITE (Sculpture In The Environment) created a sliding wall for the BEST store at Sacramento, California. Every morning when the door slides open for shoppers, it takes part of the building with it – 45 tonnes of jagged-edged engineering brick. The result is an alarmingly realistic re-creation of the aftermath of an earthquake. The break follows the angle of a crack which might occur in an earthquake and a few bricks have been cleverly removed near the point of 'impact'. Two years earlier, Wines had designed a crumbling wall facade for the BEST store at Houston, Texas. The front resembles a demolition site as a cascade of bricks pours down on to the entrance canopy, directly above the heads of the shoppers. Wines's first attempt had been at the BEST store in Richmond, Virginia, in 1972. Using special adhesive mortar, he created a brick wall which appears to be peeling away from the main concrete body.

Camelot Las Vegas style courtesy of the Excalibur Hotel (see p. 88)

● One of the finest examples of Australian kitsch is the **Big Pineapple**, a 16 m (52½ ft) high fibreglass pineapple overlooking the Sunshine Plantation near Nambour, Queensland. It serves as a visitor centre and has two floors of audio-visual displays which tell the story of the pineapple and other tropical fruit. It also contains a Polynesian-style restaurant, a tropical market and an observation area. In the same district lurk a 9.1 m (30 ft) high dairy cow, an enormous bottle of beer and an outsize lawnmower.

Further south at Coffs Harbour, New South Wales, the centre of Australia's biggest banana-growing region, is the **Big Banana** tourist complex where visitors are greeted by the sight of a 9.7 m (32 ft) long fibreglass banana. Inside the fruit are displays on the banana industry.

Another fibreglass monster towers by the roadside at Kingston, South Australia. This is **Larry the Big Lobster**, a fibreglass and steel monument to the town's major industry – rock-lobster fishing. Sheep have not been forgotten either. At Goulburn, New South Wales in the heart of sheep country, stands a 14.93 m (49 ft) high **Big Merino** with green eyes which glow ominously at night. By day, visitors can clamber inside the three-storey ram to see an exhibition on wool or watch a sheep show. In the same state, near Wauchope, is 'the world's biggest fibreglass bull', housing educational displays, an animal nursery and a restaurant. Beef is a popular item on the menu.

● Built to house the Free School of Spiritual Science, the Goetheanum at Dornach, Switzerland, is a massive concrete structure in the Expressionist style. It was designed by Rudolf Steiner who, in 1915 with Alfred Hilliger, built a bizarre boiler house near the main building. They shaped the boiler house like a tree, the rising smoke symbolizing the growth of the tree through its trunk and buds.

● Clifford E. Clinton founded his first **Clifton's Cafeteria** in 1931 in downtown Los Angeles. He called the second, which opened on Broadway in 1935, 'Brookdale' and gave the interior a forest effect. His most ambitious undertaking came four years later after a holiday in Hawaii. He immediately turned his restaurant on Olive Street, Los

Angeles, into a tropical paradise called 'Pacific Seas'. An exterior cement stucco over steel and wire mesh gave the impression of huge boulders. A waterfall rippled down the centre of the facade and, instead of windows on the second floor, he inserted tropical plants which trailed down to street level.

● In the heart of 'Crocodile Dundee' country near Ayers Rock in Australia's Northern Territory sits a new complex called the **Crocodile Hotel**. The entire building is shaped like a crocodile. The 'eyes' stick out from the reception hall, the rooms run along the 'body' to the 'tail' and the swimming pool is situated in its 'alimentary canal'.

● Lucy, a 19.5 m (65 ft) high concrete elephant weighing 90 tonnes, was built at Margate, New Jersey, United States, in 1881 by James V. Lafferty as a real-estate promotion. Much loved by the locals, she went on to become a tavern, and later

the six-storey **Elephant Hotel**, the staircases in each of her legs leading to the main rooms. She is now a national historic landmark.

● The **Excalibur Hotel and Casino** in Las Vegas, Nevada, opened in April 1990 at a cost of $290 million. Architect Veldon Simpson based his design on the theme of King Arthur, Camelot and the Knights of the Round Table and gave the hotel a centrepiece in the shape of a towered castle. The hotel stands on a 117-acre site and has over 4000 rooms.

● The £38-a-night **Ice Hotel** at Jukkasjarvi, Swedish Lapland, offers the ultimate in cold comfort – a building constructed out of ice where the average room temperature is –4°C. The beds are made from packed snow topped with spruce boughs and reindeer skins. A team of axe-wielding sculptors and artists have created ten rooms to accommodate up to 60 people, out of 2000 tonnes of snow and 1500 tonnes of ice. Many

Lucy the New Jersey elephant which measures 65 ft (19.5 m) long. The reception area is in her hind legs

rooms have individual themes. For 1994, there was a fisherman's room with an aquarium of sculpted ice fish and a hunt room featuring ice carvings of elk, wolves and bears. Guests are advised to book early since the hotel melts every April and has to be rebuilt the following winter. 'It started five years ago as an art gallery,' says creator and director Yngve Bergqvist. 'Now we have a hotel, restaurant, a cinema and an ice sauna.' The original hotel measured some 60 sq m (645 sq ft) but has grown considerably each winter. The ice complex even boasts a small sub-zero chapel for christenings and weddings, the perfect place to say 'I d-d-d-d-do'.

● Eero Saarinen designed **Ingalls Hockey Rink** at Yale University, New Haven, Connecticut, in the shape of a whale. The 'dorsal fin' undulates in the roof and under its black 'nose', the 'mouth' opens for 3000 spectators. Built in 1957, the building is known locally as the 'Whale at Yale'.

● **Jules Undersea Lodge** is an underwater hotel, five fathoms down in Bora Lagoon in the Florida Keys. A converted underwater research station, it has a restaurant and two rooms, both with private baths, and can cater for six guests at a time. It takes reservations a year in advance. An added amenity in the rooms is a giant porthole to enable guests to observe passing fish.

● Supposedly built by Squire George Ley (who died in 1716) to celebrate a gambling win, the **Pack o' Cards** public house in Combe Martin, Devon, certainly lives up to its name. It has 52 windows (the number of cards in a pack), four main floors (the number of suits) and 13 doors on the ground floor (the number of cards per suit). Many of the windows were later blocked up to escape paying window tax.

● Whereas other buildings have their functional elements tucked away on the inside, the **Pompidou Centre** at Beaubourg in Paris has them boldly displayed on the exterior. They are painted in the colours of the French Tricolore — red for the lift housing, white for the ventilation extracts and blue for other mechanical equipment.

The walls themselves are made of glass, built on a steel frame. An escalator also climbs up the building on the outside. French President Pompidou had the idea for creating a home for the arts in 1969 and, two years later, a design competition attracted 681 entries. The winning architects were Richard Rogers and Renzo Piano. Their building was completed in 1977 and has a total floor area of 107 000 sq m (1 150 000 sq ft). It is 165 m (540 ft) long, 42 m (136 ft) high and 60 m (195 ft) deep.

● A floating cinema was introduced in the United States in 1907 on the Erie Canal between Troy and Newark. Called the **Star Floating Palace**, it was a converted canal boat which gave shows at the towns along the canal.

● At the end of a quiet road in Stoke Newington, North London, stands a mighty fortress which serves as the local pumping station. It is built like a castle with huge turrets of varying shapes and sizes. There is a different design of tower at each corner. The architect was William Chadwell Mylne who, between 1854 and 1856, created it as something of a parting gift to the water company. Having already worked for the company for 43 years, he concluded that they could never actually sack him and so allowed his imagination to run riot.

● The most unlikely place to find an imitation of the Doge's Palace in Venice is an old carpet factory on Glasgow Green. The **Templeton Carpet Factory** was built between 1889 and 1892. It has a multi-coloured brick facade with tiles inlaid to simulate mosaics in brilliant reds and blues. It is a curious mix of styles. A medieval oriel window stands above an Arabic-style arch while a circular tower at one corner is juxtaposed with an octagonal tower at the next. Between the two, stands a bartizan, a form of turret. During construction, part of the building collapsed, killing 29 women working in the weaving sheds below. The building has now been converted into offices.

FOLLIES

● The **Ammerdown Park Column** is a 150 ft (45.7 m) replica of the Eddystone lighthouse. Yet it is situated 27 miles (43.5 km) inland at Kilmersdon in Somerset. Designed by Joseph Jopling to commemorate 'the genius, the energy and the brilliant talents' of Thomas Samuel Jolliffe (Lord Hylton, a descendant of Jolliffe's, had the original idea for the column), it was completed on 6 June 1853. Why Jopling chose a replica of the Eddystone remains a mystery.

● Built by wealthy solicitor Frank Crisp in 1896, the estate of Friar Park, perched on a hilltop above Henley-on-Thames in Oxfordshire, boasts many unusual features but none more startling than the 30 m (100 ft) high model of the Matterhorn which towers over surrounding trees. The replica is constructed from 20 000 tonnes of millstone grit and is topped by a piece of rock taken from the summit of the Matterhorn itself. So determined was Crisp to ensure accuracy that he forced his hapless head gardener, a Mr P.O. Knowles, to reconstruct the mountain several times.

Beneath his man-made mountain, Crisp dug a series of electrically illuminated caves linked by an underground river. Each cave was given its own theme. The Vine Cave was festooned with huge branches of glass grapes, the Ice Cave was decorated with blue icicles and a Chinese stork while the Gnome Cave was home to hundreds of garden gnomes. By the time the estate was purchased by Beatle George Harrison in 1969, some of the attractions had fallen into decay but he has successfully restored it to its former glory.

● High on the slopes of Bathwick Hill near Bath stands a sham castle. It is nothing more than a facade, with just one 12 m (40 ft) high, 30 m (100 ft) long wall consisting of two semi-circular round towers, a central gatehouse and square towers at either end. With blank windows and arrowslits, it looks blindly out over Bath. The idea for the 'castle' came from Ralph Allen, a local quarrymaster, and it was designed and built in 1762 by Richard Jones, Allen's clerk of works.

● Around 1863, the Metropolitan Railway wanted to drive its line through Leinster Terrace, Bayswater, a typical West London terrace. The authorities were keen to preserve the unity of the terrace but realized that the new line would create an unsightly gap between nos 22 and 25. The line went ahead as planned but nos 23 and 24 remained. The rear of the houses was demolished leaving just the facades propped up by heavy timbers – they still remain today.

● When the Buckinghamshire city of Milton Keynes was created in 1967, the local authorities were anxious to incorporate a green belt through the heavily built-up areas. So in a field at Bradwell, an area surrounded by roundabouts, dual carriageways and housing estates, they erected four Friesian cows and two calves made of ferro-concrete.

● An old custom in the Dalarna region of Sweden was carving wooden horses in winter which were then painted and sold in spring to augment the family income. The craft continues today with bright red the traditional colour. Standing by the roadside at the town of Avesta, dwarfing surrounding buildings and cars and painted a glowing red, is the world's biggest Dala horse, 13 m (43 ft) high, made not from wood but cast in iron and concrete.

● The 14th Lord Berners lived at Faringdon House in Oxfordshire. In 1935, he built **Faringdon Folly**, a 140 ft (42.7 m) tower designed by Trenwith Wells and Lord Gerald Wellesley. Locals complained that it would spoil the view but, undaunted, Lord Berners held a splendid opening ceremony on 5 November 1935, marked by a firework display and the release of hundreds of doves dyed red, white and blue. When asked about the purpose of the folly, he replied: 'The great point of the tower is that it will be entirely useless.' He then put a notice on it which read: 'Members of the public committing suicide from this tower do so at their own risk'.

90

● In 1795, William Beckford (see p. 12) employed a team of labourers to build a huge folly called **Fonthill Abbey** on the family estate near Hindon in Wiltshire. He wanted it to reach a height of 300 ft (91 m) to compete with the spire of Salisbury Cathedral. But Beckford was impatient and refused to wait for proper foundations to be dug, insisting that those which had already been laid for a small summer house would suffice. Ignoring the architect's plans and the protests of the builders, he pressed ahead relentlessly, boasting that he would soon be living in the tallest private residence in England. The 500 labourers worked day and night. To encourage them in their work, Beckford increased their ale ration with the result that many were too drunk to know what they were doing. Five years later, the building was still not finished. Increasingly frustrated, Beckford was determined to eat Christmas dinner there but the kitchens were by no means ready. The beams had not been secured and the mortar was not yet dry. As Beckford dined, the kitchens caved in around him and had to be rebuilt. In 1801, the Abbey was finally completed – or so it seemed. For at the first gust of wind, the tower swayed, crumbled and crashed to the ground. Beckford immediately ordered the construction of a new tower on the rubble of the old. Additional stone was brought in to strengthen it and, after another seven years' hard labour, Beckford's dream was realized. By then, however, it seemed that he had tired of it, for in 1822 he sold it. In retrospect, it was one of his wiser moves for one night in 1825, another gale sent the whole thing tumbling down again.

● Landowner, playwright and barrister G. Stuart Ogilvie had already disguised a water tower at Sizewell Court, Suffolk, as a dovecote in 1908 when he decided to repeat the idea on a grander scale at Thorpeness, 1.6 km (1 mile) further down the coast. Here he set about disguising a 18 m (60 ft) water tower by turning it into a five-storey house called 'The Gazebo'. At the top of the tower, the 136 400 litre (30 000 gallon) water tank was cleverly concealed as an ordinary clapboard house with a pitched roof, chimneys and sham windows. Early tenants were Mr and Mrs Malcolm Mason. She penned children's poems and one, inspired by her new residence, was called 'The House in the Clouds'. When she recited it to Ogilvie one evening, he was so enchanted that he insisted that the name of the building be changed from 'The Gazebo' to **'The House in the Clouds'**.

> ✳ **The Jungle** at Eagle in Lincolnshire has the facade of a ruined, uninhabitable-looking castle, behind which stands a perfectly normal modern house. Designed by Russell Collett in the 1820s and built by Thomas Lovely, the facade is made up of jagged outlines, burnt brick, thick creeper and rusticated stone. Collett used to keep kangaroos, buffalo and deer in the grounds – hence it being called The Jungle.

● Henry Hoare II, a member of the famous banking family, was an ardent royalist. So when he created a mansion and gardens at Stourhead in Wiltshire, he decided to include a tribute to constitutional monarchy. He sought initially to build a replica of St Mark's Tower, Venice, but amended his plans to a 160 ft (48.7 m) tall triangular folly tower in memory of King Alfred who, in 870, had raised his standard against Danish invaders on the same spot. The folly, which took six years to build from 1766 to 1772, is all brick apart from ten tiny stair-turret windows.

● Banker and self-styled art critic John Stewart McCaig was a much-travelled individual. Many of his jaunts took him to Italy and, on his return, he always considered it his duty to impart his learning to others less fortunate than himself, notably the humble fishermen of Oban in Scotland. McCaig had already addressed the Oban Young Men's Free Church Mutual Improvement Society when, in the last decade of the 19th century, he hit upon the idea of recreating the glory that was Rome on the west coast of Scotland. He set about building a copy of the Colosseum which, he reasoned, would not only give work to the town's unemployed masons but would also serve as a museum and art gallery. He also planned to erect a tower and statues of famous Obanites. His replica of the outer wall of the Colosseum was stunningly inaccurate. McCaig's version had pointed Gothic arches

McCaig Tower, Oban

McCaig's replica of the Colosseum at Oban

instead of round. A total of £5000 was spent on the project but when McCaig died with only the shell built, everybody lost interest. Work was abandoned and **McCaig's Folly**, as it became known, is now just a huge blackened cylinder overlooking the town. Far from housing the arts, it encloses a public garden.

● In 1738, landowner Charles Hamilton bought the estate at Painshill, Cobham, Surrey. He created a 400-acre park, modelling it on romantic Italian paintings. He built numerous follies, among them a stucco and wood Gothic temple, a Chinese bridge, a temple of Bacchus made from papier mâché, an octagonal Turkish tent, a medieval gazebo, a castle tower, a ruined abbey and a great Roman arch. But the one thing he felt would add that extra something to his park was a hermitage. So he created one in a dark secluded dell and immediately advertised for a suitable tenant. The hermit would be supplied with a mat on which to sleep, a hassock for resting his head and praying, a Bible, a pair of optical glasses, and an hourglass as a timepiece. Food and water would be brought from the house. In return, Hamilton laid down strict ground rules. The hermit had to agree to stay there for seven years, never speaking to the servants or straying beyond the boundary of Painshill. He also had to be willing to wear a camel's hair robe and would not be permitted to cut his hair, beard or nails. If the hermit stayed for the full seven years without breaking any of the rules, he would be paid the sum of £700. One hermit did commence occupation but gave up after three weeks.

● One of the great mysteries of British architecture stands in Dunmore Park in the Central region of Scotland. The bottom part of the building in question is ordinary enough – a small octagonal tower – but from the tops of the columns sprout stone, spiky leaves and the tower is transformed into a 16.1 m (53 ft) high pineapple. Each of the gently curving leaves are drained separately so as to prevent the masonry being damaged by frost. **The Pineapple** was built in 1761 at the request of 29-year-old John Murray, Fourth Earl of Dunmore, for reasons known only to himself. One suggestion is that he had it built as a summer house in which to entertain his bride of two years.

● On the banks of remote Rivington Reservoir in Lever Park, Lancashire, some 32 km (20 miles) from Merseyside is a sham ruin replica of Liverpool Castle. The real Liverpool Castle was demolished in 1720 but soapmaker Lord Leverhulme ordered work to begin on a full-size copy nearly 200 hundred years later in 1916. It had still to be completed by the time his Lordship died in 1925. In 1927, the Second Lord Leverhulme wrote of the roofless folly: 'Already the newness is wearing off . . . the uninitiated will not know that the replica is not a genuine ruin.'

● 'Mad Jack' Fuller (1757–1834) lived up to his name. The Sussex MP, who weighed 140 kg (308 lb) and was in the habit of drinking three bottles of port a day, was prone to making rash wagers. One such bet was made with a neighbour. Fuller insisted that from his home at Rose Hill, he could see the spire of Dallington church 1.6 km (1 mile) away. The distance was not the problem, more the fact that the church lay completely hidden from view in a valley. But Fuller was not one to lose a bet. So he hastily arranged for a 12 m (40 ft) high cone-shaped folly, subsequently called the Sugar Loaf, to be erected to look just like a distant church spire peeping over a hill. Such was the speed of its construction that it was described as 'nothing more than stones held together by mud'. It was later restored.

● The **Tattingstone Wonder** in Suffolk was built in 1761 by Thomas Squire White of Tattingstone Place. His father had built Tattingstone Place some 40 years earlier but the son decided to liven up the view from the house by creating an ecclesiastical eyecatcher, a fake church tower set on the roof of the end terrace of three farmworkers' cottages. The tower only has three walls but is sufficient to convince observers from the Place that it is the genuine article.

● Perched in a lime tree in the grounds of Pitchford Hall, Shropshire, is a miniature version of the 16th-century Hall. The exact date of the Tree House on stilts is unknown but it is believed to have nestled in the branches of that same lime tree for some 300 years. In 1980, it was restored to its original timbered exterior.

● A rival to Welbeck Abbey's underground tunnels (see p. 91) is the underwater ballroom at Witley Park near Godalming, Surrey, built at the turn of the century by financier and self-made millionaire Whitaker Wright. He spent £1 250 000 on improving the estate, including the construction of four lakes. In the middle of one lake, he created a small oblong island. Stairs leading directly down from the island are connected via a 400 ft (122 m) long tunnel to an 80 ft (24.4 m) high domed ballroom, built from iron and glass and cut out beneath the lake. As a break from the military two-step, dancers can observe fish swimming past. In 1904, Wright was sentenced to seven years' imprisonment for fraud but before he could be taken from the Old Bailey to begin his spell of confinement, he committed suicide by swallowing cyanide. The house at Witley Park was gutted by fire in 1952 but the underwater ballroom still remains.

HOME FROM HOME

● Occasionally, buildings arise in parts of the world far removed from their origins. Built in the 1870s, **Abercrombie House** near Orange in New South Wales is a faithful copy of a Dumfriesshire hunting lodge owned by the Duke of Buccleuch.

● At Blickling Hall in Norfolk stands a 15 m (49 ft) pyramid, the mausoleum of John, Second Earl of Buckinghamshire, and his two wives. The pyramid was built by Ignatius's Bonomi in 1794. Ignatius's brother Joseph also embraced Egyptian architecture and built the Marshall Mill, a Leeds flax mill, in the style of an Egyptian temple. The mill's flat roof used to be covered with soil for insulation whereupon the owner, John Marshall, had grass sown on to the roof and put a flock of sheep up there to graze.

Another example of Egyptian architecture in England is the **Egyptian House** at Penzance in Cornwall. The fashion for the Egyptian style was fuelled by Napoleon's campaigns in that country, and in about 1835 Plymouth architect John Foulston designed what was almost an exact copy of the 1812 Egyptian Hall that stood in London's Piccadilly. The Penzance house has a doorway flanked by lotus columns, above which are two staring, sphinx-like ladies. The building was originally intended to be a geological museum but has subsequently become The National Trust headquarters for the area.

● In 1783, the Prince Regent decided to rent a small farmhouse in Brighton to entertain his friends in private. Within four years, he asked architect Henry Holland to create something on a grander scale. Still not satisfied, in 1815 the Prince employed another architect, John Nash, to make further changes, giving the building an oriental flavour as a monument to Britain's connections with the Far East. Nash turned Holland's building into a magnificent domed palace, a mixture of Hindu, Gothic and Chinese. When the **Brighton Pavilion** was completed in 1822, the dragon chandelier in the Chinese room was the largest in the world, measuring 9.1 m (30 ft) and weighing one tonne.

✴ What is supposed to be the home of Captain James Cook (1728–79) stands in Treasury and Fitzroy Gardens, Melbourne. It was uprooted from Great Ayton, Yorkshire, and reassembled in the Australian park in 1934. But in fact the building described as '**Captain Cook's Cottage**' was home to Cook's parents not the explorer himself.

● American millionaire William Randolph Hearst was a passionate collector of art and furniture but his most extravagant purchase was that of an entire 12th-century Cistercian monastery from Spain in 1927. Not only did Hearst have to build the monks a new monastery but he also had to build a railway just to take the monastery, stone by stone, down to the Spanish coast for shipping to America. Each of the 10 000-plus stones was numbered and carefully wrapped in straw. But customs officials in the United States were horrified when they opened the crates because Spain had foot and mouth disease. So they ordered the straw to be burnt and the stones to be repacked.

The monastery lay in a Bronx warehouse until, in February 1941, desperately short of money, Hearst decided to sell it, along with some of his other prized possessions, in what was billed as 'The Sale of the Century' at Gimbels department store in New York. The new purchaser was dismayed to discover that, in the repacking of the stones, the numbering system had been ignored, leaving him to cope with a 12th-century 3-D jigsaw. The problem was solved, however, and the old Spanish monastery now stands as the **Episcopalian Church** in North Miami Beach, Florida.

● Some 13 000 km (8000 miles) from Germany stands the Bavarian town of **Leavenworth** in Washington State, USA. Originally founded on the wealth of the Great Northern Railway and the timber trade, Leavenworth was badly hit when the Great Northern yards moved to Wenatchee. The town tried to survive on its apple orchards but then, in the 1960s, it was dramatically redeveloped Bavarian-style as a tourist attraction. Now everything about Leavenworth is Bavarian. There are authentic taverns and shops selling wooden toys and clocks. There are facilities for skiing and river rafting, all conducted to the sound of alpen horns. There is even a Great Bavarian Ice Festival every January.

● Edward Anderton Reade served in India for over 34 years, reaching the position of Lieutenant-Governor of the North-West Provinces. During this time he built up a close friendship with the Maharajah of Benares whom he helped through the dangerous years of the Indian Mutiny. When Reade retired to Stoke Row in his native Oxfordshire, the Maharajah, recalling how Reade had compared the water problems of Benares to those in the Chilterns, donated funds for a well in the village.

The exotic **Maharajah's Well**, built in 1864, is cast-iron, crowned by a gilt elephant and surmounted by a splendid Mughal dome. The well shaft is more than 112.2 m (368 ft) deep.

● Sir Clough Williams-Ellis described himself as an 'architect errant'. Among his grandiose schemes was one to recreate the Italian fishing village of Portofino in Britain. He initially intended buying an island but when an uncle offered to sell him the Aberia peninsula in North Wales, he realized that it was the perfect site. For a start, the estate was already home to numerous exotic plants. Renaming the peninsula **Portmeirion**, Williams-Ellis set about adorning it with brightly coloured Italian-style architecture. He converted the existing house into a hotel and, from 1926, began building the major features of the village, including the campanile and the dome. Statues, balconies, fountains, arches, cobbles and a shell grotto were all incorporated into what Williams-Ellis called his 'home for fallen buildings'. Portmeirion acted as the setting for the 1967 television series, *The Prisoner*, starring Patrick McGoohan.

● By the side of a lake at Alresford, Essex, can be found **The Quarters**, a Chinese fishing temple built by landscape gardener Richard Woods in 1772. Woods had been commissioned to do the work by a Colonel Rebow at a cost of £343 13s 6d. The end product is extremely authentic, topped by a double-curved, concave, copper-covered roof. Colonel Rebow's successor, General Isaac Rebow, was so impressed that in 1816 he commissioned John Constable to paint the temple.

● Modelled on the 6th-century Byzantine basilica of San Vitale in Ravenna, Italy, **The Round House** was designed in 1795 by two cousins, Jane and Mary Parminter, at the end of their ten-year long Grand Tour of Europe. Situated a mile north of Exmouth, Devon, the Round House has 16 sides, small diamond-shaped windows and tiny triangular rooms hidden behind sliding panels. The walls are adorned with painted birds, which have real feathers, and the narrow staircases are encrusted with shells and fossils. It took the cousins 11 years to decorate.

● With its galleried, rectangular hall and with both a portico and a steeple, **St John's Church, Calcutta**, is almost an exact replica of St Martin-in-the-Fields, London. That was the intention of its designer, James Agg, a young officer in the Royal Engineers who was posted to India in 1779. St John's was consecrated in 1787.

PRIVATE HOMES

● As an industrialist flew into Durban, South Africa, in 1971, he was horrified to look down and see what appeared to be a crashed plane lying on the ground. Only later did he discover that it was, in fact, Dookie Ramdarie's new **Aeroplane House**, a dwelling built in the shape of an aircraft, the bedrooms being housed in the wings. Despite initial objections from the local authority, Ramdarie's house was allowed to stay and he proceeded to sprinkle further transports of delight around Durban. His second effort was a bus factory in the shape of a bus and then, in 1981, he designed the **Ship House**, a house in the form of a ship, complete with funnel and lifeboats.

● In the High Street at Haddenham, Buckinghamshire, is **The Bone House**, the exterior walls of which are decorated with the bones of dead sheep. Knuckle-bones have been formed into patterns to make animals, faces, tools, hearts, diamonds and the date – 1807. Unfortunately, the designer omitted to write his name in bones.

● As well as his work on La Sagrada Familia, Antonio Gaudi also created two remarkable houses in Barcelona. Between 1905 and 1907, he worked on **Casa Batlló**, a house which combines images of bones, skulls, seaweed, lava, clowns, sequins, fish and a dragon. Gaudi remodelled an existing building and covered it with an intricate mosaic. He also inserted slender columns in the windows, earning it the nickname of 'House of Bones'. The tiled roof sparkles and undulates like the Mediterranean but also possesses a dragon-like quality with glazed scales, while at the rear of the house, a procession of helmeted clowns point towards the sky. The image Gaudi was creating was that of the dragon, Spain, being slain by the Christian cross and sword of Barcelona's patron, St George. Below, the skulls and bones of martyrs are visible in the balconies and general structure. Gaudi's other masterpiece was **Casa Milà** (1905–10). The building as a whole has been likened to a Henry Moore sculpture. The exterior features continuous undulating walls, the horizontal edges of which resemble eyebrows or lips. These are pierced only by windows which preserve the expression of human eyes or mouths. Towards the end of his career, Gaudi proclaimed that the straight line belonged to man, the curved one to God.

✱ Designed by John Lautner, the **Chemosphere**, built in 1960, bears an uncanny similarity to a hovering spacecraft. Set on a steep hill site in Los Angeles, the 204 sq m (2200 sq ft) octagonal house is built on a stout pedestal with steel bracing. Its unusual shape affords the occupant a 360-degree view over the San Fernando Valley.

✱ The smallest house in Britain is a fisherman's cottage at The Quay, Conwy, Gwynedd, built in the 19th century. It comprises just two rooms and a staircase. It has a 183 cm (72 in) frontage, is 310 cm (122 in) high and measures 254 cm (100 in) from front to rear.

● In the outback of South Australia, north of Adelaide, is the town of **Coober Pedy**. The name is Aboriginal and means 'white fellow's hole in the ground'. It aptly describes the place since a sizeable proportion of the population live in dugouts to shelter from daytime temperatures which can exceed 50°C and bitterly cold winter nights. Many of the early dugout homes were old opal mines but now they are often cut specifically as residences. Another reason for carving out homes underground is the serious shortage of timber in the area for building conventional homes. Some of the homes are open to the public, including one with an indoor swimming pool. There is also an underground Catacomb Church plus The Desert Cave, Australia's first underground five-star hotel!

● Timothy Dexter (1747–1806) was a self-made New England millionaire who had made his fortune from a series of unlikely ventures such as exporting woolly mittens to the tropical West Indies and coal to Newcastle. But one thing still irked him – the local businessmen refused to take him seriously. As a grand statement, he purchased a Georgian mansion overlooking the sea at Newburyport, a harbour town 64 km (40 miles) from Boston. He decorated the roof with Eastern minarets and golden balls, erected a huge golden eagle as a weather vane and, from 1801, filled the garden with life-size wooden statues of famous men, declaring loudly that they were 'better company' than his condescending neighbours. He built up a collection of 40 statues, among them Napoleon, George Washington and Venus, but towering above them all was one of Dexter himself. Following his death, the house became first a hotel and then a library. A violent storm destroyed most of the statues although some were sold. Dexter's was put on a bonfire.

● In the early 1960s, three American 'drop-outs' built **Drop City**, a curious settlement near Trinidad, Colorado. The former students of the University of Kansas bought four acres of goat pasture and started to build, modelling their creations on the geodesic dome of American architect Richard Buckminster Fuller. Their materials were by-products of the industrial society they had abandoned – scrap timber, car windscreens and waterproofed tar paper, all painted sky blue. The finished houses had a patchwork effect with windows tilted at 45°.

● American architect Buckminster Fuller's own dream house was called the **Dymaxion House** (standing for 'dynamic plus maximum efficiency'). Shaped like a flying saucer with a fin on top, the house was portable and was designed to be dismantled and transported should the occupants ever need to move to a different location. He wanted the house to be circular – because that was the most economical – and to be built from lightweight aluminium so as to facilitate transportation. Fuller drew up his plans in 1927 but the first Dymaxion House was not built until 1946 when a special aluminium alloy developed for aircraft during the Second World War finally made construction possible. It was certainly lightweight, occupying an area of 100 sq m (1075 sq ft) yet weighing only 2722 kg (6000 lb), little more than some cars. Fuller intended to mass-produce the houses but in the end only the two prototypes were ever finished. For not only did Fuller have problems securing sufficient financial backing for the project but rumours persisted that the Dymaxion House was leaky and cold. Kansas entrepreneur William L. Graham bought both prototypes and lived in one from 1946 until 1972. The other was never assembled. Both of Fuller's dream houses are now with the Henry Ford Museum at Dearborn, Michigan.

● Tucked away in a natural bowl formed by crags of sandstone rock on three sides, **Eagle Rock** is a house shaped like a huge glass and steel bird. It was built in Sussex in 1983 by Ian Ritchie for a retired lady botanist who wanted the house to reflect its unusual setting. The 'body and wings' form the living accommodation, the 'head' is a loft housing the water and central heating systems, the 'beak' is a car porch and the 'tail feathers' a conservatory. The roofs of the 'wings' have solar control blinds to imitate bird feathers. In her book, *An Album of Curious Houses*, Lucinda Lambton notes: 'One of the most exciting details of Eagle Rock is that the "wings" are actually suspended from the central spine of the house, making you feel that it could suddenly heave into life and flap away.'

● In 1919, American newspaper magnate William Randolph Hearst decided to build a simple bungalow for himself and his movie-star girlfriend, Marion Davies. He found a spectacular site – 250 000 acres in the Santa Lucia Mountains overlooking the Pacific – and instructed architect Julia Morgan to come up with something elegant but spartan. The result, nearly 20 years and $8 million later, was an exotic fantasy castle, **The Enchanted Hill** (*La Cuesta Encantada*) at San Simeon, California. The complex was modelled on the Spanish Renaissance cathedrals. Hearst scavenged Europe for treasures to fill the mansion's 100-plus rooms and was known to dismantle entire suites from Spanish palaces and reconstruct them at San Simeon. The main dining-hall was furnished with 500-year-old choir stalls from Catalonia. The Enchanted Hill might have been even more enchanting had Hearst not run out of building money in 1937.

● In 1950, American architect Bruce Goff designed a highly innovative house near Norman, Oklahoma, for sculptor Eugene Bavinger and his wife Nancy. The Bavingers detested conventional box-shaped houses and opted instead for an undivided, open space in which they could move freely and practise their hobby – plant breeding. They also wanted to keep building costs below $5000. They managed this by doing much of the work themselves and by using airline scrap as part of the house. The building has no rooms in the accepted sense – they are replaced by flat, circular elements, built from aircraft noses covered with velour. These stand in space like oversized cocktail glasses or are hung from the ceiling as 'living lamps'. The different levels of the house are connected by fragile stairways. The central mast of the house is the pipe of an oil drill while the roof hangs from biplane struts.

Twenty years later, Goff designed a house for Glen and Luetta Harder near Mountain Lake, Minnesota. The wood-frame building has a roof covered with bright orange weatherproof carpeting and in the middle of the living-room is a circular, fabric-covered flower bed with fountain. The Harders ran a turkey farm and at one stage insemination tubes found a place in the decor.

● Arguably the most unusual sight in Britain is that of an ordinary small terraced house at Headington, Oxford, with a 25 ft (7.6 m) fibre-glass shark buried nose-down in the roof. The sculpture was erected by the house-owner Bill Heine as a protest against man's inhumanity. It became a great tourist attraction but involved Heine in a six-year battle with Oxford City Council. At first they ordered its removal but Heine appealed. The then Enivironment Secretary Michael Howard ruled that it could stay, accepting that the shark did no demonstrable harm to visual amenity. Junior minister Tony Baldry added: 'Any system of control must make some small space for the dynamic, the unexpected and the downright quirky'. Thus in 1992, Oxford City Council relented, deciding that to discourage creativity and expression was contrary to the city's long history as an educational centre.

Ernest Trobridge's castle-like council houses in Kingsbury, London – enough to keep any rent collector at bay

● Architect Ernest Trobridge dreamed of council estates where the homes consisted of mini castles and timber-framed cottages. Encouraged and financed by the success of a prefabricated house he had exhibited at the 1920 Ideal Home Exhibition, he purchased ten acres of land at Kingsbury, north-west London, and set to work on creating his Utopia. He built houses that looked like medieval castles with battlements in the form of round-turreted chimney towers, arrowslits and even dry moats. Trobridge's buildings possess evocative names such as Whitecastle Mansion and Highfort Court, the latter being enhanced by an entrance which sweeps, drawbridge-like over the dry moat running around the basement to a front door framed beneath an imposing arch. All that is missing is a portcullis.

● The world's first rotating house was completed in 1984 in the village of Saint-Isidore near Nice. The brainchild of French inventor François Labbé, the house is constructed entirely of metal and can be turned to face sun or shade at the press of a button.

● English poet Rev. Robert Stephen Hawker (1803–75) (see p. 26) had the six chimneys of his vicarage at Morwenstow, Cornwall, modelled on his favourite church towers − except for the kitchen chimney which is a copy of his mother's tomb. When designing the chimneys in 1837, he based five on church towers where he had previously lived − Stratton, Whitstone, North Tammerton and two in Oxford. The sixth, he wrote, 'perplexed me very much till I bethought me of my mother's tomb; and there it is, in its exact shape and dimensions'.

✳ When the water level is particularly low at Ladybower Reservoir in North Derbyshire, a curious sight protrudes above the surface − a church spire. It is the only visible remnant of the villages of Ashopton and Derwent, both of which were flooded when the reservoir was filled in 1943 to quench the thirsts of Derby, Sheffield, Leicester and Nottingham. The occupants of the villages were rehoused at nearby Yorkshire Bridge.

✳ A house in Rockport, Massachusetts, is made entirely from recycled newspaper. The walls have 215 reinforced layers of newsprint. Heating is a problem and, not unreasonably, smoking is prohibited inside.

● At Potter Heigham in Norfolk stands a house made out of the top of a helter-skelter which used to be on Yarmouth's Britannia Pier before the First World War. As the helter-skelter dwindled in popularity with holidaymakers, it is said that a local bookmaker bought it and converted the top storey into a holiday home.

● Two Americans, Lucius Beebe and Charles Clegg, purchased an abandoned pullman car from the Great Northern Railroad in 1955 and converted it into a magnificent travelling home called The Virginia City. The car, which weighed over 90 tonnes, was 26.2 m (86 ft) long and 2.89 m (9½ ft) wide, had run on the route between Chicago and the West Coast before going out of service in the 1940s. Beebe and Clegg took it to a private siding in Reno, Nevada, and decorated it in the flamboyant style of the 19th century. Clegg said: 'We designed the car to capture the elegance of the Doge's Palace in Venice'. When completed, the pullman housed two bedrooms, a kitchen, dining-room, bathroom and drawing room.

● Retired salesman John Halstead moved to Rochdale, Lancashire, in 1936 and bought a house in Broad Lane. He spent the next four years, until his death in 1940, decorating the outside walls with shells, broken plates and saucers, even cows' horns and the parts from an old bedstead. In the centre, he arranged pieces of blue and white pottery to form the words 'Tempori parendum', meaning 'We move with the times'. The abode was christened 'Shell House' and local children would collect bits and pieces which he would then cement on to the walls. On his death, his daughter sold the house for £25.

● Sir Thomas Tresham was educated in England as a Catholic during the Protestant Reformation and became obsessed with the power of numbers.

In 1597, he ordered the building of a **Triangular Lodge** at Rushton, Northamptonshire, in which everything relates to the number three – a homage to the Trinity. It has three sides, each of which measure 33 ft (10 m), three gables on each side, three storeys and triangular or hexagonal rooms decorated with trefoils or triangles in groups of three. All of the Latin inscriptions have 33 letters.

● Alexander Wortley was a fiercely independent individual who resented having to pay any form of taxation. In a bid to avoid the taxman's clutches, he chose to live in a small green wooden box, 0.9 m (3 ft) wide, 1.2 m (4 ft) long and 1.5 m (5 ft) high, which, because it was on wheels, he was able to take all over the country. It had an arched metal roof and interior furnishings consisting of an old bus seat and a few shelves. Wortley lived in it until his death at the age of 80 in 1980. He spent the last 20 years of his life as caretaker of a cottage in Buckinghamshire and parked his box at the bottom of the garden.

✱ Among Grade II listed buildings in England is a small black and yellow AA Box near Grasmere in the Lake District, described as being of architectural and historic interest. Ernie Smith's three-seater outside lavatory at Bishop's Tawton, North Devon, falls into the same category.

Sir Thomas Tresham's Triangular Lodge at Rushton, Northamptonshire – a homage to the Trinity

TOWERS

✱ Between 1889 and 1907, Austrian Josef-Maria Olbrich created his Artists' Colony on the Mathildenhohe at Darmstadt, Germany. In 1905, the wedding of Grand Duke Ernst Ludwig of Hessen presented Olbrich with the opportunity of crowning his colony with a tower. And so he built the 48 m (157 ft) high **Wedding Tower**, the top of which is shaped like a hand with five concrete fingers pointing towards the sky to signify the happy event.

✱ In 1549, Hugh de Freston arranged for the building of a six-storey brick tower on his Suffolk estate overlooking the Orwell estuary. The **Freston Tower** was intended to further the education of his daughter Ellen who was to be taught a different subject on a different floor each day of the week. On Monday on the ground floor, she pondered the virtues of charity; Tuesday on the first floor, she learnt tapestry; Wednesday on the second floor, it was music; Thursday on the third floor, she studied classics; Friday on the fourth floor, English literature; Saturday on the fifth floor, art; and on Sunday, she studied astronomy on the roof.

✳ Work was begun on the famous **Leaning Tower of Pisa** in Northern Italy in 1173 as a bell tower for the nearby cathedral. It first started to tilt when construction reached the third storey, as a result of which the upper tiers were built out of line with the rest in a vain attempt to straighten it out. The tower was not completed until 1350. The reason for the tilt is generally attributed to inadequate foundations rather than some amazing feat by Bonanno Pisano, the first of three architects to work on the tower. For although the tower is 179 ft (54.5 m) high, 62 ft (18.9 m) in diameter and weighs 14 453 tonnes, the foundations are only 10 ft (3 m) deep. Consequently, the top is about 17 ft (5 m) out of true.

✳ The **Perky Bat Tower** at Florida Keys was built in 1929 as the brainchild of Richard C. Perky. He hoped to control the local mosquito population by importing insect-devouring bats to live in his highly desirable wooden tower which was immaculately louvred in pine. Although the bats never came, the tower still stands.

✳ For many years, the most useless lighthouse in the world was that at Rubjerg Knude, North Jutland, Denmark. It is backed by mountainous dunes which rise 73 m (240 ft) above sea-level and are visible as a landmark many miles away. But the dunes are so high that they hide the lighthouse from the sea! The lighthouse is now disused and has been converted into a Sand Drift Museum.

✳ Infuriated by the fact that Germany's highest mountain, Zugspitze, was only 2964 m (9724 ft) high, mountaineer Wolfgang Gorter built a concrete tower on the summit to give Germany a 3000-metre mountain.

UNBUILT STRUCTURES

✳ In 1758, French architect Charles Ribart planned a curious addition to the Champs Élysées in Paris – a three-storey building in the shape of an elephant. It was to be constructed where the Arc de Triomphe now stands and was to contain a ballroom with air conditioning, and furniture which folded into the walls. Entry was to be via a spiral staircase in the elephant's underbelly while the building's drainage system would be incorporated in the trunk. The French government greeted Ribart's idea with a resounding 'Non'.

✳ Also in the 18th century, another French architect, Jean-Jacques Lequeu, came up with an idea for a vast stable in the shape of a cow. The hayloft was to be ventilated and lights would shine through the eyes. The plans were dropped.

✳ The Isaac Newton Monument was the brainchild of Anglo-German artist George Scharf in 1834. He planned a 12 m (40 ft) high pyramid, sliced off two-thirds of the way up to make a platform for a huge stone globe. The idea was simply to enclose Newton's old house in Westminster but the size of the monument would have been such that had it been built, it would have engulfed the whole of the south side of Leicester Square.

6

HISTORY

BATTLES

● On 28 May 585 BC, a total eclipse of the Sun blacked out the sky over Mesopotamia during a battle between the Medes (from what is now known as Iran) and the Lydians (from modern Turkey). Horrified at what they saw as an omen, both forces laid down their arms and made peace on the spot.

● Before going into battle, Roman generals used hens to find out whether the portents were good. The hens were carried around in cages. If they ate quickly, it was supposed to be a good omen. If they ate slowly, it was a bad omen. If they had no appetite, disaster was on the horizon. Wise generals deliberately starved the birds before any conflict so that they would eat readily, thus ensuring victory. Prior to the sea battle of Drepana (250 BC) during the First Punic War, the consul P. Claudius Pulcher became angered when the hens refused to eat. In a fit of rage, he had them hurled into the sea, declaring: 'May they drink if they won't eat'. The drowned hens had the last laugh as Pulcher lost the battle, losing 20 000 men.

Left Japanese Lt Hiroo Onoda continued to fight the Second World War singlehandedly until 1974 from a remote island in the Philippines (see p. 112)

● When Viking leader Harald Hardrada, King of Norway since 1047, invaded England in 1066, he soon saw off the northern militia at Fulford, Yorkshire. But the big showdown would be with King Harold II whom Hardrada thought was still on the south coast of England waiting for the Normans. Four days after Fulford, on 25 September 1066, Hardrada and his men camped on meadows either side of the River Derwent at Stamford Bridge. In the glorious weather, many of the Vikings removed their armour and, not anticipating any activity for many days yet, indulged in a spot of sunbathing. They did not even rouse themselves when they saw approaching soldiers, presuming them to be a detachment of Vikings. By the time they discovered that it was the English army, force-marched up from London, it was too late. The Vikings were overrun, many without having been able to don their armour, and Harald Hardrada was killed.

● In 1183 at the mighty fortress of Kerak in the kingdom of Jerusalem, 11-year-old Princess Isabella married Humphrey of Toron, six years her senior. But there threatened to be an uninvited wedding guest. For the princess's guardian, Reynald of Chatillon, had been launching raids from Kerak on the Muslim armies under Saladin. Now Saladin sought revenge and began bombarding Kerak with the intention of killing Reynald. Remarkably, the wedding celebrations continued inside the castle while Saladin started his siege. Lady Stephanie, mother of the groom, even sent food from the bridal feast out to the enemy. Saladin was so touched that he asked in which tower of the castle the newly-weds were to live and ordered that it should not be attacked. Otherwise the siege continued in all its ferocity until the royal army from Jerusalem arrived, forcing Saladin to retreat towards Damascus and allowing the wedding guests to go home.

● On 22 May 1499, as part of the Swabian War, the Swiss canton of Grisons, with some 6000 men, defeated an Austrian army of 12000 in the Calvendefile near Taufers. But an even more astounding victory against the odds occurred in 1538 when the entire Inca empire was toppled by just 180 men under the Spaniard Francisco Pizarro. The Inca empire stretched over a 4000 km (2500 mile) area of the Andes but its troops were exhausted after seven years of civil war and suffering with illnesses introduced by the Spaniards when they landed in 1532. With an army of thousands of men, the Inca ruler Atahualpa faced Pizarro (with his 180 men and 37 horses) for the first time at Cajamarca in Peru. Pizarro kidnapped Atahualpa, and the Inca warriors, unnerved by their first encounter with firearms and cavalry, fled in terror. The Spaniards had thus conquered the Inca empire within six years of their arrival. Atahualpa was garrotted by his Spanish captors in 1533.

✳ At the Battle of Lepanto in 1571, the Austrians under Don John defeated the Turks, thus ending Turkish power in the Mediterranean. In the course of the battle, the Turks ran out of ammunition and their troops were seen pelting the enemy with oranges and lemons.

● At Vigo in Spain on 12 October 1702, a British naval force under Sir George Rooke attacked the French and Spanish fleets. A boom had been placed across the mouth of the harbour but the *Torbay*, a ship of 80 guns commanded by Sir Thomas Hopsonn, managed to break under it. An enemy fireship then set the *Torbay* ablaze but the flames were almost immediately put out by the *Torbay*'s cargo – a massive quantity of snuff. The snuff proceeded to have an adverse reaction on the crews of the French warships who had to dive into the sea for relief after inhaling it. Thanks to this unlikely source of inspiration, the British were able to capture treasure at Vigo estimated at over £2 million.

✳ It was purely by chance that Gibraltar ever became a British colony. In 1704, during the War of the Spanish Succession, Sir George Rooke was sent to capture the French port of Toulon but, being unable to do so and not wishing to return to Britain empty-handed, he took Gibraltar instead.

● In the course of the Battle of Soor in 1745, Frederick the Great of Prussia had his baggage train seized by Austrian Hussars commanded by General Nádasti. The Austrians made off with all of his clothes, horses, money, silverware – even his favourite flutes – but the biggest loss was his beloved pet whippet bitch, Biche. When peace negotiations began after the battle, Frederick discovered that, far from having been killed by the Hussars, Biche was being held captive by Nádasti's wife who wanted to keep her. Frederick insisted that there could be no end to the war unless his whippet was safely returned. The Austrians agreed to his demands and man and dog were reunited.

● The Prussian armies of the 18th century were not exactly renowned for their excellent eyesight. In 1757, the forces under Prince Augustus William were forced to abandon the safest escape route when they saw the road blocked by what they took to be batteries of Austrian artillery. The Austrian guns turned out to be nothing more deadly than a herd of cattle. The same army panicked later on spotting what they thought were more guns. This time they burned all their own transport and pontoon bridges before realizing that the 'guns' were really tree trunks. In the same year, another Prussian leader, Field Marshal

Seydlitz, had managed to trap a French cavalry force in a hollow near Rossbach, only for one of his officers to fail to close the trap, mistaking young fir trees for French infantry advancing to the rescue.

● January 1795 was part of the coldest winter for a century in Holland, enabling a French cavalry troop to cross the thick ice on the salt waters of the Zuider Zee and surround the Dutch fleet which was helplessly frozen in. Shocked at seeing French cavalrymen riding around their ships, the Dutch commanders had no option but to surrender.

● By 1814, a small band of Chilean patriots had been struggling for four years to free their country from Spanish rule. Their leader was one Bernardo O'Higgins (c. 1776–1842), the illegitimate son of a Spanish officer of Irish origin. Their cause looked lost when O'Higgins was wounded by a Spanish bullet, but he immediately ordered his men to round up all the animals they could find – sheep, mules, goats and dogs. The Chileans then frightened the animals so that they stampeded towards the Spanish. Forced to move aside, the Spanish unwittingly allowed the Chileans to escape behind the charging herd. The Chileans headed for the mountains where, reprieved by the animal intervention, they continued their struggle. They reorganized their forces and three years later the Spanish were finally defeated, enabling O'Higgins to become the first ruler of independent Chile.

● The Battle of Karansebes (1788) witnessed one of the biggest self-inflicted wounds in military history when over 10 000 Austrian troops were

French hussars capture the Dutch fleet on the frozen Zuider Zee in January 1795

105

killed or injured by their own colleagues. Flanked by regiments of hussars, the Austrian columns were marching towards the distant Turkish enemy when, as night fell, they crossed a bridge near Karansebes. Some of the hussars stopped to buy alcohol from onlooking peasants but when a number of infantrymen tried to do the same, the hussars forced them back. Instant dissent broke out in the Austrian ranks with the irate footsoldiers firing shots into the air and attempting to frighten the hussars by shouting 'Turci! Turci!' as if the enemy were upon them. The drunken hussars joined the call, also yelling 'Turci!' and firing shots. By now the rear columns of the Austrian army were approaching the bridge and, hearing the pandemonium and shooting, they panicked and started firing at each other in the darkness. Realizing what was happening, officers raced up and down the lines calling 'Halt!' but to the hysterical soldiers, it sounded like 'Allah!' Convinced that the Turks were about to slaughter them, the baggage handlers and transport workers at the rear attempted to drive their wagons through the mass of troops ahead, in the process sending soldiers plunging into the river and creating a mighty stampede. It was not until first light that the Austrians realized there were no Turks at all and were left to count the cost of their folly.

● A strange irony surrounded the German mine-layer, the *Konigin Luise*, which on 5 August 1914 became the first naval casualty of the First World War. Sighted off Southwold, Suffolk, by a trawler which reported a suspicious vessel 'throwing things overboard', the *Konigin Luise* was sunk by two British destroyers, *Lance* and *Landrail*, and the light cruiser, *Amphion*. The German crew were taken on board the *Amphion* but not before they had planted 180 mines. The following morning, the *Amphion* struck one of the mines and sank so quickly that 151 men drowned including many of the prisoners from the *Konigin Luise*.

● When, on 8 December 1914, British troops set about breaching the Medina railway north of Alexandretta, Turkey, thereby cutting the links between Constantinople and the Turkish forces stationed in Arabia, they expected fierce resistance from the Turks. Instead, and for no apparent reason, the Turks happily assisted the enemy in their sabotage, even shunting up locomotives to be dynamited. The Turks did draw the line at being commanded by a foreigner but were quite willing for the British officer in charge of the operation to become a Turkish officer for the day. Once he had become an 'Anglo-Turk', the Turks obligingly helped to wreck the railway. Mission accomplished, the British officer promptly resigned his commission and returned to his ship.

✳ At Christmas 1914, an unofficial truce came into effect along certain sections of the Western Front. On Christmas Day, near Houplines in France, the Saxons and the Seaforth Highlanders played football for an hour in the area of No Man's Land which divided the opposing forces. With the Germans leading the Scots 3–2, the German commanding officer ordered his men back to the trenches. The following day, they were once again fighting bitterly on the battlefield.

● The Battle of Tanga (1914) in East Africa saw 8000 British troops pitted against the might of the German army yet the outcome was decided by a swarm of bees. The British were supported by untrained Indian troops who between them spoke 12 different languages. Communication was thus not easy. Already alarmed by the clouds of smoke which emanated from the Germans' black-powder rifles, the Indians were soon in for a greater shock. For hanging from trees across the battlefield were numerous hives containing particularly large and aggressive African bees. Angered by the noise and the bullets, the bees emerged from the hives and swarmed all over the advancing Indian troops. In panic, the Indians retreated to the sea, still pursued by the bees. One soldier was stung 300 times. The British were forced to evacuate. In total, over 1000 British were killed and 500 wounded at Tanga as a result of the confusion caused by the bees.

● Fort Douaumont at Verdun, France, was reputed to be the strongest in the world. Yet in 1916 it was captured by a solitary German soldier. The fall of the fort was a result of the absent-mindedness of French General Chrétien. In February 1916, he had been ordered to reoccupy the fort (it had previously been evacuated) and defend it to the last man, but when he went on leave he forgot to pass the message on to his successor. So at the start of the German assault on Verdun, Douaumont was manned by just 56 gunners. On 25 February 1916, German Sergeant Kunze led his troops to seize the fort. Encountering no resistance, he entered alone. In the corridors he arrested four French gunners and then stumbled into a room where a lecture was taking place and arrested 20 more. The capture was completed by three more German officers, alerted by Kunze. The fort remained in German hands for six months, only being retaken by the French at a terrible cost.

Below right Captain Robert Jenkins displays his severed ear to the House of Commons in 1739, thus provoking The War of Jenkins' Ear

● On 19 November 1941 off Shark Bay, Western Australia, the Australian cruiser *Sydney* encountered the German surface-raider *Kormoran*. The former, having been torpedoed by the latter, managed to sink her opponent by gunfire before she herself blew up. So both the hunter and the hunted went down. There were no survivors among the *Sydney*'s crew of over 700.

● The Russians had a cunning plan of their own during the Second World War – the invention of the 'dog mine'. The idea was to train dogs to associate food with the underneath of tanks. Then, with bombs strapped to their backs, the animals were supposed to dart hungrily beneath the advancing German Panzer divisions, blowing the enemy to pieces. Unfortunately, the dogs tended to associate food solely with Russian tanks and forced an entire Soviet division to retreat. The masterplan was scrapped on the second day of the Russians' involvement in the war.

BIZARRE WARS

✱ In the early 18th century, British ships used to conduct illicit tax-free trade with Spanish colonies, much to the annoyance of the Spanish King, Felipe V, who ordered his ships to stop and search any suspicious British vessels. In 1731, British Captain Robert Jenkins sailed his brig *Rebecca* past Cuba en route from London to Jamaica. Off Havana, he was stopped by a Spanish customs and excise boat commanded by Captain Fandino. Jenkins was to claim that Fandino seized the cargo which he had bought legally in Jamaica and then cut off the Englishman's ear. For his part, Fandino maintained that Jenkins was a tax-evader who had vowed to defend his cargo 'with his life' until the Spanish sword had silenced him. Seven years later, King George II heard about the incident, Jenkins producing a jar containing his ear pickled in alcohol as proof. In 1739, Britain declared war on Spain in what became known as The War of Jenkins' Ear. The conflict lasted for nine years.

* In 1859, the United States and Britain almost went to war over a pig. The animal was the property of Englishman Charles Griffin who lived on San Juan Island, just off the Pacific coast of Canada near Vancouver. It had a tendency to stray on to the potato patch of an American neighbour, Lyman Cutler, who responded by shooting it. Griffin protested to the British Government and troops from both countries moved into the area. Nobody could decide whether the pig had been poking its snout in American or Canadian soil for the pig had unwittingly exposed a flaw in the 1846 Treaty which had established the US–Canadian border. At the western end, the treaty fixed the border along the 49th parallel of latitude to 'the middle of the channel' separating Vancouver Island from the mainland. But with so many straits and islands in the channel, the two sides were unable to agree on precisely which channel was being referred to. The Pig War dragged on for 13 years during which time American and British troops remained stationed at opposite ends of the island. No shots were ever exchanged. The dispute was finally settled by arbitration in 1872 when the German Kaiser, Wilhelm I, awarded the island to the United States.

* When General Mariano Melgarejo became President of Bolivia in 1865, he held a celebration feast to which he invited the recently appointed British Minister for his country. During the meal, Melgarejo introduced his mistress to the guests and ordered that they stand and salute her. The British Minister refused, whereupon Melgarejo had him stripped naked and made him ride out of town, his hands tied, on the back of a donkey as thousands lined the streets to watch. Queen Victoria was furious to hear of this insult to the British Empire and instructed the Royal Navy to send six gunboats to Bolivia and sink its fleet. Her admirals quietly pointed out that Bolivia had no coast and therefore no fleet, at which the Queen sent for a map and a pair of scissors and cut Bolivia from the world. She ordered Bolivia to be removed from all maps. On the huge map of the world hanging in the House of Commons, all sign of Bolivia was completely blacked out. To British eyes, Bolivia did not exist again until June 1871 when Melgarejo was assassinated.

* Following a State visit to Paris, word got back that Spanish King Alfonso XII (reigned 1874–85) had been insulted by the French. Don Miguel Garcia Saez, the Mayor of Lijar, a small town in southern Spain, took such exception to this that he immediately declared war on France. The town's 300 citizens supported the call to arms but over the next 93 years of warfare, no shots were fired. It was only after King Juan Carlos, Alfonso's grandson, had been favourably treated on a visit to France that, in 1981, the town council of Lijar decided to suspend hostilities 'in view of the excellent attitude of the French'.

* The quickest defeat suffered in any war was by Said Khalid, the pretender Sultan of Zanzibar, in 1896. On 27 August, the British fleet arrived to deliver an ultimatum, Rear Admiral Harry Holdsworth Rawson demanding that Khalid vacate the palace. When he refused, fighting broke out at 9.02 a.m. Precisely 38 minutes later, it was all over. Zanzibar's only warship, the ageing *Glasgow*, was sunk by just two shells and the palace was totally destroyed.

* A postage stamp printed in 1932 started a war between Bolivia and Paraguay. The Paraguayan stamp featured a map in which the Chaco territory, situated between the two countries and claimed by both, was labelled 'Chaco Paraguayo'. The stamp also bore the words, *Ha sido, es, y serà* (Has been, is, and will be).

On 15 June 1932, the incensed Bolivians attacked Paraguay, beginning a war which continued until 12 June 1935. A total of 100 000 people were killed in the war. In 1938, the two countries signed a peace treaty under which Paraguay was given 90 per cent of the disputed territory.

CHARACTERS IN HISTORY

● **King Pepi II** (aka Phiops II) ruled Ancient Egypt for some 94 years after being crowned at the age of 6 (*c.* 2294 BC). He owed his long life to a healthy outlook which included a novel way of discouraging troublesome insects. To deter flies from landing on the royal personage, the King always kept a supply of naked slaves handy, their bodies smeared with honey.

● As a result of switching from the Roman republican calendar to the new Julian calendar, the year 46 BC lasted 445 days. The old republican calendar had become hopelessly out of step with the seasons. The spring equinox, which should have marked the end of March, was occurring in the middle of May. So in 46 BC, **Julius Caesar** commissioned Greek astronomer Sosigenes to devise a new calendar based on the solar year with a 365-day year and an extra day every fourth year. The average year of the old calendar had been 366 and a quarter days. However, before the new system could be introduced, the discrepancy between the seasons and the date had to be sorted out. Part of Caesar's solution was to add 67 days in the form of two extra months between November and December. Not surprisingly, it became known as the Year of Confusion.

> ✳ **Pope Stephen II** was elected on 23 March 752 but he died the following day. As he was never consecrated, his name was omitted from Vatican records and given to his successor.

● **Charlemagne** (*c.*742–814), emperor in the west of the area now known as the Holy Roman Empire, was zealous in the cause of education and, in addition to founding many schools, he did much to restore the popularity of Latin as a language. Yet Charlemagne himself never learned to write properly. Towards the end of his life, he used to keep writing materials under his pillow to practise but his handwriting remained little more than a childlike scrawl.

● Since his wife, a Christian slave named Itimad, had never seen snow but was fascinated to know what it looked like, Arab **King Almotamid**, who ruled the region around Seville in Spain in the middle of the 11th century, arranged for an entire hillside near Cordoba to be planted with almond trees. In spring, the falling petals from the trees turned the slopes white. It was the nearest thing to snow that Itimad would ever see in southern Spain.

● **King John** (reigned 1199–1216) had an unusual servant, Solomon Attefeld, who went under the title of the Royal Head Holder. He was rewarded with large pieces of land for performing his duty – holding the royal head when the King went to sea to prevent him being seasick.

● During the Hussite Wars of the 15th century, blind **General Jan Zizka** (1360–1424) successfully defended his native Bohemia in the face of overwhelming odds. On his death-bed, he gave instructions that his skin should be used to cover a drum so that it could continue to beat out defiance to his enemies. The drum survived for a number of centuries and was sounded at the outbreak of the Thirty Years War in 1618.

● **King Charles VIII** of France (reigned 1483–98) was born in 1470 with six toes on his left foot. Another French King, Louis XIV (reigned 1643–1715), also had toe trouble. His started to rot towards the end of his 72-year reign, a fact discovered when his valet found a toe in one of the royal bedsocks. Nevertheless, it was syphilis which finished him off in 1715.

● Spaniard **Sebastian del Cano** is probably the only mutineer in history to have been rewarded with a coat of arms and a statue. He was a member of the expedition of five ships under the command of Portuguese navigator Ferdinand Magellan which set sail from San Lucar de Barrameda, just north of Cadiz, on 20 September 1519. At Port St Julian in Patagonia, Magellan had to quash a mutiny, one of the ringleaders of which was del Cano. But del Cano's skill as a pilot made him too valuable to be executed. When

Magellan was killed by natives on the Philippine island of Mactan, del Cano assumed command and safely steered the *Vittoria* back to Seville at the end of July 1522, the only ship to complete the circumnavigation of the globe. As a result, del Cano was honoured by King Charles V of Spain with a statue in his home town of Guetaria.

● Young **King Edward VI** (reigned 1547–53) was not always the best behaved child at school but, being royal, it was not permissible to cane him. So whenever Edward was to be punished, another boy, Barnaby Fitzpatrick, stepped in to provide a substitute bottom and take the beating while His Royal Highness looked on.

● Born in 1640, **Philippe, Duke of Orleans**, son of King Louis XIII of France, was forced to wear pretty dresses and play with dolls because his mother had longed for a daughter. It was no great shock that Philippe grew up to be somewhat effeminate.

● Following his unsuccessful attempt to snatch the English crown, **James, Duke of Monmouth** (1649–85), bastard son of Charles II, was beheaded. It was only after the execution that the Keeper of King's Pictures discovered that there existed no official portrait of Monmouth. So the decapitated head was stitched back on and the dead Monmouth was placed in a chair to have his portrait painted by German-born artist Sir Godfrey Kneller.

● When Russian ruler **Peter the Great** (reigned 1682–1725) discovered that his wife Catherine had been unfaithful, he had the head of her lover, his own chamberlain William Mons, chopped off and inserted in a large jar of alcohol. Peter then placed the jar with its gruesome contents on Catherine's bedside table to remind her of her unfaithfulness.

✳ **Louis XIV** of France (reigned 1643–1715) hated washing and took only three baths in the whole of his adult life. But he loved beds and owned 413 of them.

✳ **Philip, Prince of Calabria,** the eldest son of Charles III of Spain (1716–88), owned scores of pairs of gloves and was known to wear 16 pairs simultaneously.

● **Augustus II**, the Elector of Saxony who became King of Poland in 1697, fathered over 300 children in his 63 years. But only one, Frederick Augustus, was legitimate and it was he who was crowned Augustus III in 1734 following the War of the Polish Succession.

● **George II** (reigned 1727-60) was very precise. At one minute to nine every night, he would stand outside his mistress's bedroom, holding a fob watch in the palm of his hand. At exactly nine, he would enter, pull down his breeches and have sex – often, it is said, without bothering to remove his hat.

● **Sultan Mustapha III**, who ruled Turkey from 1757 to 1774, fathered 582 children, all of them boys. At one stage, he became so desperate that he offered the position of Empress to any woman who presented him with a daughter – but none did.

● **George IV** (reigned 1820–30) clipped off a tiny lock of hair from each woman he slept with and put them in individual envelopes, each bearing the owner's name. Some 7100 such envelopes were found in his bedroom cupboard after he died.

● After the location of his body had remained a mystery for nearly 200 years, the decapitated corpse of **Charles I** was stumbled upon by workmen in St George's Chapel, Windsor Castle, in 1813. The Royal Physician, Sir Henry Halford, was called in to identify the remains and at the same time secretly removed the severed vertebra from the King's neck. He then had it set in gold and for the next 30 years he and his family used it as a salt cellar. The ornament was confiscated in 1843 when Queen Victoria got to hear about it and ordered that the bone be returned to the royal coffin.

CHILD RULERS

✳ **Alfonso XIII** of Spain, who reigned from 1886 to 1931, was actually born a king after his father, Alfonso XII, had died without an heir but with a wife, Maria Christina, who was three months pregnant. She filled in as a 'child-bearing Regent' for six months until Alfonso was born on 17 May 1886. The new king survived several assassination attempts before fleeing the country in 1931 as civil war threatened. When General Franco became Spanish dictator in 1936, he reinstated the king as a 'private citizen'. But Alfonso never returned to Spain alive and died in Rome in 1941.

✳ **John I** of France lived and reigned for just five days, 14–19 November 1316. His father, Louis X, had died on 5 June 1316 when his second wife, Clemence of Hungary, was four months pregnant. John was born but died five days later. His uncle took the throne as Philippe V.

✳ **Mary, Queen of Scots** became Queen of Scotland in 1542 at the age of one week. A widow at 18, following the death of her husband, Francis II of France, she was beheaded in 1567.

✳ Born on 6 December 1421, **Henry VI** was just eight months old when he became King of England on 1 September 1422. Seven weeks later, on 21 October, he was also proclaimed King of France upon the death of his insane grandfather Charles VI. Henry's uncle, John, Duke of Bedford, was made Regent of France while his uncle Humphrey, Duke of Gloucester, became Protector of England. Henry, head of the House of Lancaster, did not enjoy a happy reign. He inherited his grandfather's insanity and, although he recovered, the crown was seized in 1461 by the Yorkist Edward IV during the Wars of the Roses. Weak and monk-like, Henry was supposedly murdered in the Tower of London in 1471.

✳ **Petronilla of Aragon** was aged less than a year when she became queen in 1137. She reigned until 1163. Alfonso XI of Leon and Castile was a year old when he acceded to the throne in 1312. He ruled until 1350 when he was killed by the Black Death. Joanna I of Navarre became queen in 1273 at the age of one. She reigned until 1305. James V of Scotland (reigned 1513–42), James VI of Scotland (reigned 1567–1625), who also, in 1603, became James I of England, and John II of Leon and Castile (reigned 1406–54) were each only one year old when becoming king of their respective countries.

✳ When **Harald IV** of Norway died in 1136, his two-year-old son, Sigurd II, became joint-ruler with his half-brother, Inge I, who was only one year old. They reigned together until 1155 with Inge, who was known as 'The Hunchback', continuing for a further six years.

✳ **Isabella II** of Spain was three when she came to the throne in 1833. She assumed control of the Spanish Government at the age of 13 but three years later married her half-witted impotent cousin, Don Francisco de Bourbon. In 1868, she was deposed in a coup led by a former lover, Serrano.

✳ The following rulers were all aged three when assuming power – Otto the Great of the Holy Roman Empire (reigned 983–1002); Frederick I of Sicily (reigned 1197–1250); Sebastian of Portugal (reigned 1557–78); and Ivan IV 'the Terrible' of Russia (reigned 1533–84).

✳ **Isabelle**, daughter of Charles VI of France, was only seven when she became the second wife of England's 29-year-old King Richard II in 1396. Three years later, she was a widow at the age of ten.

✳ **Benedict IX** was known as 'the boy Pope'. He was only 11 or 12 when first elected Pope in 1032 and, before his death in 1056, had two other terms in office. His first spell as Pope was from 1032 until 1044. He became Pontiff again in 1045 and between 1047 and 1048 was named anti-Pope, set up in opposition to the canonically elected Pope, Clement II.

✳ **Shih Huang Ti**, the first sovereign emperor of the Qin dynasty, came to power in China as a 13-year-old boy. He lived in a huge palace, which covered an area 1½ miles (2.4 km) by ½ mile (0.8 km) and was surrounded by 270 smaller palaces, all linked by a network of tunnels. He ruled by fear yet was himself so afraid of assassination that he slept in a different palace each night.

He ruled for 15 years until 207 BC, during which time he was responsible for completing the Great Wall.

● In her later years, **Queen Victoria** (reigned 1837–1901) was so weak that when being photographed holding one of her grandchildren, it was feared that she might drop the child. So a servant (presumably female) was often secreted beneath the royal skirt to hold up the baby.

● **Prince Christian of Schleswig-Holstein** was blinded in one eye after being accidentally shot by Queen Victoria's son, Prince Arthur, while out hunting in 1892. So the remorseful Victoria bought him several glass eyes in different colours. His favourite was deliberately bloodshot and, right up until his death in 1917, he wore it to match the other whenever he had a cold.

● **Crown Prince Luis Filipe of Portugal** was mortally wounded at the same time that his father Charles was killed by a bullet which severed his carotid artery in the streets of Lisbon on 1 February 1908. He was technically King of Portugal (Dom Luis III) for about 20 minutes.

✳ A stickler for punctuality, **George V** (reigned 1910–36) kept the hundreds of antique clocks at Sandringham House, Norfolk, 30 minutes fast so that he would never be late for an appointment. Thus 'Sandringham Time' was always different to the rest of the world.

● In 1944, **Hiroo Onoda**, a 23-year-old second lieutenant in the Japanese army, was posted to Lubang Island, 121 km (75 miles) south of Manila, to perform guerrilla and intelligence duties. His orders were to carry on fighting even if his unit was wiped out. Onoda obeyed the orders to the letter – and continued to fight the Second World

Queen Victoria seen with great-grandchildren in 1900. On the cushion is the young Duke of York, who, because of the Queen's failing strength, was supported by a maid hidden beneath the vast royal dress

War for the next 30 years. During that time, he resisted all attempts to make him surrender for he was convinced that stories that the war was over were nothing more than United States propaganda. Leaflets dropped on the island signed by Onoda's chief of staff and announcing Japan's surrender were dismissed along with loudspeaker attempts by friends, relatives and old comrades to talk him out of hiding. Search parties and Japanese police were greeted with a hail of bullets.

Switching hideouts to avoid detection, he lived on a diet of bananas and coconuts. He took care to conserve his ammunition although he would sometimes snipe at islanders or take pot shots at an imaginary enemy. In 1974, Onoda stumbled across Norio Suzuki, a Japanese student on a camping holiday. Onoda was about to shoot him but Suzuki said he knew all about him and recounted how concerned the Emperor and the people of Japan were for his safety. Onoda replied that he would only lay down his arms if ordered to do so by his commanding officer. So Major Yoshimi Taniguchi temporarily left his job as a bookseller to fly to Lubang where, at 3 p.m. on 10 March 1974, Hiroo Onoda was finally persuaded to stop fighting. It was Onoda's 52nd birthday.

STRANGE DEATHS

✳ For years, **King Mithridates VI** of Pontus in Asia Minor took small doses of poison in order to develop a resistance should anyone try to poison him. He built up such a strong immunity that when he tried to take his own life in 63 BC to escape the clutches of the Romans, the poison he took had no effect. So instead he ordered a slave to kill him with a sword.

✳ At the age of 27, **Edmund Ironside**, who had only been King of Southern England for eight months in 1016, was murdered while sitting on the toilet. One evening in November, he sat on the long wooden lavatory box in his house to empty his bowels. Little did he know that one of his knights, Edric Streona, was lurking in the pit below. As Edmund sat down, Edric twice thrust a sword into him. Streona was later beheaded.

✳ **Henry I** (reigned 1100–35) died on 1 December 1135 after eating a surfeit of lampreys (small eel-like creatures) at a banquet in France. A similar excess befell **King John** who on the night of 18/19 October 1216 perished at an abbey in East Anglia after devouring a quantity of peaches and cider.

✳ At Nottinghamshire in 1290, **Edward I** (reigned 1272–1307) was lying gravely ill. Poison had set into a battle wound. Showing little faith in the royal doctors, his 50-year-old Queen, Eleanor, proceeded to suck all the poison from the wound. Her actions saved the King's life but killed her. Edward was so moved by her devotion that he had large crosses erected at each of the 12 places where her coffin stopped during its journey by coach to London. These memorials became known as the 'Eleanor Crosses'. Three still stand – at Geddington, Northampton and Waltham.

✳ **Charles VIII** of France was renowned for his impeccable manners. On entering a tennis court at the Chateau d'Amboise in 1498, he bowed to his wife and allowed her to proceed first. As he brought his head up from his magnanimous gesture, it crashed against a low wooden beam, fracturing his skull and killing him.

✳ In the late 19th century, to prove he had something to offer to the arts, Prussian **General von Hülsen** dressed up as a ballerina and performed a *pas de ballet* in the presence of the Kaiser. However, the General's 56 years caught up with him and he suffered a fatal heart attack at the height of his performance.

✳ **Alexandros I** of Greece (reigned 1917–20) died in 1920 at the age of 27 from blood poisoning after being bitten by his pet monkey.

✳ **King Haakon VII** of Norway (reigned 1905–57) died in September 1957, aged 85 years, when he slipped on the soap in his marble bath and struck his head on one of the taps.

✳ Having been nominally Queen of Scotland since 1286, seven-year-old **Margaret, the 'Maid of Norway'**, sailed from Norway in

September 1290 to claim her new kingdom. But on the journey across the North Sea, she suffered terrible sea-sickness and died in the Orkneys before ever reaching the Scottish mainland.

✳ The unhappy **Edward II** (reigned 1307–27) had been held prisoner in Berkeley Castle, Gloucestershire, for eight months when he met the most terrible end in September 1327. One night, the 43-year-old King was seized by three assassins, hired by Lord Berkeley on the orders of Edward's Queen, Isabella, and her lover, Roger Mortimer. While two held him down, the third rammed a long, open-topped deer's horn up the King's backside. Once this was firmly in position, the red-hot tip of a long-handled poker was pushed through the horn and deep into Edward's bowels. The poker was then withdrawn, reheated and reinserted at least once more. Edward's screams resounded through the castle but the following day his body, which bore no visible marks of foul play, was put on display to convince the public that he had died in the night from natural causes.

Edward II relinquishes the throne in 1327. He soon came to a painful end

TREATIES

✳ When drawing up the Versailles Peace Treaty at the end of the First World War, the parties concerned forgot all about the tiny Pyrenean state of Andorra whose army comprised one officer, six privates, four general staff and no artillery. So in 1939, Andorra found itself fighting two World Wars simultaneously. The situation was resolved by the signing of a private peace treaty with Germany, formally concluding the First World War.

✳ Over the centuries, the border town of Berwick-upon-Tweed has changed hands between Scotland and England 13 times. Consequently, it was customary to refer to it as a separate entity in all State documents. At the outbreak of the Crimean War, Britain declared war on Czarist Russia in the name of Victoria, Queen of Great Britain, Ireland, Berwick-upon-Tweed and all British Dominions. But when the war ended two years later in 1856, the Paris Peace Treaty omitted to mention Berwick. So Berwick was officially at war with Russia for another 110 years until in 1966 a Soviet official, realizing the gravity of the situation, visited the town to declare peace. The Mayor of Berwick, Councillor Robert Knox, replied: 'Please tell the Russian people that at last they can sleep peacefully in their beds!'

✳ In 1809, the Council of Huescar, a small village in southern Spain, was so angry at Denmark's decision to side with France against Britain in the Napoleonic Wars that it boldly declared war on the Danes. Denmark remained blissfully unaware of the fact and it was not until 11 November 1981 that a formal armistice was signed by the warring factions to bring an end to 172 years of hostilities.

✳ For 335 years, the Scilly Isles and the Netherlands were at war. In 1651, Dutch Admiral Maarten Tromp had declared war on the Scillies because its residents had engaged in acts of piracy during the English Civil War. In 1986, following three centuries of inactivity, the conflict was officially ended.

LAW AND ORDER

● Roman Emperor Caligula (ruled AD 37–41) was so upset by the death of his sister Drusila that he imposed a year of mourning, during which everyone in the empire was forbidden to dine with his family, laugh or take a bath. The penalty for transgression was death.

● Under the laws of Alfred the Great, King of Wessex (reigned 871–901), anyone caught fighting in the presence of a bishop had to pay 100 shillings in compensation. The fine rose to 150 shillings if an archbishop was present.

● In 1349, Edward III banned all sport in England except archery because his soldiers needed more practice. The English archery laws compelled all able-bodied men under a certain rank to practise with the bow on Sundays and holidays from childhood to the age of 60. Archery butts had to be set up in all villages. Edward also banned the game of football 'under pain of imprisonment'.

● Acts were passed in England in 1388 and 1410 prohibiting the playing of tennis by servants and labourers. The penalty was six days' in prison.

● In Nuremberg, Germany, in 1503, a law was passed prohibiting children from playing marbles except after a church service.

● Swimming in England was strongly discouraged during the reign of Elizabeth I (1558–1603). At Cambridge University, undergraduates were forbidden to swim and were threatened with flogging or expulsion should they do so. Elizabeth also made the wearing of hats compulsory for anyone over the age of seven on Sundays and holidays. Failure to do so would result in a fine of 3s 4d.

● In 16th- and 17th-century Turkey, anybody caught drinking coffee was liable to execution.

● Shortly after the First World War, King Amanullah of Afghanistan stayed at London's Ritz Hotel where he became fascinated by English traditions. The visit made such an impression on him that when he returned to his native country, he tried to pass a law requiring all of his male subjects to wear bowler hats. It was not a popular move and Amanullah was forced to abdicate.

● The City Council of Chico in California once banned nuclear weapons. Anyone caught detonating a nuclear device within the city limits was liable to a fine of $500.

AMERICA'S STRANGE LAWS

The method of legislature in the United States allows for a number of bizarre laws from states, counties and towns eager to preserve their identity.

✳ In Alaska, it is illegal to look at a moose from the window of an aircraft or any other flying vehicle.

✳ A law at Kirkland, Illinois, forbids bees to fly over the town.

✳ Carrying fishing tackle in a cemetery is illegal in Muncie, Indiana.

✳ A law in Kansas reads: 'When trains meet at a crossing, both shall come to a full stop and neither shall proceed until the other has gone'.

✳ In Milwaukee, people must keep their pet elephants on a leash while walking them on public streets.

✳ At International Falls, Minnesota, it is illegal for a dog to chase a cat up a telegraph pole. Owners can be fined or arrested.

✳ In Waterloo, Nebraska, barbers are prohibited from eating onions between 7 a.m. and 7 p.m.

✳ 'Profane, vulgar or indecent language' is forbidden on the streets of Raritan, New Jersey. The penalty is a possible 90-day jail sentence and a $300 fine.

✳ At Greene, New York State, it is against the law to walk backwards while eating peanuts during a concert.

✳ An Ohio law states that pets have to carry lights on their tails at night.

✳ In inland Oklahoma, it is illegal to attempt to catch whales or get a fish drunk.

✳ It is a criminal offence in the United States to alter the tune of 'The Star Spangled Banner'.

✳ It is illegal to carry an ice-cream cone in your pocket in Lexington, Kentucky.

TRIALS

● In 1471 at Basle, Switzerland, a cockerel was found guilty of laying an egg 'in defiance of natural law'. The bird was sentenced to death and burnt at the stake as 'a devil in disguise'.

● At Stelvio in northern Italy, a warrant was issued in 1519 for the arrest of a number of moles after crops had been badly damaged. The moles were required 'to show cause for their conduct by pleading their exigencies and distress'. For some reason, they failed to appear in court and, in their absence, were sentenced to exile. In its mercy, the court promised them safe conduct 'and an additional respite of 14 days to all those which are with young'.

● French lawyer Bartholomew Chassenée successfully defended a number of rats which were charged with destroying a barley crop in 1521. When the rats failed to appear in court to answer the charges, Chassenée claimed that his clients had been intimidated by 'evilly disposed cats' belonging to the prosecution and demanded a cash undertaking that the cats would not attack the rats on their way to court. When the prosecution refused to guarantee the rats' safety, the case was dismissed.

● John Lee of Babbacombe, Devon, was known as the man they could not hang. Lee, aged 19, was convicted of murdering Emma Keyse, a former maid to Queen Victoria, at her home on 14 November 1884. He was sentenced to die at Exeter Jail on 23 February 1885 but three times he was placed on the hangman's trap and three times the trap refused to drop even though the mechanism was found to be in perfect working order. The official explanation was that rain had caused the trap door to swell but there was also a suggestion that the builder of the gallows had rigged the trap to be jammed by the weight of the chaplain standing next to the condemned man. Whatever the cause of the failure, it saved Lee's neck for his death sentence was commuted to life imprisonment. He was released after serving 22 years in jail and later emigrated to the United States where he died.

● On 7 February 1894, young Will Purvis was led to the gallows to be hanged for the murder of a farmer in Columbia, Mississippi. The trap door opened but the noose became unknotted and slipped over Purvis's head. The deputies were keen to try again but a 3000-strong crowd, believing they had witnessed a miracle, wanted Purvis spared and he was led back to his cell. Eventually, a new date of execution was set – 12 December 1895 – but a few days beforehand, he was sprung from jail by friends. He surrendered to the authorities on 12 March 1896, still protesting his innocence, and was granted a pardon and freed in 1898. In 1917, a man named Joseph Beard confessed to the murder on his death-bed. In the course of the trial, Purvis had been so appalled at being found guilty that he had yelled at the 12 jurors: 'I'll live to see the last one of you die!'. Purvis died on 13 October 1938, three days after the death of the last juror.

● Emperor Menlek II of Abyssinia was so impressed by stories telling of the efficiency of the electric chair that in 1890 he ordered three from New York – even though at the time Abyssinia had no electricity. The fact did not seem to connect in the Emperor's mind and it was not until they arrived that he realized they would not work. He threw two of the chairs out and used the third as his throne.

7

TRANSPORT

AVIATION

● Attempts to fly date back to around 1020 when Oliver of Malmesbury, an English Benedictine monk, tried to fly from Malmesbury Abbey, Wiltshire, using wings. He broke both legs.

● On 8 August 1709, Father Bartolomeu de Gusmao (1685–1724) demonstrated a model hot-air balloon in the Ambassador's drawing-room at the Casa da India, Terreiro do Paco, Portugal, to King John V of Portugal and other assembled dignitaries. The balloon rose to a height of 3.6 m (12ft) before being destroyed to prevent it setting the Embassy curtains on fire.

● One of the most intrepid of birdmen was 62-year-old French nobleman, the Marquis de Bacqueville, who, in 1742, prepared to fly across the River Seine in Paris with paddles fitted to his arms and legs. At the last minute he got cold feet and asked a servant to try them out first. The servant, sensing that refusal would mean unem-

Left François Barathon's ingenious pedal-driven lifebuoy of 1895 (see p. 130). The shipwrecked survivor was supposed to sit on the bag and pedal to safety

ployment, diplomatically pointed out that a valet could not possibly precede his master. The Marquis was outfoxed and, with a big crowd gathered below, realized there was no backing out. From a window ledge on the top floor of his house he leaped out and began flapping vigorously. He plummeted to the ground like a stone, narrowly missing the pavement but landing instead on a pile of old clothes in a washerwoman's boat which had been moored on the riverbank to enjoy the spectacle. The clothes cushioned the Marquis's fall and he sustained nothing more than a broken leg.

● In 1772, Canon Desforges of the Collegiate Church of Saint Croix d'Etampes in France devised an intricate flying machine. It comprised a wickerwork basket, manually operated wings and a vast fabric canopy to help support it in the air and also, it was hoped, to prevent the contraption from crashing. The whole thing, including the Canon, weighed 96.6 kg (213 lb) but, nevertheless, he was confident that it could reach speeds of up to 96 km/h (60 mph) and planned to fly from Etampes to Paris. When launched from a building in Etampes, the Canon's wonder machine crashed straight to the ground, disintegrating on impact.

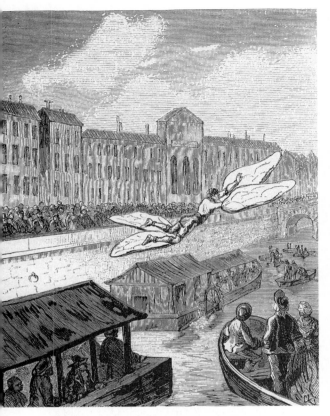

The ingenious flying device of the Marquis de Bacqueville (see p. 119)

English Channel, from England to France. He persuaded a wealthy American, John Jeffries, to pay all his expenses and to join him on the flight. Ten kilometres (6 miles) out from Dover, the balloon began to float perilously close to the sea so the duo decided to jettison the flapping wings and rudder which were attached to the basket. They continued to fly dangerously low and so, in a further attempt to lighten the load, the two men tossed their coats into the sea. This was still not enough. There was only one thing for it – they would have to remove their trousers. This desperate measure proved successful and they landed 20 km (12 miles) inland in the Forest de Felmores, wearing only their underpants.

● In 1865, an anonymous US designer wrote to a science magazine with the suggestion that a device powered by ten eagles could be used to carry a man through the air. He designed a harness for the birds, each tethered to the rim of a circular frame, with the passenger seated in a basket in the centre. The birds would be steered by ten sets of reins and a set of cords was provided to adjust the eagles' altitude. The one thing the inventor did not appear to have considered was how to catch the eagles in the first place.

● Few flying machines were as bizarre as that invented by Belgian shoemaker Vincent de Groof. His equipment – 'a device with bat-like wings' – was part flapper, part parachute. The framework was made of wood and rattan and the 12 m (40 ft) wings were covered with waterproof silk and controlled by three wooden levers worked by the arms and legs. The tail, also covered with strong silk, was 6 m (20 ft) long. On 9 July 1874, de Groof planned a flight over London. He was to be taken to an altitude of 300 m (1000 ft) by balloon and then released. The ascent went smoothly; the descent was less successful. Released over the Thames, de Groof and machine plunged into a street in Chelsea when the wing frame failed. De Groof was killed.

● The 1870s also saw Monsieur A. Goupil's aerial velocipede. The Frenchman's machine resembled a unicycle beneath a zeppelin. The balloon-type

The Canon suffered several broken bones.

● On 27 August 1783, Jacques Alexandre César Charles released a 3.6 m (12 ft) diameter unmanned balloon from Champ-de-Mars, Paris. It made a 45-minute flight to Gonesse but, on landing, it was attacked and destroyed by violent villagers who thought it was a monster. Their fears were reinforced by a curious odour coming from a puncture in the balloon.

● In 1785, two years after the Montgolfier brothers had made the first manned balloon flight, Frenchman Jean-Pièrre Blanchard had the idea of being the first person to fly across the

❋ Pilot Douglas Corrigan took off in dense fog from New York in 1938 with the intention of flying west to California. However, he got his bearings sadly wrong and instead flew due east for 28 h, eventually landing in Ireland. His escapade earned him the nickname 'Wrong-Way Corrigan'.

balloon-type structure was made of wood, covered with silk, and weighed 100 kg (220 lb). The aeronaut perched on the pedals of the unicycle which was linked to the balloon by connecting rods. From this vantage point, he operated the pedals and a rudder. A description of M. Goupil's brainchild in the *Chronique Industrielle* explained: 'As the apparatus obtains velocity its weight diminishes on account of the increase of the vertical reaction of the current and, finally, it ought to ascend and maintain itself aloft'. It is not known whether the aerial velocipede ever lived up to its billing.

● In 1885, Dr W.O. Ayres of New Haven, Connecticut, designed a forerunner of the flying bedstead. His contraption was driven by seven propellers, six for lift and one for propulsion. Foot pedals provided the drive for two of the lifting propellers while compressed-air motors drove the other four. The propulsion screw was operated by a hand crank as were the rudder and elevator controls. The doctor's device never threatened to take off.

● In the 1900s, a Parisian, Count de Guiseux, is said to have achieved modest hops with his Aeroplane Bicycle in which large wings were fixed to a bicycle. A propeller was situated in kite-shaped

Dr W.O. Ayres and his magnificent flying machine driven by seven propellers

compartments which assisted lift-off when there was a breeze. The propeller was linked to the drive chain of the back wheel and the bicycle was so highly geared that it turned at a much faster rate when the Count pedalled. He had to pedal furiously to have any hope of elevation, making any form of sustained flight an exhausting prospect.

❋ A paper aircraft built by 17 pupils from four high schools at Hampton, Virginia, USA, had a wing span of 9.29 m (30 ft 6 in). Launched indoors from a 3 m (10 ft) high platform at the NASA Langley Research Center Hangar at Hampton on 25 March 1992, it flew a distance of 34.97 m (114 ft 9 in).

BICYCLES

● The invention of a Mr Revis from Cambridge in 1839, the Aellopedes was a type of enormous tricycle, 3.6 m (12 ft) long with two rear wheels 1.8 m (6 ft) in diameter and a guide wheel at the front around half that size. The rider propelled it by stepping backwards on treadles connected to the axle and it was claimed to be able to attain speeds of 48 km/h (30 mph). Priced at about £30,

it was described by *The Mirror* of 23 March 1839 as 'a carriage light and elegant in form' and noted that the 'Gentlemen of the University of Cambridge adopted it as a means of exercise'. The article added that Mr Revis 'has made offers to the heads of the post-office department, with a view to a speedier and more economical transmission of the cross-mails'.

● An Englishman named Mr Trinden hated falling off his bicycle and hated cycling up hills. He decided to solve both problems with his 1869 invention, the Balloon Velocipede. His bicycle was attached to a giant balloon, the idea being that the balloon would give an upward pull and fight gravity going up a hill. It would also reduce the risk of falling off. Mr Trinden appeared to have overlooked the fact that he might float off into the clouds on a windy day.

Cycling rose to new heights with the Eiffel Tower model in the 1890s

● In the United States in 1869, a monocycle was brought out in which the rider had to sit inside the 2.49 m (8 ft 2 in) single wheel on the axle.

● A three-wheeled vehicle powered by dogs was invented in the 1880s by a Monsieur Huret from France. Inside the two huge rear wheels were treadmills driven by the revolving dogs. Although M. Huret no doubt considered his machine to provide valuable exercise for the hounds, the idea was scrapped following protests from animal-lovers.

● Under a law of 1888, every cyclist in Britain had to ring the bell on his bicycle non-stop while the machine was in motion. The law was not abolished until 1930.

● In 1897, Frenchman Léon Bollée designed his motor tricycle, a curious mix of wheelchair and motor cycle. Another oddity was that the passenger sat in front of the driver in a wickerwork bathchair with the driver in tandem, furiously occupied with the hand-operated steering, the gears, the clutch and the brakes.

● Around 1899, Britain's Humber Cycle Company produced the Eiffel Tower, a two-wheeled machine with the seat some 3.6 m (12 ft) above ground. The rider reached this precarious perch with the assistance of a companion who held the whole thing steady. It was used primarily for advertising, display boards being strapped to the high-sided frame.

● A curious British machine of the 1930s was the Allworth Triplet Tandem which had three seats and an attached Watsonian sidecar. It was designed to transport the entire family and measured 2.4 m (8 ft) in length.

● Neville Patten of Gladstone, Queensland, Australia, constructed a bicycle with wheels just 19 mm (0.76 in) in diameter and rode it for a distance of 4.1 m (13 ft 5½ in) on 25 March 1988. Jacques Puyoou of Pau, Pyrénées-Atlantiques, France, has built a tandem 36 cm (14 in) long which has been ridden by him and Madame Puyoou.

● In 1979, Pedaalstompers Westmalle of Belgium built a 20.39 m (66 ft 11 in) long tandem for 35 riders. It weighed 1100 kg (2425 lb). Parking was considered something of a problem.

● Californian Steve Roberts has invented a highly technological bicycle that is equipped with computers, sophisticated communication equipment and a global positioning system, using satellites, to locate itself anywhere in the world. The computer screen and keyboard enable him to write while he rides. The bicycle has 105 gears and is also fitted with its own talking burglar alarm that knows when the machine is being used by a stranger. In case of theft, it announces loudly: 'I am a bicycle. I'm being stolen.' In ten years, Roberts has travelled some 7000 miles (11 265 km).

MOTORCARS, CARRIAGES, BUSES AND TRAMS

● The world's first horseless carriage was the Fardier, a three-wheeled road steamer, designed in 1769 by French artillery engineer Capitaine Nicolas-Joseph Cugnot (1725–84) to move guns. It had a top speed of 3.6 km/h (2¼ mph) but its small boiler meant that stops had to be made every 15 minutes to top it up with water.

● Born in 1719, the son of a Northamptonshire rector, Captain Philip Thicknesse became a successful author with his account of an economy version of the Grand Tour, undertaken in 1775. He and his wife, three children and assorted pets travelled around France and Spain in a two-wheeled Cabriolet, drawn by Callee the horse. Their spaniel ran alongside, a parakeet nestled in Mrs Thicknesse's ample bosom while Jocko the monkey, wearing a red jacket, a riding hat, jackboots and a detachable pigtail, sat perched on the horse's back. Local peasants were suitably puzzled.

● In 1834, a French sail carriage called L'Eolienne (after Aiolos the Greek god of the winds) was tested in Paris. It had two masts fixed to the top of a conventional carriage, each with two or three square sails. Horses were not used at all. The wind-powered coach was fast but extremely dangerous, being impossible to steer along winding roads. A crew of sailors was needed to man the rigging and when they went up to raise or lower the sails to control the speed, the whole carriage became hopelessly unbalanced. Also the brakes were not strong enough to bring it to a halt. All in all, it was little surprise that it soon gave way to the steam carriage.

● The Locomotives on Highways Act, passed in 1865 and popularly known as the Red Flag Act, insisted that any self-propelled carriage on an English highway have a crew of three, one of whom had to walk in front with a red flag as a warning of its approach, especially to horse-carriage drivers.

● The first attempt at installing traffic lights took place in London's Parliament Square in 1868. Revolving red and green lanterns, illuminated by gas, were manually operated by the police.

No doubt there were many volunteers among the constabulary for such gentle duties – until, that is, the operating officer was badly injured when the gas apparatus exploded. The experimental lights were soon removed.

Electric traffic lights were introduced in Cleveland, Ohio, in August 1914 and in the UK in 1926 at the junction of St James's Street and Piccadilly in London. They did not make it to Albania until October 1993.

● The appearance of the first steam trams in San Francisco in the 1870s caused total pandemonium. Horses panicked with the result that horse-drawn vehicles started careering in all directions. Then an inventor named S.R. Mathewson came up with an ingenious idea – he built a steam tram in the shape of a horse. Patented in 1876, it had a huge equine figure at the front and a small carriage at the rear. It reached speeds of up to 8 mph (12.8 km/h) and because the engine was gas-fired, there was no smoke to frighten the horses.

✳ In 1914, French General Gallieni used a fleet of taxis, the drivers still wearing their caps, to ferry his troops from Paris to the Battle of the Marne. The soldiers slept in the backs of the cabs.

● American silent movie star Buster Keaton owned 20 cars simultaneously. The biggest was 30 ft (9.1 m) long and had sleeping accommodation for six, two drawing rooms, a kitchen and an observation deck. Built to resemble a yacht, it was 'captained' by Keaton dressed in an admiral's uniform.

Flamboyant pianist Liberace owned a 1931 Cadillac Roadster. It was plain black when he bought it, but over the years he had the exterior covered in gold leaf and the pedals lined with mink.

The Maharajah of Nabha, India, had his Rolls-Royce customized in the shape of a swan. Exhaust fumes were discharged through the 'beak'.

● The early 1930s was a grim period in Canadian history. Some 1.5 million Canadians were out of work and many farmers hitched horses to their cars simply because they could not afford either to license or run them. These strange vehicles were called 'Bennett buggies' after R.B. Bennett who was Prime Minister during the worst years of the Depression.

> ✳ In 1972, a small van was converted into a thatched cottage to advertise the 14th-century Tudor Rose Inn at Fordingbridge, Hampshire. The sides of the van were painted black and white to give a half-timbered effect and the roof of the vehicle was thatched.

● During the early 1970s, Mrs Helen Ireland of Auburn, California, managed to fail her driving test in the first second. She got into the car, bade the examiner 'good morning' and started the engine. Alas she mistook the accelerator for the clutch and shot straight through the wall of the Driving Test Centre.

For many years, the driving test in Egypt simply consisted of driving 6 m (20 ft) forward and the same distance in reverse. Then, in 1979, accurate reversing between two rubber traffic cones was added to the test but repeated damage to the cones soon led to them being replaced by white lines.

● A familiar sight on the streets of southern California in the 1970s and 1980s were 'erotic vans' created by disabled war veteran Ken Jones. By 1984, following 'The Dark Room' and 'The Massage Parlour', 62-year-old Jones was driving his ultimate erotic vehicle which he christened 'The Harem'. Inside he had installed crystal chandeliers, mirrors, tasselled rugs, curtains, sub-

> ✳ A multi-seat Mini 6.1 m (20 ft) long was created at BMC's Cowley, Oxford, plant and displayed in the window of the company's Piccadilly showroom at Christmas 1964. The vehicle had standard Mini halves at the front and rear and proved so popular that seven people rang in to place orders!

dued lighting, a television, a refrigerator, a cocktail bar, a large bed and dozens of velvet cushions.

● Bill Harding of Kansas City customized his 1966 Buick Le Sabre by giving it a green covering of Manhattan perennial rye. He believed his grass car symbolized the delicate balance between nature and machines. 'You can't have perfect technology or pure nature', he said in 1984. 'It has to be a balance of those two things for the world to work.'

● One of the most adaptable cars is the Volkswagen Beetle. In 1963, an open-topped Beetle body with a 2.1 m (7 ft) high chair in place of the rear seat was exhibited in London. It was billed as 'the biggest armchair in the world'.

Advertisements for Rolo featured a 3.2 m (10 ft 6 in) wide Beetle.

The Lintas advertising company had two convertibles sawn apart. The left convertible inner half, its right front wheel and the rear side bodywork were all cut out and then the two halves were welded together, the entire operation costing £12 000. The result was a near double-width car with five wheels, two at the front, three at the back. This special Beetle could accommodate six people in the front.

A Beetle 7.2 m (23 ft 6 in) long made its only journey through the Swiss town of Schaffhausen carrying 21 young men on their way to medicals for military service. The vehicle, which took months to weld together, had its gear stick 4 m (13 ft) behind the driver so gears were changed by shouting instructions.

Two more Beetles have ended up as 4.6 m (15 ft) high roller boots. Converted in California in 1979, the two-seater boot-shaped Beetles were made as a pair. The left 'boot' has a left-hand drive; the right one has a right-hand drive. They have been

✻ Traffic congestion is so bad in Bangkok, the capital of Thailand, that drivers are advised to carry food, water and even portable toilets when travelling to work in the city. The average journey to the office takes five hours.

used mainly for promotional purposes – the right is in Germany while the left has been advertising a roller-skating rink in Derby.

● In January 1990, French inventor Jacques Calvel introduced a collapsible vehicle called 'Golfe'. Originally designed for use on a golf course, it could be folded up like a briefcase, transforming it into a parallelepiped 1.75 m (5 ft 9 in) long and 1.09 m (3 ft 7 in) wide. Driven by a bicycle motor, it weighed 60 kg (132 lb) and was capable of a speed of 30 km/h (18½ mph).

● In 1990, HE Sheik Hamad Bin Hamdan Al Nahyan of Abu Dhabi, United Arab Emirates, built a two-wheeled, two-storey caravan containing eight bedrooms and bathrooms and four garages. The caravan, which could store 24 000 litres (5280 gallons) of water, measured 20 m (66 ft) long, 12 m (39 ft) wide and weighed 120 tonnes.

● In 1994, a French company based at Thenay produced the Hobbycar, an amphibious four-seater. With its 1.9-litre diesel turbo engine, the Hobbycar can reach 112 km/h (70 mph) on dry land and the fitting of twin hydrojets and an inflatable skirt enable it to power through the water. Commercial director Maurice Danton enthuses: 'If there's a crowd at St Tropez and the Hobbycar is parked next to a Ferrari, the Hobbycar gets all the attention. It's also much better for picking up girls

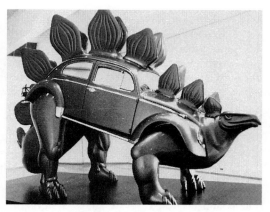

In order to show how modern cars would, to future generations, look as old as dinosaurs do today, Professor Patricia Renick, an artist at the University of Cincinnati, USA, converted a Volkswagen Beetle into a stegosaurus

if you tell them it goes on water as well.'

● Jay Ohrburg of Burbank, California, has designed a 100 ft (30.5 m) long 26-wheeled limousine. Its features include a swimming pool with diving-board and a king-sized water bed. It is designed to be driven either in one piece or to bend in the middle. Its main purpose is for use in films and exhibitions.

✻ At Brannockstown, County Kildare, in 1972, a single-decker bus became a drive-away church. The bus was converted into a church and painted in Gothic, blue-stone aluminium. The destination sign read 'Churchmobile'.

RAILWAYS

● In 1825, British railway pioneer George Stephenson (1781–1848) deliberately lied to a parliamentary inquiry conducted into the speed of trains. He told MPs that trains would never travel faster than 12 mph (19 km/h) even though he knew they were capable of achieving twice that speed. The reason for the deceit was to allay public fears that trains exceeding 12 mph would bring about mental disorders among passengers and might also cause suffocation since the speed would suck the air from their lungs.

● The first US transcontinental railroad was completed on 10 May 1869 at Promontory, Utah, where the Central Pacific and Union Pacific railroads were united. A meeting point had not been established beforehand and since the companies were receiving up to $48 000 in Federal loans for each mile (1.6 km) of track they laid, the rival gangs happily passed one another. The Union Pacific gang carried on constructing 225 miles (362 km) of parallel grading before they were finally stopped.

● The old Ghan railway from Adelaide to Oodnadatta, South Australia, was built in the wrong place. When work on the 610 mile (981 km) line commenced in 1877, designers decided that since all of the creek beds north of Marree were bone dry and because nobody could remember seeing rain, there would not be any rain in the future. They laid the initial stretch of line right across a flood plain and when the rains did come, the tracks were washed away. The whole line was a mess. The foundations were flimsy, the sleepers were too light, the grading too steep and it meandered hopelessly. Consequently, top speed was just 18 mph (29 km/h). Early rail travellers went from Adelaide to Marree on a broad gauge line, changed at Marree to narrow gauge as far as Oodnadatta and then on to Alice Springs by camel. The line was eventually extended the 280 miles (450 km) to Alice Springs in 1929 but still trains were frequently stranded by heavy rain, necessitating the dropping of supplies to passengers by parachute. Once the Ghan rolled in ten days late, something which even British Rail has yet to accomplish. Finally in 1980, a new line was laid – in an area free from flooding.

✳ The only railway to travel to the top of a volcano was opened on Mt Vesuvius, Italy, in 1880. It took passengers to the summit station at 1223 m (4012 ft), just below the crater. The railway was destroyed by the eruption of 20 March 1944 and was replaced by a chair lift.

● Between November 1896 and January 1901, visitors to Brighton, Sussex, could travel on a railcar on stilts. It belonged to the Brighton and Rottingdean Seashore Electric Tramroad, a 2¾ mile (4.42 km) stretch of track built along the seashore by Magnus Volk. At high water, the four rails were submerged beneath 15 ft (4.6 m) of water, as a result of which the railcar, built by the Gloucester Railway Carriage and Wagon Company Ltd, stood on legs 23 ft (7 m) high. It had a cabin like a ship and was the only railcar which carried a lifeboat and lifebelts as standard equipment.

● It is not often that a boat and a train collide but this was the case in February 1913 on the Memphis branch of the Louisville and Nashville Railroad. The area was severely flooded at the time and in the dark, a freight train collided with the shallow-draught packet-boat *Lochie S* which was sailing above the tracks at Cumberland, Texas. Nobody was injured and liability for the damage was never settled.

● The first escalators at a London Underground station were installed at Earls Court on 4 October 1911. Two 12 m (40 ft) Seeberger escalators linked the District and Piccadilly lines. To reassure the public about the safety of the new device, a man with a wooden leg, 'Bumper' Harris, was hired to ride up and down the escalators for the day. When passengers saw that Bumper came to no harm, they too decided that it was safe to travel by escalator.

● Odd fuels have been used for steam locomotives to keep railways running in difficult times. On a branch of the Arica–La Paz Railway in Chile, llama dung and dried moss have been burned, while in Brazil, during a crop surplus, coffee beans were used. In 1919 when there was a shortage of coal in Russian Turkestan, dried fish was used as locomotive fuel. For this purpose, the Soviet government requisitioned 8000 tonnes from Aral Sea fishermen.

● The highest standard-gauge passenger railway in the world runs between Lima and Huancayo in the Peruvian Andes. The station at Ticlio is 4680 m (15 350 ft) above sea level and at places the track rises to 4818 m (15 806 ft). It takes four hours for the train to climb from Lima, at sea-level, to Ticlio.

Magnus Volk's electric trolley car successfully navigates high tide on the run between Brighton and Rottingdean

The change in altitude is so rapid that some passengers have difficulty breathing in the thin air. Accordingly, attendants join the train at around 4000 m (13 000 ft) (by which time the pressure has dropped to 415 millibars compared to 765 millibars at the point of departure) to administer oxygen to those feeling faint. Gradients on the line reach 1 in 25. On the steepest slopes, there is no room for the line to curve back and forth so the track has been laid out in zigzag sections called switchbacks. At the end of each section is a short siding so that the train alternately steams forward and reverses across the slope as it climbs.

● The world's smallest public railway is the 15 in (381 mm) gauge Romney, Hythe and Dymchurch Railway in Kent. It is 22.2 km (13.8 miles) long and from Hythe to New Romney is double track. Trains reach speeds of 32 to 40 km/h (20 to 25 mph). The railway has ten steam locomotives designed by Henry Greenly and was built between 1925 and 1931. It opened on 16 July 1927.

✳ In 1971, Mr and Mrs William Farmer of Margate, Kent, travelled to Wales for their summer holiday. At the start of the week, they joined a British Rail mystery tour . . . which promptly took them straight back to Margate. Declining the proposed tour of the town, they popped home for a cup of tea instead.

SHIPS AND CANALS

● In ancient Sumeria in southern Mesopotamia, traders used collapsible boats to transport goods by river. Upstream, they constructed boats of hides stretched over light wooden frames. After being loaded with the cargo plus the requisite donkey, the boats then drifted downstream to their destination. At the other end, the cargo was unloaded, the boat taken to pieces and the frame sold on for timber. The hides were loaded on to the donkey and the crew walked back, finding that preferable to having to propel the boat upstream against the current. Once back at their base, they would build a new frame, cover it with the existing hides and set off with the next cargo.

● One of the earliest attempts at building a submarine was by Dutchman Cornelius van Drebbel. In 1620, he built a wooden frame covered with greased leather to make it watertight and fitted it with oars and managed to row 15 ft (4.5 m) below the surface of the River Thames.

● Pressure of work meant that Sir Henry Bessemer (1813–98), British inventor of the revolutionary steel-making process, needed to make frequent trips overseas. Unfortunately, Sir Henry was a bad traveller, prone to bouts of sea-sickness. So he devised a swinging saloon which, with the help of naval architect R.J. Reed, was incorporated in a new cross-channel steamer, the *Bessemer*. The idea was that the saloon, balanced amidships on a central pivot, would remain on an even keel regardless of the ship's motions. Instead it rolled violently. So Bessemer introduced a hydraulic brake, operated by a man who sat watching a spirit level. When this too failed, he had the saloon locked in position and the ship used as a conventional steamer. However, the *Bessemer* was virtually unsteerable. On her first trip, she collided with the pier at Calais and repeated the feat on her return to Dover. Sir Henry ended up selling the ship for scrap, but his swinging saloon found its way into the Horticultural College at Hextable, Kent, where it was destroyed by a German bomb during the Second World War.

✳ In the early 19th century, insanity in the Royal Navy was seven times the national average. Eminent surgeon Sir Gilbert Blane concluded that this was due to head injuries sustained by the men constantly banging their heads in the confined space between decks, something they were particularly apt to do after consuming copious quantities of rum.

● In 1840, a construction company built a canal between Lakes Corrib and Mask in western Ireland. Since they built it entirely on porous limestone, no sooner had the water been poured in than it drained away. So a clay bed was laid instead. Everything progressed smoothly until, with the canal almost completed, it was discovered that one of the lakes was several feet lower than the other. It suddenly dawned on the workmen that they were asking water to flow uphill. At that, the whole project was abandoned.

● The strangest ship ever built was the *Connector*, assembled in England in 1863. It was constructed in three sections which were loosely hinged together to allow the ship to ride comfortably through heavy seas with an undulating motion. The three parts were detachable, each part being an independent vessel, which would thus allow the sections to be loaded and unloaded at separate wharves. Despite its undoubted ingenuity, the *Connector* was singularly unsuccessful.

● When the 739-tonne ship *Athens* was caught in a gale in Table Bay off South Africa on 16 May 1865, she broke moorings and was wrecked on rocks near Moville Point. All 29 people on board drowned, the only survivor being a pig which was miraculously washed up alive.

● On the night of 25 November 1875, the *Royal Adelaide*, an iron sailing ship of 1320 tonnes bound from London to Sydney, was driven ashore on Chesil Beach, Dorset. The impact caused her to break up and hundreds of cases of spirits were washed from her holds on to the shore. Six of the 67 passengers drowned in the wreck but there

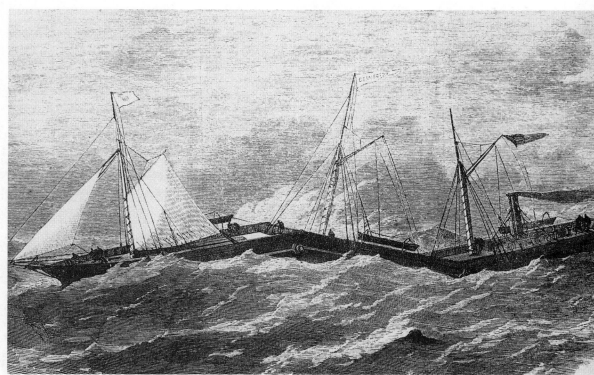

The curious SS *Connector* on its maiden voyage across the Thames from Blackwall to Erith Reach in July 1863

were greater casualties among the thousands of onlookers, 20 of whom were dead by the morning after drinking too much of the washed-up cargo.

● The first man to sail solo around the world was a non-swimmer. Nova Scotia-born Captain Joshua Slocum, aged 51, set out from Newport, Rhode Island, on 24 April 1895 in his 36 ft 9 in (11.2 m) sloop, *Spray*. He returned on 3 July 1898, having completed a round trip of 46 000 nautical miles. Slocum embarked on a new voyage in *Spray* at the age of 65, leaving Rhode Island in November 1909, but neither he nor the boat were ever seen again.

● In 1895, a German inventor by the name of Najork came up with a cross between a bicycle and a dinghy. The Najork Foot Motor Boat, as he called it, was a conventional boat with a bicycle in the centre. It was powered by feverish pedalling and the bicycle was connected to the boat's rudder so that the rider could steer the craft at the same time. Possibly because it looked so strange, it never caught on.

Also in 1895, Frenchman François Barathon invented a pedal-driven lifebuoy. It comprised a saucer-shaped metal dish containing an inflatable rubber bag and some complex machinery. The shipwrecked survivor was supposed to sit on the bag and work two sets of cranks, one with his hands, the other with his feet. The cranks turned two propellers, one of which was set vertically in order to keep the craft stable and the other to push from behind. Progress was further aided by the attachment of a small sail.

● A ship called the *Resolute* once made a 1000 mile (1609 km) journey without any crew. The *Resolute* was part of an expedition commanded by Sir Edward Belcher which left England in 1852 to search for Sir John Franklin who, seven years earlier, had set off in a quest to find the elusive North-West Passage. Now Franklin had vanished, along with 129 officers and men and his two ships, the *Erebus* and the *Terror*. The salvage expedition fared little better and in May 1854, the *Resolute* was abandoned, stuck fast in the ice at the western end of Barrow Strait off the northern coast of Canada. The *Resolute* was next seen 474 days later by the commander of an American whaler, having presumably drifted through Barrow Strait, Lancaster Sound and Baffin Bay. Apart from shipping a little water, she was in excellent condition.

● German engineer Anton Flettner invented one of the most curious vessels of the 20th century – the rotor ship. From 1922, he had been conducting experiments at the University of Göttingen and had concluded that the wind pressure on a revolving disc was much greater than on a conventional sail. Putting this theory into practice, he designed a ship with two rotors, each turned by a small engine at the base. When the rotors were turned at four times the speed of the wind, the pressure exerted proved to be 15 times greater than on a sail of the same size. His prototype ship, the *Baden-Baden*, was launched in 1925, propelled by two huge rotating towers, 19.8 m (65 ft) high and 3 m (10 ft) in diameter. When it first arrived in New York from Hamburg, the *Baden-Baden* was greeted with wild enthusiasm. Rotor ships were seen as the way ahead. They were 80 per cent cheaper to run than sailing ships, could attain higher speeds (up to 17 knots) and needed fewer crew members. Yet within 20 years, all of the Flettner rotor ships had been condemned to the scrapyard. The incessant vibration of the rotors had caused insurmountable mechanical difficulties and the total dependence on wind power made the ships notoriously unreliable.

● The British liner the *Queen Mary*, launched in 1934, was supposed to have been called the *Queen Victoria*. Prior to the launch, Sir Thomas Royden, a director of shipbuilders Cunard, met King George V to obtain permission to call the new liner the *Queen Victoria*. Unfortunately, Royden made his request in rather flowery language, requesting if the vessel could be named 'after the

✱ The 'Snake Boat' Nadubhagóm from Kerala, southern India, is 41.1 m (135 ft) long and has a crew of 109 oarsmen plus nine 'encouragers'.

* The completion of the Panama Canal in 1914 was marked by a special display. Among those invited to attend by the US State Department was a representative of the non-existent Swiss Navy! The US ambassador to Switzerland, Pleasant A. Stovall, issued the invitation to the Swiss Foreign Office but when the Americans realized their geographical blunder, the offer was withdrawn.

greatest Queen this country has ever known'. The King misunderstood and, visibly moved, answered: 'That is the greatest compliment ever paid to my wife. I shall ask her.' The King's wife, Queen Mary, readily assented, leaving Cunard with little option but to revise its plans.

● On 28 November 1994, Scotsman Tom McLean, veteran of five solo Atlantic crossings including two in a rowing boat, unveiled his latest craft for reaching New York – a 60-tonne boat shaped like a whale. Depending on the success of ocean trials, McLean is planning to offer regular transatlantic trips in the diesel-powered vessel. Christened *Moby*, it comes complete with a huge mouth and large eye. There is a false bulkhead in the nose to deal with stray icebergs.

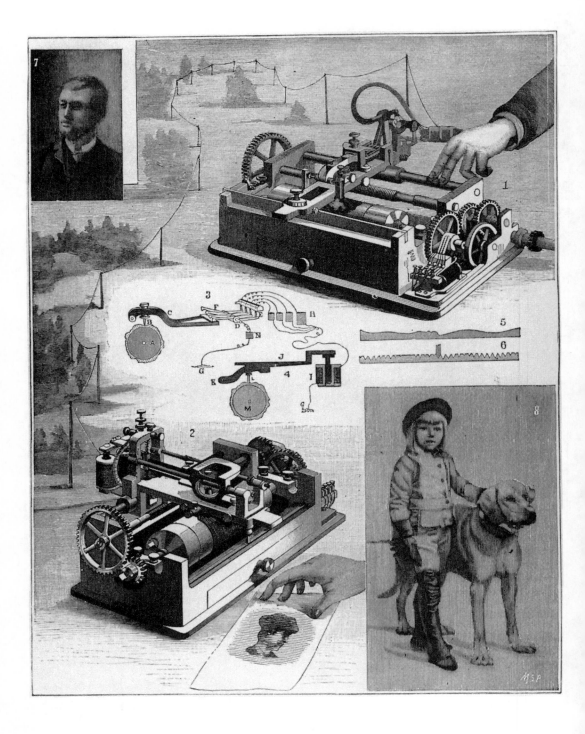

8

SCIENCE AND TECHNOLOGY

INVENTORS AND INVENTIONS

● The very first pair of roller skates were put together by Belgian musician Joseph Merlin. Eager to impress guests at a masked ball in London in 1760, Merlin made a grand entry on the skates while playing a violin. But, unable to stop or change direction, he shot across the ballroom straight into a full-length mirror. The mirror and the violin were broken and Merlin badly injured.

● The stethoscope was born out of the shyness of a young French physician, René Laennec (1781–1826). One day in 1816, Laennec was consulted by a young woman whom he suspected might be suffering from a heart disorder. He felt uncomfortable about following the usual procedure of placing his ear next to the patient's naked chest in order to listen to the heartbeat and so used a rolled-up newspaper instead. He was astounded to discover that the tube magnified the sounds and went on to construct a 30 cm (1 ft) long cylinder of wood – the first true stethoscope.

Left A 19th-century facsimile or copying telegraph system, this one made by Amstutz of Cleveland, Ohio, USA

● The fax machine was invented before the telephone. Patents for a fax machine date back to 1843 and messages were being faxed over 30 years before Bell's telephone. One of the pioneers was Scottish clockmaker Alexander Bain (1818–1903) who, in 1840, shortly after the invention of the telegraph, produced a crude method of sending pictures over telegraph wire. Bain's machine used swinging pendulums connected at either end of the telegraph line. For a character to be sent by wire, it first had to be made out of metal. At the sending side, a pendulum tipped with a metal stylus swung back and forth over the character. At the receiving end of the line, a similar pendulum swung to and fro across chemically treated paper. Each time the sending pendulum struck the metal, it completed an electrical circuit and sent an electric pulse through the wire. Reaching the swinging pendulum at the receiving end, the electricity discoloured the chemically treated paper, leaving a trace on the paper whenever contact was made. Clocks incorporated at either end were intended to advance the metal characters and the paper a fraction of an inch in unison but Bain encountered problems in synchronizing both pendulums and clocks. As a result, his machine was

133

consigned to obscurity and it was left to an Italian priest, Giovanni Caselli, to invent the first commercial fax system. Caselli greatly improved Bain's machine, removing the need for the original to be scratched in metal. He also installed a separate clock in the transmitting end which synchronized the pendulums. Caselli helped establish a fax line between Paris and Lyons for five years between 1865 and 1870. In the modern fax machine, the swinging pendulums have been replaced by light beams.

● German chemist Christian Schönbein (1799–1868) founded the modern explosives industry in his wife's kitchen. It was while working there in 1845 that he inadvertantly spilt a mixture of nitric and sulphuric acid on to a cotton apron. He hung the apron up to dry but as soon as it dried out, it exploded. As compensation for the loss of his apron, Schönbein had accidentally discovered nitro-cellulose. By 1890, nitro-cellulose, in the form of gun cotton, had replaced gunpowder as the most efficient military explosive.

● James Clerk Maxwell (1831–79), the Scottish physicist who, in the early 1860s, predicted in mathematical form the existence of electromagnetic waves 20 years before they were discovered by German Heinrich Rudolf Hertz (1857–94), was in the habit of conducting deep scientific conversations with his dog Tobi. Maxwell often tested his theories and formulated new ideas this way – even in the middle of a crowded party.

● American inventor Thomas Alva Edison (1847–1931) was the man responsible for the first practical electric light, the microphone and the forerunner of the record player. By his death, he held nearly 1300 patents. Yet he had only three months of formal schooling in his entire life. In 1855, at the age of eight, he attended a Michigan school run by a disciplinarian clergyman, the Reverend G.B. Engle, but ran away three months later after a teacher described his brain as 'addled'. Edison received little parental support either. His father thought young Thomas was stupid.

● The structure of benzene came to German scientist Friedrich Kekulé (1829–96) in a dream. Kekulé knew that the atoms in any molecule are linked by chemical hooks called valency bonds. Carbon has four hooks, hydrogen one. Benzene is a hydrocarbon in which six carbons are linked with six hydrogens, a state of affairs which puzzled Kekulé who could not work out how the atoms could be linked in a chain without leaving some hooks unattached – a chemical impossibility. Then in 1862, while working as a professor at Ghent, Belgium, he had a dream in which he saw a snake suddenly wriggle into a circle and swallow its tail. The dream told him that the carbon atoms in benzene were arranged in a ring.

● In the early 1870s, American schoolboy Horatio Adams was helping his father Thomas perform a series of experiments with chicle, the dried sap from a Mexican jungle tree. Thomas Adams was hoping to make rubber from it, but when that attempt failed he and his son started chewing pieces of chicle while contemplating their next move. It was as they did so that they chanced upon the perfect use for chicle – and quickly set up business to manufacture chewing gum.

● The founder of intelligence tests, pioneer of fingerprinting and cousin of Charles Darwin, English 19th-century scientist Sir Francis Galton (1822–1911) had a penchant for statistics – particularly those belonging to women. He conducted a survey to compile a 'Beauty Map of Britain' and invented a pocket counting device for recording the number of pretty women he met in the streets in various parts of the country. He concluded that London had the highest proportion of beautiful women, Aberdeen the lowest. Another survey took him off to Africa to ascertain why Hottentot women had the biggest bottoms. Not wishing to anger them at close quarters, he achieved his results by measuring the ladies' posteriors from a distance with a sextant.

● A factory builder by trade, Englishman Hubert Cecil Booth was watching an unsuccessful demonstration of railway carriage cleaning at Lon-

Hot on the heels of Hubert Cecil Booth, J.S. Thurman devised a cleaning method whereby compressed air was passed through a pipe and nozzle and the dust blown into a bag. The motor and compressor were housed on a horse-drawn van in the street. The picture shows a Parisian house being cleaned in 1904.

don's St Pancras Station in 1900 when he came up with the idea for the vacuum cleaner. The carriage was being cleaned by compressed air, a huge air blower having been placed over one open carriage door to blow dirt into a bag located over another. The result was nothing more than a cloud of dust. Discussing the incident in a restaurant in Victoria Street with other witnesses, Booth suggested that the solution was to suck dirt into a receptacle rather than try to blow it away. He demonstrated his theory by placing a handkerchief over the back of his plush seat, putting his lips to it and sucking. He nearly choked but a ring of black spots on the handkerchief proved the principle to be sound. In 1902, Booth formed the Vacuum Cleaner Company Ltd but, rather than sell his cleaners to the public, he chose to provide a service. It was just as well since his first model, nicknamed the 'Puffing Billy', was so large that it needed a team of men to operate it. Having the carpets cleaned necessitated the stationing of a horse-drawn van outside the customer's house. Mounted on the back of the van was a powerful vacuum pump,

driven by a petrol motor, and from which 800 ft (244 m) long hoses snaked their way through the windows to remove the offending dust. In addition to being cumbersome, the appliance was extremely noisy and frightened passing horses, which led to Booth being sued by cab proprietors.

In 1907, J. Murray Spangler, an asthmatic janitor from North Canton, Ohio, tried to simplify his job by inventing a labour-saving cleaning device. Powered by an electric motor, it consisted of a tin can, a broomstick and an old pillow-case as a dust bag. This odd contraption was the forerunner of the modern upright vacuum cleaner and soon attracted the attention of harness-maker H.W. Hoover who, fearing that the arrival of the automobile would hit the carriage trade, was looking for alternative ventures. Spangler sold the design to Hoover and in 1908, Hoover marketed it as the Electric Suction Sweeper, priced at $75. In 1927, two old vacuum cleaners plus other odds and ends formed the prototype iron lung!

135

● At 3 a.m. on Easter Sunday 1921, German-American physiologist Otto Loewi (1873–1961) had a vivid dream. 'It was the design of an experiment to determine whether or not the hypothesis of chemical transmission that I had uttered 17 years ago was correct. I got up immediately, went to the laboratory, and per-formed a simple experiment on a frog heart according to nocturnal design.'

Loewi's experiment proved that it is not nerves but the chemicals they release which directly affect the heart – a discovery that led to him winning the Nobel Prize for Medicine in 1936.

FAILED INVENTIONS

✳ Some inventions were simply too crazy to succeed. Take the self-tipping hat of 1896. In those days, it was customary for a man to raise his hat to a lady but this presented a problem if the man were laden down with goods. So James Boyle of Washington State came up with the self-tipping hat. The wearer only had to nod to activate a clockwork lifting mechanism in the crown. In spite of Boyle's suggestion that the hat could also be used for carrying advertising placards, it never took off.

✳ A similar fate befell Natalie Stolp's 1914 device to discourage men from rubbing their thighs up against those of a lady on a crowded train or carriage. Mrs Stolp from Philadelphia patented a spring attached to the lady's under-skirt which responded to male pressure by releasing a short, sharp point into the offender's flesh.

✳ In the 1980s, three French women, Dominique Peignoux, Yvette Guys and Francoise Dekan, marketed a musical nappy whereby a contrap-tion was tucked inside the baby's nappy and played 'When the Saints Go Marching In' as soon as it became wet.

✳ Helium-filled furniture was the brainchild of William A. Calderwood of Peoria, Arizona. His 1989 patent envisaged furniture floating to the ceiling when not in use, thereby allowing extra floor space. When required, the furniture would be pulled back down to the floor by a rope.

✳ Few inventors are as creative as Kenji Kawakami, President of Chindogu, the Useless Invention Society of Japan. Among his re-cently unveiled products are a tie which, in wet weather, transforms into an umbrella; a back-scratching T-shirt; a commuter chin-rest on a tripod to stop weary commuters falling asleep on the passenger next to them; a two-headed mop on a long pole which cleans the floor and the ceiling at the same time; a rubber glove with stick-on chopsticks that enables diners to hold chopsticks at precisely the right angle; and an umbrella which also acts as a clothes line, garments being pegged around the rim. The idea is that the clothes dry as the umbrella is rotated, Kawakami choosing to ignore the fact that the device with its swirling wet socks and blouses would actually make the owner wetter than if he or she were exposed to the elements.

● Until the 19th century, false teeth were made from animal bones. Hippopotamus bones were the most widely used since they were the strongest. But not only did they become worn and turn brown, they also emitted a distinctly unhygienic odour. Consequently, they had to be changed every couple of years. As an alternative, human teeth were sometimes used instead. English dandies wore 'Waterloo teeth', extracted from skulls dug up from the 1815 battlefield and later teeth from those killed in the American Civil War (1861–5) were also shipped to England.

● For a month in 1934, Anna Manaro, a young woman from the village of Pirano in Italy, baffled medical science by developing a curious condition. Whenever she fell into a deep sleep, the area around her breasts started to glow a vivid electric blue, the colour soon spreading to other parts of her body. The colour seemed to be glowing through her skin as if emanating from inside her body. On 11 April, Dr Protti from Padua University observed this incredible phenomenon at first hand, in company with five other medical experts. They found that during the few minutes in which she glowed, her heartbeat and respiratory rate both doubled. Otherwise, she suffered no adverse effects. Theories were advanced about radiant blood but, when Anna Manaro's complaint vanished as suddenly as it had arrived in May, the finest medical minds were none the wiser as to the cause.

METEOROLOGY

FREAK WEATHER

● The winter of 1435 in Britain was cold enough for the River Thames to bear waggons as far as Gravesend, Kent, and for wine to freeze in Scotland. In 1684, a bottle of ink froze indoors at Oxford and over 7 cm (3 in) of ice formed on a pond in one night.

● At Spearfish, South Dakota, on 22 January 1943, the temperature rose by 49°F (27.2°C) in just two minutes from −20°C (−4°F) to 7.2°C (45°F) between 7.30 a.m. and 7.32 a.m.

● A freak blast of hot air swept over the towns of Figueira da Foz and Coimbra, Portugal, on 6 July 1949. It only lasted two minutes but a naval officer at Figueira da Foz reported that in that time, the temperature shot up from around 100°F (37.8°C) to 158°F (70°C). A number of farmyard fowl were killed and the Mondego River was said to have dried up in several places.

● Lightning has been known to strike out of a clear sky. In September 1966, a lightning flash from a clear sky felled 30 workers who were picking peppers at Alfrida, Arizona. Three of the workers were killed. On 2 June 1976, a single, blinding flash of lightning occurred at Myrtleford in the Australian state of Victoria on a cloudless night. A fireball was seen to explode over three houses, causing a television set to blow up and telephones to be put out of order. A large area was blacked out and a nearby shed had a burn hole in it the size of a tennis ball.

● Parts of the Atacama Desert in northern Chile have had no rain in 400 years. The nearby town of Calama is said to be the driest in the world. Yet on 10 February 1972, torrential rain fell on the town, causing floods and landslides. Mud swept down from the hills, electricity supplies were short-circuited in the town and in local mines, and Calama was cut off by water.

● On average, two hurricanes a year develop over the Arabian Sea. On 27 October 1972, the first time for 75 years, such a storm travelled along the Gulf of Aden. It caused 230 mm (9 in) of rain in Djibouti (mean annual rainfall 127 mm (5 in)) and 152 mm (6 in) in Aden where the mean annual rainfall is 25 mm (1 in).

ODD SPOTS

* Culbin was once a wealthy estate on the shores of the Moray Firth in Scotland. But much of the coarse binding grass in the area had been taken for roof-thatching which meant that by the 1690s, the sand dunes had started to shift. In the autumn of 1694, a deep depression produced a yellow sand blizzard which lasted all night and drifted high against the houses. Residents had to dig themselves out. Eventually, the entire village became submerged in sand. Over the years, subsequent storms have reshaped the sand and during the 19th century, the tips of some houses were visible.

* Lochranza, a village on the Isle of Arran, stretches for 1¼ miles (2 km) along a NW–SE axis and has three hills rising sharply between 750 and 1600 ft high (299–488 m). Each winter between 18 November and 8 February, these hills block out the sun from the landward part of the village.

* Mount Wai-'ale-'ale on the island of Kauai, Hawaii, is 1569 m (5148 ft) high. The island is situated at latitude 20°N, on the fringe of the equatorial low pressure convergence zone, at longitude 156°W, in the middle of the Pacific Ocean, and is therefore constantly enveloped in warm, moist air. The mean average rainfall on Mount Wai-'ale-'ale is 11455 mm (451 in) and rain falls on average 335 days per year, sometimes as much as 350 days. Yet just a few miles away at sea-level areas on Kauai, there is as little as 500 mm (20 in) of rain per year.

* A renowned frost hollow in England is Rickmansworth, Hertfordshire, where a natural valley is further blocked by a railway embankment which acts as a dam against the free flow of cold air. Temperatures fell to –8.3°C (17°F) as late as 17 May in 1935.

* Seasonal temperature fluctuations are at their most dramatic in the centre of land masses, producing long, cold winters and short, hot summers. Verhoyansk in north-eastern Siberia has recorded a lowest temperature of –68°C (–90.4°F) but a summer maximum of 37°C (98°F).

STRANGE DOWNPOURS

● At Dubuque, Iowa, on 16 June 1882, hailstones up to 12 cm (5 in) in diameter fell during a 13-minute storm. In two of the stones, small living frogs were found. The frogs had been carried up in the vertical currents of a storm and had acquired coatings of ice before becoming heavy enough to fall to the ground.

On 11 May 1894, at the height of a hailstorm, a gopher turtle encased in ice fell on Bovina, 13 km (8 miles) east of Vicksburg, Mississippi. During the same storm, a small block of alabaster, also encased in ice, fell on Vicksburg itself.

At Essen, Germany, in 1896, freshwater carp fell from the sky, inside blocks of ice.

'Human hail' fell in Germany over the Rhön mountains in 1930. Five glider pilots, caught in a thundercloud, baled out of their gliders and were carried up and down within the super-cooled cloud until they fell to earth, frozen within ice prisons. Only one survived.

● Ice meteors are large chunks of ice which occasionally fall from the sky. The favoured explanation is that they fall from aircraft which have flown through super-cooled cloud, the water thus turning to ice. A carpenter working on the roof of his house near Düsseldorf, Germany, on 10 January 1951 died after being impaled by a shaft of ice 1.8 m (6 ft) long and 15 cm (6 in) in diameter which had fallen from the sky.

On 2 January 1977, a block of ice weighing about 50 kg (110 lb) smashed through the roof of

FISH SHOWERS

Rain sometimes carries strange objects which have been swept aloft by strong air currents in shower clouds. Fish have been recorded in many cases.

✻ On the morning of 9 February 1859 at Aberdare, Mid-Glamorgan, rain brought a downpour of fish. Minnow and smooth-tailed stickleback covered an area of the ground measuring some 80 × 12 m (240 × 36 ft).

✻ On 16 February 1861, Singapore was shaken by a violent earthquake, followed by six days of torrential rain. When the rain finally stopped, locals were seen filling their baskets with a species of catfish, *Clarias batrachi*, which had fallen during the storm.

✻ In October 1947, US marine biologist Alan Bajikov observed a fall of fish while having breakfast with his wife in a cafe at Marksville, Louisiana. Sunfish, minnows and black bass plummeted from the sky during a gentle shower. There was no report of any whirlwinds which could have swept the fish up from the nearest stretch of water, the Gulf of Mexico, over 130 km (80 miles) away.

✻ Another fall of fish was recorded at Chilatchee, near Uniontown, Alabama, in the spring of 1956. A small dark cloud was seen forming in the sky, followed by a 15-minute shower in which rain fell over an extremely small area – no more than 60 sq m (200 sq ft). As the rain fell, the cloud turned almost white. Three types of fish fell – catfish, bass and bream – and were seen flopping around on the ground. Again, no whirlwinds, tornadoes or other unusual weather was reported in the area.

✻ When a severe storm hit the St. John's district of Worcester on 28 May 1881, hundreds of periwinkles crashed to the ground with the rain, some with such force that they buried themselves in the earth. Locals rushed out to collect the shellfish. One large shell was found to contain a living hermit crab. On the same day in another part of town, beach pebbles fell through the skylight of a shop. Yet Worcester is some 110 km (70 miles) from the sea.

✻ During heavy rain, several hundred sand eels fell over one-third of an acre in the Sunderland suburb of Hendon on 24 August 1918. Not only were the eels dead but, when gathered up shortly after the downpour, they were found to be stiff and hard.

a house in Ponders End, Middlesex.

'Blue ice' is a frozen cocktail of flushed toilet waste that forms on the outer hull of an aircraft when a leak occurs in the plane's sewage system. It freezes as it emerges and grows in size, remaining in place until the plane hits warmer air. Then it crashes to the ground, often on unsuspecting houses situated below the flight path. A fall of blue ice hit a house in Billericay, Essex, in August 1994, breaking roof tiles. At lower altitudes, blue ice falls in liquid form which causes less damage but is considerably more unpleasant.

● In 1578, large yellow mice were recorded as falling on Bergen in Norway. The following year, a precipitation of lemmings hit the same town.

● Lumps of burning sulphur, some the size of a man's fist, dropped from the sky on to the roof of Loburg Castle, near Magdeburg, Germany, in June 1642.

● Following several weeks of drought, a fierce storm broke one Sunday afternoon in August 1814 over Fremontiers, near Amiens, France. In the rain which accompanied the storm were dozens of tiny frogs which proceeded to hop around on the ground.

Live frogs also fell on Leicester, Massachusetts, on 7 September 1953. As children gathered them up in buckets, many frogs were found in gutters and on roofs, proving that they had not simply hopped on to the streets from an overflowing pond.

● Lumps of meat, 7 to 10 cm (3 to 4 in) square fell from a cloudless sky over an area 90 m (100 yd) long and 45 m (50 yd) wide in Bath County, Kentucky, on 3 March 1876. When examined, the meat proved to be lung and muscle tissue, either from a child or a horse. The popular belief at the time was that the meat had been disgorged by buzzards. But it would have taken a vast number of buzzards to disgorge sufficient meat to cover 4000 sq m (5000 sq yd) of land and none had been seen in the region.

Equally baffling was the early-morning deluge of dead birds which tumbled from a clear sky on to the streets of Baton Rouge, Louisiana, in November 1896. The only plausible explanation was that the birds, which included wild ducks, catbirds and woodpeckers, had been driven inland by a storm on the Florida coast and had been killed by a sudden change of temperature over Baton Rouge.

● A rainfall of thousands of living snakes reportedly fell over the southern part of Memphis, Tennessee, in 1877. They measured between 30 and 40 cm (12 and 18 in) in length.

On 22 June 1991, a resident of Rebenacq, France, covers his roof with a tarpaulin after a violent storm producing hailstones the size of tennis balls had destroyed the slate roofs of all 150 houses in the small Pyrénéan village

● A 0.6 m (2 ft) long alligator fell from the sky at Evansville, Indiana, on 21 May 1911, landing on the front doorstep of the home of Mrs Hiram Winchell. When the hapless creature tried to crawl indoors, it was clubbed to death by Mrs Winchell and several other women with bed slats.

● In the course of a storm over the Gorkiy area of the Soviet Union on 17 June 1940, silver coins worth several thousand copecks fell from the sky. Thousands of 1000 franc notes fluttered down on

Bourges, France, in 1957. In December 1975, dollar bills fell from the sky over Chicago, Illinois – a total of $588 was collected and handed over to the police. In January 1976, paper money fell over Limburg, West Germany.

● On 26 October 1956, the dead body of a small monkey was found in the back garden of a house at Broadmoor, California, by Mrs Faye Swanson. The 10×10 cm (4×4 in) post holding her clothes-line had been damaged, presumably by the falling monkey. The only possible explanation for the incident was that the monkey had fallen from an aircraft, yet the local airport maintained that no planes had been carrying such cargo that night.

● A crop of peaches, hard, green and the size of golf balls, fell on a building-site at Shreveport, Louisiana, on 12 July 1961. The workmen were able to confirm that the peaches were coming from the sky and not simply being thrown. Although there was a thick black cloud overhead, weathermen said that the conditions that day were not conducive to the fruit having been lifted in strong winds.

● A fall of maggots accompanied a heavy storm at Acapulco, Mexico, on 5 October 1968. Craft assembled for the Olympic yachting events were covered in maggots about 2.5 cm (1 in) long.

● Hundreds of golf balls fell from the sky over Punta Gorda, Florida, on 3 September 1969 and were found rolling in the streets.

● During the 1930s drought in the United States, which created the Dust Bowl of the central plains, dust was frequently carried aloft and transported at high altitudes. It was then deposited to the ground with falls of rain or snow, creating strange colouring effects. The Great Duststorm of 12–13 November 1933 carried dust from Montana State right across to the Atlantic coast. 'Black rain' fell in New York State, 'brown snow' in Vermont.

In Europe, on 14 October 1755, 'blood red rain' fell at Locarno, Switzerland, turning to 'red snow' up in the Alps. It is thought that the coloured dust which fell that night over an area of 930 sq km (360 sq miles) originated in North Africa. It is estimated that of the 230 mm (9 in) of rain, 25 mm (1 in) was dust.

On 2 November 1819, 'red rain' fell on Blankenberge, Belgium. But the theory of fine red dust or sand being transported via a whirl-wind cut no ice on this occasion. For when 4082 g (144 oz) of the Belgian rain were reduced by evaporation to 113 g (4 oz), there were no traces of sand. Further analysis of the rain mysteriously revealed the presence of a chloride of cobalt. How it came to be there baffled meteorological experts.

WEATHERMEN

● American Charles Hatfield was a professional rainmaker. For more than 30 years, he offered his services to those in need of water – saving crops, breaking droughts and filling lakes. He offered to rid London of its smogs and to water the Sahara but his most remarkable achievement was re-served for California. In December 1915, in return for a payment of $10 000, he volunteered to fill the huge reservoir at Morena Dam which supplied water to San Diego. The reservoir could hold 15 billion gallons of water but, since its construction, had never been more than one-third full. So confident was Hatfield of success that he came up

with the terms, no rain, no pay. The San Diego City Council accepted his offer and, on 1 January 1916, Hatfield started erecting a wooden tower, on the top of which he placed large galvanizing trays containing his secret moisture-attracting substance. Within four days, it was raining. On 10 January, it began to pour with rain – and did not stop for ten days. Hatfield's popularity was on the wane as streets were flooded, highways closed and phone lines cut off. Rivers overflowed, washing away 200 bridges, and houses were demolished by a 12 m (40 ft) high wall of water when the nearby Lower Otay Dam crumbled. Fifty people lost their

lives. A brief respite was followed by yet more rain so that by 26 January, the water level at the Morena Dam was rising by ½ m (2 ft) an hour. It finally came to a halt just 12 cm (5 in) from the top of the dam, thus averting a disaster of calamitous proportions. Hatfield considered that he had fulfilled his part of the bargain but the Council flatly refused to pay him, insisting that the deluge was an act of God.

● Former park ranger Roy C. Sullivan of Virginia, US, was a veritable human lightning conductor. He was first struck by lightning in 1942 but suffered nothing more than the loss of a big toe-nail. In July 1969, he lost his eyebrows and in July 1970, his left shoulder was seared. On 16 April 1972, his hair was set on fire by lightning; on 7 August 1973, his new hair caught fire and his legs were seared. On 5 June 1976, he sustained an ankle injury, but his seventh strike, on 25 June 1977, saw him taken to Waynesboro Hospital with chest and stomach burns after being hit while fishing. After surviving so much, Sullivan committed suicide in September 1983, apparently rejected in love.

Left Human lightning conductor Roy Sullivan shows off another lucky escape

NUMBERS

● In 1225, to solve a puzzle about the breeding rate of rabbits, Leonardo Fibonacci (*c.* 1170–1240), an Italian mathematician from Pisa, published an arithmetical sequence in which each number is the sum of the preceding two numbers. The series begins 1, 1, 2, 3, 5, 8, 13, 21, 34, 55, 89. In the 19th century, this simple sequence was found to occur in nature and was named the Fibonacci sequence. For example, on the outside of a pineapple there are usually eight spirals in one direction and 13 in the other. These are both Fibonacci numbers as is their total, 21. Similarly, the florets on the head of a sunflower form two overlapping spirals, one clockwise, the other anti-clockwise. There are 21 florets in the clockwise spiral and 34 in the anti-clockwise. These are consecutive Fibonacci numbers.

As the series progresses, the ratio of each number to its predecessor becomes ever closer to 1.618033989:1, the figure known as the Golden Ratio. Known to mathematicians since at least 300 BC, the Golden Ratio is a rectangular proportion of height to width which can be seen in such classical buildings as the Parthenon in Athens. If a Golden Ratio rectangle is divided into a square and a rectangle, the smaller rectangle repeats the same proportion. If the smaller rectangle is divided again, the yet smaller rectangle retains the same proportion, and so on. If corresponding points on the various rectangles are joined in a certain way, they form a logarithmic spiral which is exactly the same spiral as that found in natural structures such as the shell of a snail.

● A group of numbers with unique properties are the prime numbers. A prime number has no proper factors – it cannot be divided by any natural numbers other than itself and 1. Examples of prime numbers are 2, 3, 5, 7, 11, 13, 17, 19, 23. In January 1994, computer scientists David Slowinski and Paul Gage, working at Cray Research Inc., Minnesota, discovered a prime number containing 258 716 digits.

● The mathematicians of ancient Greece devised a series of perfect numbers. A perfect number is one which is equal to the sum of all its divisors other than itself. The lowest perfect number is 6 (its divisors are 1, 2 and 3 which add up to 6). The second is 28 (1 + 2 + 4 + 7 + 14).

The Greeks knew only two other perfects – 496 and 8128 – but over 1500 years later, in the 15th century, a fifth perfect number was found – 33 550 336. The 33rd perfect number, discovered in 1994, has 517 430 digits.

● Isaac Newton named seven colours in the spectrum although indigo is barely distinguishable as a separate colour and even orange is doubtful. But Newton included them because seven was his favourite number.

● One sum is always the same, whatever the numbers. Take any three-figure number in which the first figure is larger than the last – for example 901. Then reverse it, making 109, and subtract the smaller number from the larger, making 792. Finally add that to the same number reversed, in this case 297. The answer is 1089 and will be 1089 whatever the starting number, as long as the numbers are treated as having three figures, e.g. 635 (635 − 536 = 099, 099 + 990 = 1089).

SCIENTIFIC CURIOSITIES

● Lights of different wavelengths have different colours. Long-wave light looks red, middle-wave light looks green and short-wave light appears to be blue. It would therefore seem to follow that objects and surfaces acquire their colour by virtue of the dominant wavelength reflected from them so that a blue object looks blue because it reflects more short-wave light. When objects are viewed in different conditions of illumination, the wavelength composition of the light reflected from them alters accordingly. Yet if something like a banana were to be viewed in a room lit by different forms of lighting and at varying stages of daylight, it would continue to look yellow. This phenomenon is a departure from the belief that there is a straightforward relationship between the colour of a surface and the wavelength composition of the light reflected from it. For when a surface forms part of a complex, multi-coloured scene, there is no simple and obvious relationship. The phenomenon is called colour constancy. Some thought the reason for it was

memory (we remember what colour a banana is) but in fact the only condition when the colour of a surface does bear a simple and straightforward relationship to the wavelength composition of the light reflected from it is a reduction screen or aperture condition where a small area is viewed in isolation.

● Heiligenschein (German, meaning holy aureole) is the name for the strange whitish ring of light which surrounds the shadow of a person's head on dew-covered grass. It is most often seen early in the morning when the sun is still low in the sky, thus casting elongated shadows, and the grass is heavy with dew. The phenomenon, also known as Cellini's halo, is generally attributed to the reflection of incident sunlight by the dewdrops. The light reflected from such a drop is at its most intense in the backward direction, the intensity diminishing as the angle of reflection deviates from 180°. The shadow of the observer's head encompasses the precise 180° line, thus preventing the reflection of any light from that direction. But if the shadow is far enough away, the light reflected from the drops immediately surrounding the observer's head-shadow back to the observer's eye will be reflected through almost 180°. The further away the shadow, the nearer the angle gets to 180°. Under these conditions, the reflected light surrounding the shadow of the head will be exceptionally bright, hence the halo.

● Water has many unique properties. For example, a skin forms where water meets other materials. This is caused by water molecules being more attracted to each other than to other substances, as a result of which they squeeze together to form a dense layer – a phenomenon known as surface tension. The same attraction of molecules also enables water to climb uphill, unlike other liquids. Capillary action, as it is called, causes water to move upwards through the ground to the roots of plants and through stems and leaves. Another property of water is that it absorbs more heat than almost any other substance without a vast increase in temperature. When a kettle of water is boiled, it is subjected to a temperature that would cause many substances either to melt or burst into flames. But the water soaks up the heat until a temperature of 100°C (212°F) is reached. At that point, water boils and steam bubbles burst through the surface tension. Water also has the ability to float when frozen and although it expands at freezing point, it becomes less dense. Fresh water starts to freeze at 0°C (32°F) when in bulk. But in the form of drops, it can exist in clouds at temperatures as low as –40°C (–40°F). This is known as supercooling. Even so, these droplets freeze instantly on contact with ice crystals or other particles of sub-zero temperatures.

● If you swing a bucket of water round and round over your head, the water will stay in it even when the bucket is upside down. The reason is that its inertia tells the water to continue rushing through space at a steady speed in a straight line and, having been started in one direction by the swinging bucket, to carry on in that direction. Since the bucket is made to follow a circular path, the water is forced to accelerate to get round the corners. This gives it 'artificial gravity' which enables it to stick to the bottom of the bucket even when the bucket is upside down. First studied in depth by Isaac Newton, inertia is responsible for many of life's little curiosities. A passenger on a bus with coins in his pocket will find that the coins, which possess this same inertia, go on forcing themselves forward after the bus has stopped.

● Helium is a colourless, odourless and tasteless gas which becomes liquid at –286.6°C (–452°F). It has two liquid forms. Helium I, stable from 2.19 to 4.22 kelvins, is an ordinary liquid, used as a refrigerant. Below 2.18 kelvins, it becomes helium II which is a superfluid with no viscosity. This lack of viscosity means that, when placed in a container, helium II will 'crawl' over the side as a film.

● If pure oxygen is breathed at more than two and a half times atmospheric pressure, it can be poisonous, causing convulsions and even fatality. Consequently, deep-sea divers usually breathe compressed air (of which only about 20 per cent is oxygen) or a mixture with an inert gas such as helium, rather than just pure oxygen. At atmospheric pressure, pure oxygen can harm only new-born babies when it may cause a form of blindness called retrolental fibroplasia. So pure oxygen is used only in incubators with special monitoring equipment.

● In certain circumstances, kitchen utensils and even fillings in teeth act as radio receivers. In locations near a big transmitter with a large field strength, the saliva in the mouth reacts with the metals in the tooth filling to make a junction, acting like a decoder in a conventional radio receiver. If a saucepan has corrosion on its base, the dissimilar metals can produce the same effect – again provided a large transmitter is nearby. This has led to instances of people suddenly getting Radio 1 on their frying pan or tuning in to someone who has just been to the dentist to listen to the news report.

SPONTANEOUS HUMAN COMBUSTION

● In January 1932 at Bladeboro, North Carolina, a cotton dress being worn by Mrs Charles Williamson suddenly and unaccountably burst into flames. She was not standing near any kind of fire nor had her dress been in contact with any flammable substance. Her husband and daughter ripped off the blazing dress with their bare hands yet remarkably none of the trio was even slightly burned. As the family recovered from the drama, a pair of Mr Williamson's trousers, which were hanging in the wardrobe, also suddenly caught fire. Then a bed went up in flames as did a pair of curtains in an unoccupied room of the house. Over the next four days, various articles throughout the house were found burning with bluish jet-like flames, yet adjacent objects remained unaffected. The flames, which had neither smoke nor smell, could not be extinguished. They simply vanished after the particular article had burnt out. After five days, the fires stopped abruptly, never to return. This series of mystery fires left the experts baffled.

● On the morning of 2 July 1951, Mrs Mary Reeser, a 67-year-old widow from St Petersburg, Florida, was found reduced to ashes in an apartment which showed little sign of damage. That morning, her landlady, Mrs Pansy Carpenter, taking a telegram to Mrs Reeser's room, found the doorknob hot. Anxiously, she summoned a painter from across the street and as he entered the room, he immediately felt a blast of hot air. He saw no sign of Mrs Reeser. The bed was empty and although there was a little smoke, the only fire was a small flame on a wooden beam over a partition dividing the living-room and the kitchenette. When the fire brigade arrived and inspected the premises, they discovered a charred area some 1.2 m (4 ft) in diameter in the middle of the floor. This area contained a number of blackened chair springs and the remains of a human body. All that could be identified were a charred liver attached to a section of the spine, a shrunken skull, one foot, still wearing a black satin slipper, and a small pile of ashes. Tremendous heat must have been necessary to incinerate

the body yet only the chair and the table next to it were damaged. The carpet on which the chair stood had not even burned through. Part of the ceiling was coated with soot but a pile of newspapers in the room remained intact. The laboratory found that Mrs Reeser's estimated weight of 79.4 kg (175 lb) had been reduced to just under 4.5 kg (10 lb). Experts could not determine the cause of the fire – there were no blown fuses to indicate an electrical fault. Dr Wilton M. Krogman, a physical anthropologist at the University of Pennsylvania's School of Medicine and a noted authority on the effects of fire on the human body, remarked: 'They say truth often is stranger than fiction and this case proves it'.

● One October evening in the late 1950s, 19-year-old Maybelle Andrews was dancing with her boyfriend, Billy Clifford, in a London dance hall when she suddenly burst into flames. The fire blazed from her back and chest, enveloping her head and igniting her hair. She died on the way to hospital. Billy Clifford's testimony said: 'I saw no one smoking on the dance floor. There were no candles on the tables and I did not see her dress catch fire from anything. I know it sounds incredible, but it appeared to me that the flames burst outwards, as if they originated within her body.' The verdict was 'death by misadventure, caused by fire of unknown origin'.

● Former actress, 75-year-old Olga Worth Stephens of Dallas, Texas, was sitting in a parked car in October 1964 when witnesses saw her burst into flames. She was killed but the car was not damaged and contained nothing that could have started the fire. A similar incident occurred on 9 October 1980 when Jeanna Winchester, riding in a car in Jacksonville, Florida, suddenly burst into bright yellow flames. The car crashed as the driver endeavoured to beat out the flames, but although the victim sustained severe burns, she did manage to survive her ordeal. Examination of the car revealed little or no fire damage. There was no spilt petrol, the victim was not smoking and the car window was up, ruling out the theory that something could have been thrown into the vehicle. Officer T.G. Hendrix commented: 'The white leather seat she was sitting on was a little browned and the door panel had a little black on it. Otherwise there was no fire damage. I've never seen anything like it in 12 years in the force.'

STRANGE EXPERIMENTS

● In 1950, N.E. Collins conducted experiments to determine the responses of a young chick when its brain is removed. He concluded that a decerebrated chick will not move towards a clucking or retreating object. He did however discover that leaving the basal portions of the cerebral hemispheres intact did not interfere with the chick's social responses, a comfort to us all.

● In 1952, W.H. Gantt proved that, in regulated doses, alcohol can cure neurotic dogs of premature ejaculation. Pursuing this theme with some vigour R.S. Ryback wrote a 1969 paper 'The Use of Goldfish as a Model for Alcohol Amnesia in Man' and after seven more years of research was able to conclude that the short-term memory of a mildly inebriated goldfish is better than that of a sober fish. So next time you see a goldfish coming back from the pub, expect it to be able to remember exactly how much it has had to drink.

● Founder and editor of the esteemed journal, *Worm Runner's Digest*, James V. McConnell had been experimenting with flatworms at the University of Texas for over three years when in 1956 he began to contemplate what effect chopping a worm in half would have on its memory. Testing the worm's memory by observing its reaction to an electric shock sent through water, he found that regenerated worms did indeed retain knowledge. He then split a number of worms' heads down the middle and allowed each half to regenerate. The resultant two-headed worms proved to be faster learners than one-headed worms, proving conclusively that in a worm's world, two heads are better than one.

● In 1980, Miss P.A. Mitford undertook a doctoral thesis on 'The Perception of Laughter and its Acoustical Properties'. A group of 15 men and 15 women were tested on four different types of laughter – social laughter, tension-releasing laughter, humour-provoked laughter and tickling-induced laughter. Miss Mitford concluded that women on a diet are less influenced by the laughter of others in an audience than women not on a diet.

● In 1984, D. Porter and A. Neuringer conducted tests on the musical appreciation of pigeons. By rewarding the birds for the correct identification of the composer of music played to them, the experimenters taught the pigeons to discriminate between one-minute excerpts of Bach flute music and Hindemith viola music. Two pigeons excelled themselves, achieving a success rate of over 80 per cent. A recording contract surely beckons.

THE UNIVERSE

● Unlike other planets in the solar system, Venus spins east to west instead of west to east. It also takes longer (243 days) to spin on its axis than it does to orbit the Sun (224.7 days) with the result that a Venusian 'day' is longer than a Venusian 'year'.

● Jupiter spins through a 'day' in 9 h 50 min and takes 11.9 Earth years to complete its orbit around the Sun. So a Jupiter 'year' is nearly 10 400 Jupiter 'days' long.

● While most planets spin along their orbits (the Earth is tilted at only 23½°), Uranus is tilted on its axis at around 98° – almost on its side. This creates the longest seasons in the solar system – winters and summers that are 21 Earth years long.

● Although Mercury has daytime surface temperatures as high as 430°C (800°F), a radar study of the planet revealed ice at its poles. It appears that despite the fact that the poles are bathed in scorching sunlight, the light hits at a shallow angle. Consequently, some craters remain permanently in shadow, forcing temperatures there below zero. So any ice which formed billions of years ago during the planet's creation, when water boiled on its surface and then condensed as frost, would still be there.

● Temperatures in the outer part of the Earth's core, 1200 km (745 miles) from the centre of the Earth, match those to be found on the surface of the Sun – 5800°C (10 500°F). The temperature of the Earth increases with depth, on average by 30°C (140°F) per mile (1.6 km). The heat is thought to be caused by radioactivity within the Earth's core and possibly by rock movements and chemical changes taking place under extreme pressure.

● The land and ocean floor of the Earth rest on a number of separate plates, each made of rock between 64 and 96 km (40 and 60 miles) thick. The plates, which are borne on a sea of molten rock, move across the globe at a rate of between 1 and 15 cm (½ in and 6 in) a year. A vast shift has taken place over the ages — Africa was once over the South Pole while parts of the United States were to be found over the North Pole. Every year, the New World moves a little further away from the Old as a result of the widening bed of the Atlantic Ocean. A chain of underwater mountains, known as the Mid-Atlantic Ridge, runs down the centre of the Atlantic. Along its length, molten rock constantly wells up and cools to form a new crust which forces the Continental plates apart. Due to this movement, Iceland, which sits astride the ridge, is getting bigger each year. In a million years' time, it is estimated that the Atlantic will be 40 km (25 miles) wider. Else-

where, equal amounts of crust are being destroyed. In the Pacific, sections of sea-bed plates are returning to the Earth's molten interior so that South America is slowly drawing closer to New Zealand.

● Britain's geography is also changing. It is tilting along a line running from Devon, through South Wales and across central England to North Yorkshire. The land to the north and west of the line is rising while that to the south and east is sinking. The reason is that northern Britain is slowly springing back into position after being weighed down during the Ice Age. Consequently, other areas are sinking slightly. Geologists calculate the rise or fall to be no more than 12 cm (5 in) every 100 years. An example of the shift is Harlech Castle in West Wales. When it was built by Edward I in 1286, the watergate led directly from the castle walls into the sea. Now, because the area is lifting slowly, the castle is about ½ mile (0.8 km) inland.

● Due to the Earth's rotation, all things that move over the face of the Earth tend to drift from their appointed paths, to the right in the Northern Hemisphere, to the left in the Southern Hemisphere. This phenomenon was examined by French mathematician Gustave-Gaspard Coriolis (1792–1843) and was subsequently named the Coriolis effect. During the First World War, a huge German gun christened Big Bertha was used to bombard Paris from a site 115 km (70 miles) away. Since the shells took three minutes to reach their target, the gunners had to adjust their aim to allow for the Coriolis drift to the right which, over that distance, totalled a whole mile (1.6 km).

● A blue Moon can occur when particles of critical size scatter light at the red end of the rainbow spectrum more than the blue. When this happens, red light disappears against the blackness of the night sky but the unscattered light shining through makes the Moon look blue. Scattering is the change in direction of light rays produced by the molecules of air. Scattering is greater for light rays of shorter wave length (violet) than for rays of longer wave length (red). The sky appears blue and the Sun yellow when light from the Sun travels through a depth of clean, dry atmosphere. Blue, the shortest wave band of the visible spectrum, is scattered by the molecules of the atmosphere and the remainder reaches the eye. But when smoke particles from forest fires in Alberta, Canada, were blown over to Britain on 26 September 1950, more red light was scattered than blue. The result was a blue Moon. It is a very rare occurrence – hence the expression 'Once in a blue Moon'.

● Aurorae, luminous displays of colours, are caused by electrical solar discharges in the upper atmosphere and occur most frequently at high latitudes. They are created in a similar way to the pictures on a television screen which are produced by a beam of electrons being focused on to a fluorescent screen by electromagnets. The Earth's magnetic field has the same effect on charged particles coming from the Sun and focuses them on to the sky above the North and South Pole. The sky acts as a screen. The magnetic fields are shaped like a funnel at the poles and, as the particles spiral down, they excite atoms in the upper air. These atoms cause the lights of the aurora. Oxygen atoms produce red, green and yellow lights, nitrogen produces violet, blue or green. The aurorae of the Northern Hemisphere are called Aurora Borealis or the Northern Lights. In the Southern Hemisphere, they are known as Aurora Australis. Although usually only seen in polar regions, they are occasionally seen at lower latitudes, as at Cuzco, Peru, on 2 August 1744 and Honolulu, Hawaii, on 1 September 1859.

● Noctilucent clouds are clouds which, because of their great altitude (up to 85 km (52 miles)), remain sunlit long after the sun has gone down. They appear silvery or bluish white and are visible only on summer nights at high latitudes. They are believed to consist of ice crystals or meteoric dust. For despite the thinness of the air and therefore the scarcity of water vapour, ice crystals form because that level is the coldest in the entire upper atmosphere.

● Mirages occur when layers of air of different temperatures and different density are superimposed. The light waves are bent and refracted irregularly as they pass from an object through the unequal layers. In a superior mirage (where the image is seen above the real object), the light from the object bends downwards when travelling through a layer of very cold dense air before reaching the eye. The effect can bring into view objects which are normally below the horizon and accounts for repeat sunsets in polar regions. Refraction not only brings objects below the horizon into view, it sometimes appears to project them high into the sky. The 3078 m (10 100 ft) mountain peak Cerro La Encantada, on the peninsula of Baja California in Mexico, is not usually visible from Puerto Penasco, 187 km (116 miles) away on the other side of the Gulf of Mexico. But about an hour before sunset, the sea breeze drops and cold air settles over the bay, and a mirage of La Encantada rises up in the sky.

Fata Morgana is a complex superior mirage caused by distortion of light, both vertically and horizontally, when passing through several layers of air of different density. In 1913, a US expedition led by Donald MacMillan set out to discover a mysterious Arctic mountain range that had been sighted by explorer Robert Peary six years earlier. Peary had called it Crocker Land. MacMillan's party sailed as far as they could through the ice floes, then continued on foot until the vast mountain range described by Peary came into view. But as the men moved towards it, the mountains receded and when the men stood still, so did the mountains. Finally, at sunset, the mountains dissolved to nothing. It was a Fata Morgana mirage.

An inferior mirage is seen below the real object when light refracts and internally reflects at the boundary of an intensely hot layer of low density air, such as exists over a desert or a tarmac road in summer. The image seen is always in the direction along which light enters the eye, irrespective of previous distortion, so the reflection of the sky appears on the ground. Due to the convection activity near the ground, the reflection shimmers and the brain reacts by concluding that the reflection of the sky must be the more familiar phenomenon of water. In 1798, Napoleon's army in Egypt saw a blurred landscape with lakes that vanished and blades of grass which became palm trees. The mystified soldiers are said to have fallen to their knees in prayer, believing that the end of the world was nigh.

TALES OF FOOD AND DRINK

✳ During the Second World War, American pilots in the Pacific were given asparagus as part of their emergency rations. However, the reason was not to give them a taste of *haute cuisine* but to help them catch fish. The plan was that pilots who found themselves marooned on desert islands should eat the asparagus and then urinate into the sea. Asparagus contains strong chemical attractants called mercaptans which would pass into the urine, spread through the water and prove irresistible to fish. Once lured into the area, the fish could then be caught by the hungry pilot for food.

✳ The practice of eating earth is called geophagy. In a village north of Accra, Ghana, some 5000 tonnes of rock are mined each year and turned into food. The clay is crushed, sieved and mixed with water into an edible dough. The fine brown earth around the Mississippi is also a popular delicacy, having a texture – if not a taste – like sherbet. Fearful of starvation, slaves in the United States used to eat earth – often with fatal results. They would become addicted and eat so much that their bowels would become blocked.

✳ High in protein and minerals, insects are a popular dish in many parts of the world. As long ago as 1885, Vincent M. Holt listed sample menus in his booklet 'Why Not Eat Insects?' He suggested, to start, either slug soup or boiled cod with snail sauce; a choice for the main course of wasp grubs fried in the comb, moths sautéd in butter, braised beef with caterpillars or new carrots with wire-worm sauce; and for dessert, either gooseberry cream with sawflies, devilled chafer grubs or stag beetle larvae on toast. The first insect restaurant to open in the United States, the Insect Club in Washington, DC, offers such delights as cricket pizza (with extra cricket), mealworms in a blue cheese sauce wrapped in puff pastry and grasshopper burgers in woodlice sauce.

✳ More commonly used on toast, Marmite yeast extract was once prescribed in the Eastern tropics as a cure for burning feet and beriberi. The British Medical Research Council's 1951 report on 'Deficiency Diseases in Japanese Prison Camps' stated that Marmite had also proved effective in the treatment of scrotal dermatitis.

✳ In August 1979, a racehorse called *No Bombs* snatched a Mars Bar from his stable boy on the way to Ascot racecourse in Berkshire and went on to win by eight lengths. But the horse was subsequently disqualified after a routine dope test revealed traces of caffeine and theobromine, two mild stimulants naturally present in cocoa beans, which are guaranteed to make anyone run faster. It emerged that the Mars Bar was to blame. The horse's trainer, Peter Easterby, called it 'the most expensive Mars Bar ever'. It had cost £4064 in prize money.

✳ For centuries, Dutch merchants had been able to demand high prices for the nutmeg spice of which they had the world monopoly. So it came as a bitter blow when their lucrative trade was wrecked by pigeons. Until the late 18th century, the nutmeg tree, *Myristica fragrans*, grew only on the Dutch-owned Indonesian islands of Banda and Amboina, giving the Dutch total control over the sought-after spice which comes from the tree's seeds. But by 1900, pigeons feeding on the seeds had scattered them to neighbouring islands which were not under the Dutch flag. Thus the monopoly ended and prices tumbled.

✳ When advertising men for Pepsi-Cola had their slogan 'Come alive with Pepsi' translated into Mandarin Chinese, it came over as: 'Pepsi brings your ancestors back from the grave'.

✳ Humans eat more sharks than sharks eat humans, this despite the fact that shark meat spoils rapidly, releasing quantities of ammonia. The flesh of the Greenland or sleeper shark can have particularly odd side-effects. Unless boiled in several changes of water and dried after each boiling, it produces symptoms of drunkenness known among Eskimos as 'shark sickness'.

✳ Mr Whitekey's Fly-by-Night Club at Anchorage, Alaska, is described as 'a sleazy bar serving everything from the world's finest champagnes to a damn fine plate of Spam'. It offers anything with Spam at half price when you order champagne and, even more tempting, any dish with Spam free if you order Dom Perignon.

✳ The belief, promoted by manufacturers and Popeye alike, that spinach makes you strong is based on a printing error. In 1870, a misplaced decimal point in a set of published food tables made spinach appear to contain ten times more iron than other vegetables. In truth, it has much the same iron content.

✳ Strictly speaking, the strawberry is not a fruit at all. The botanical definition of a fruit is a seed-bearing structure which grows from a flower's ovaries whereas a strawberry is merely the swollen base of the strawberry flower. The plant's true fruits are the tiny, hard pips that are embedded around the outside of the flesh and which contain the seeds.

✳ Right up until the 19th century, urine was often used as an early-morning mouthwash. Because urine is warm and acidic, it neutralized the decaying action of the cold, damp secretions from the pituitary gland which flow from the brain into the mouth.

✳ Foods like yoghurts which coalesce are an essential ingredient for space travellers. For in the weightless environment of space, while the spoon may float off, the yoghurt will stay on it.

✳ In 1626, English philosopher Francis Bacon (1561–1626) conducted one of the earliest experiments into frozen food by stuffing a chicken with snow in order to observe the effect of the cold in preserving its flesh. Alas he caught a chill from the snow and died soon after.

✳ Villagers in Denby Dale, West Yorkshire, bake a giant pie to mark special occasions. The first was produced in 1788 to celebrate George III's reported recovery from insanity (two weeks later, he was once again certified insane). The second pie was baked to mark Wellington's victory at Waterloo in 1815 and the third, in 1846, was to celebrate the repeal of the Corn Laws. This pie required 13 horses to pull it, contained the meat from five sheep, one calf, 14 rabbits, seven hares, two brace each of pheasant and partridge, two guinea fowl, two ducks, two turkeys, two geese, six pigeons, four hens, 63 small birds and 45 kg (100 lb) of beef. The fourth, to mark Queen Victoria's Jubilee in 1887, went a bit 'off' and had to be buried in quicklime. In 1964, a pie was baked to commemorate four royal births in one year. It contained three tonnes of beef, one and a half tonnes of potatoes and over half a tonne of gravy and seasoning. Baked in a steel dish 5.5 m (18 ft) long, 1.8 m (6 ft) wide and 0.5 m (18 in) deep, it fed 30 000 people. The ninth pie in the series, baked on 3 September 1988 to mark the bicentenary of Denby Dale pie-making, weighed a colossal 9.03 tonnes (19 908 lb).

✳ Admiral George Dundas, who died in 1820, struck a bet with a group of friends that he 'and one other' could consume 16 lb (7.3 kg) of tripe at a single sitting. Bets were taken and Dundas sat down to begin the repast. After eating about an eighth of the total, he set down his knife and fork and sat back as friends led in a large bear who promptly devoured the remainder. A committee of officers conferred to decide whether or not the bet had been won and in the end decreed that the bear did count as 'one other'. Thus Dundas gained a large sum of money but not indigestion.

Room for one more on top. The poor female common toad sometimes has to carry a dozen males during mating. No wonder she often suffocates

9

THE NATURAL WORLD

ANIMAL KINGDOM

AMPHIBIANS

● The ears of the male and female **American tree frog** (*Eleutherodactylus coqui*) are tuned differently. Thus while humans can hear the frog's entire call of 'coqui', the male frog is only able to hear the first part, 'co', which warns him of another male in the area, and the female can only hear the second part, 'qui', which informs her of the presence of a potential suitor.

● The male **Darwin's frog** (*Rhinoderma darwini*), found on the southern coast of Chile, swallows the eggs his mate lays and keeps them in a sac under his chin. He swallows the eggs two weeks after the female has laid them and can carry up to 17 tadpoles. When the tadpoles are big enough, the male opens his mouth and releases them into the big wide world.

● The **flying frog** (*Rhacophorus pardalis*) lives in Borneo and has long toes with wide webs between them. When it leaps, it spreads out its webbed fore and hind feet to make flat gliding surfaces. Sticky pads on the toes help it to grip on to objects when landing. Some flying frogs possess an additional oddity – they lay their eggs in trees.

● The **paradoxical frog** (*Pseudis paradoxa*) of South America is smaller as an adult than as a tadpole. The tadpole grows up to 25 cm (10 in) in length but when it turns into a frog, it shrinks. The adult is never more than 7 cm (3 in) long.

● The **common toad** (*Bufo bufo*) suffers from the fact that there are more males than females. During courtship, the male, desperate to keep the female, clings on fiercely to her back and may be carried around for several days before the eggs are laid. In the meantime, he has to fend off rival males who are eager to dislodge him. If a male is dislodged, others frantically climb on to the female, often forming towers of up to ten toads. Not surprisingly, the female sometimes suffocates under the weight, although the males may hang on for several days while her body decomposes beneath them. If the lovelorn males are unable to find a female, they will try to mate with just about anything – including sticks, water-lilies and even goldfish.

● When threatened, the **fire-belly toad** (*Bombina variegata*) throws itself on to its back to reveal a bright yellow belly, covers its eyes with its paws and holds its breath until the danger has passed. To deter potential attackers further, it also emits a mildly corrosive white fluid.

● The female **Surinam toad** (*Pipa pipa*) uses her back as an incubator for her eggs. Her flat back contains tiny depressions where each egg rests, protected by a thin layer of tissue. The young remain there throughout the tadpole stage for as long as four months, only emerging after changing into the immature toad form.

● The **axolotl salamander** of Mexico (*Ambystoma mexicanum*) is the Peter Pan of the amphibian world – it never grows up. For as long as it lives in water (which can be for life), it retains its youthful appearance of feathery external gills and larval tadpole-like shape. It can even breed in this

The axolotl is the 'Peter Pan' of the natural world. It remains in larval form, only ever becoming an adult salamander if its pond dries up

form. But if the lake in which it lives dries up, the axolotl can change into the adult form of a salamander with lungs in place of gills.

BIRDS

● The **wandering albatross** (*Diomedea exulans*) can glide for six days without beating its wings and can even sleep in mid-air while gliding at 55 km/h (35 mph). The adult albatross not only has the largest wing-span, nearly 12 ft (3.6 m), of any living bird, its egg also takes longer to hatch – up to three months – than any other bird.

● The male **bower-bird** (*Ptilonorhynchus*) of Australia builds love bowers to attract a female. The male gathers a number of twigs and builds a structure like a small hut. He then decorates the hut with flowers and colourful objects such as feathers, fruit, shells, pebbles, even glass or paper if the nest is near civilization.

The male atlas bower-bird goes as far as painting the walls – by dipping bark or leaves into the blue or dark green saliva he secretes. The bower-bird spends months building and sometimes changes the decor each day by removing certain ornaments and replacing them with new ones. When finally satisfied with his handiwork, he performs a love dance outside the bower, frequently offering the female a pretty item from his collection in a bid to impress her.

● According to the laws of aerodynamics, some flying birds are too heavy to fly. The upper weight limit for a flying bird is around 18 kg (40 lb). If the body mass were increased further, the flight muscles required to provide power output would take up a higher proportion of the weight than the bird could afford consistent with maintaining all its other functions. The world's heaviest flying birds are the **Kori bustard** or paauw (*Ardeotis kori*) of north-east and Southern Africa and the **great bustard** (*Otis tarda*) of Europe and Asia. By rights, neither should be able to get off the ground. The Kori bustard has weighed in at 19 kg (42 lb) while there is an unconfirmed report of a 20.9 kg (46 lb 4 oz) male great bustard shot in Manchuria which was indeed too heavy to fly, thus making it an easy target for hunters.

● The young **hoatzin** (*Opisthocomus hoazin*), which lives in swamplands and along the river banks of the Amazon and the Orinoco in South America, has claws on its wings. It has a claw on the leading edge of each wing, at the point of the thumb and another at the end of each wing tip. By using these claws and its beak, the bird is able to clamber about in the thick undergrowth of its habitat. The hoatzin looks like a cross between a chicken and a secretary bird and is a throwback to archaeopteryx which lived some 140 million years ago and also had three claws on each wing.

● The home of the **Great Indian Hornbill** (*Buceros bicornus*) is a prison. When the female is ready to lay her eggs, she hides in a hole in a tree. The male then seals up the hole, leaving just a narrow slit through which he passes food. Although she is unable to get out, the female has the consolation of knowing that the eggs are safe from predators such as snakes and monkeys. The female stays in there until the chicks are a few months old. She then breaks out and helps the male with the feeding.

● The ruby-throated **hummingbird** (*Archilochus colubris*) appears to defy the laws of physics by propelling its tiny body on a non-stop 800 km (500 mile) flight from North America across the Gulf of Mexico to South America each autumn. Metabolic tests suggest that the bird, which weighs just 2.8 g (0.1 oz), is simply too small to store sufficient energy for the arduous journey. The hummingbird, the largest of which is no more than 2 cm (0.8 in) long, also has the distinction of being the only bird that can fly backwards, a feat it performs as it beats its wings up and down at great speed (some have a wing-beat of 80 per second) while hovering in front of flowers, ready to dip its beak in the nectar.

● The national bird of New Zealand, the **kiwi** (*Apteryx australis*), is the only bird with nostrils at the tip of its beak. Whereas other birds hunt by sight or hearing, the kiwi uses the nostrils at the end of its 15 cm (6 in) long beak to sniff out food at night, plunging the thin, curved beak deep into rotten wood or the ground to find worms and grubs. Although the kiwi is only about the same size as a chicken, it lays an egg which is ten times larger than a hen's. No other bird lays a bigger egg in proportion to its size.

● The **quetzal** (*Pharomachrus mocino*) from Central America has such a long tail that it cannot

take off from a branch in the usual way without ripping its tail to shreds. Instead it has to launch itself backwards into space like a parachutist leaving an aircraft. From beak to tail, the bird measures only 35 cm (14 in) but the tail is another 0.6–0.9 m (2 to 3 ft) long, like a bridal train. It nests in hollow trees but has to back itself into the hole. Inside, the tail is then curled over its head and out of the hole at the front.

● Most birds use body heat to incubate their eggs but the **mallee fowl** (*Leipoa ozellata*), a member of the brush turkey family from Australia and the Pacific Islands, keeps its eggs warm by burying them in a compost heap of rotting vegetation. As well as tending the eggs, the male continually checks the temperature of the incubator with his bill. His aim is to ensure that the inside of the mound mains almost constantly at 33°C (91°F) and he achieves this by adding or removing a layer of sand when necessary. Ironically, after such care and devotion, once the eggs are hatched the parents totally ignore the chicks which are forced to fend for themselves immediately.

● Since there is no vegetation in Antarctica to build nests, the male **Emperor penguin** (*Aptenodytes forsteri*) incubates the egg on its feet for 64 days, during which time it is unable to feed or even move. The egg is kept warm under a flap of skin below the penguin's belly.

● According to ancient observers, that lethal killing machine the crocodile will only allow one creature within snapping distance – the **Egyptian plover** (*Pluvianus aegyptius*) which wanders in and out of the giant reptile's mouth to pick bits of decaying food from between its teeth. However, this behaviour has yet to be witnessed by modern naturalists. Just as the plover is said to act as the crocodile's dentist, so the African oxpecker (family *Buphagus*) searches the backs of elephants, rhinos and cattle, removing the ticks which burrow in their skin.

● Despite its long legs, the **secretary bird** (*Sagittarius serpentarius*) is unable to run. Instead it hops along the African scrubland in search of its staple diet of snakes and lizards. The bird derives its name from the 20 black crest feathers behind its ears which suggest quill pens once used by secretaries, and is the only bird of prey with terrestrial habits.

● The **tailorbird** (family *Orthotomus*), found throughout the Old World, uses its sharp beak to pierce holes along the edges of two leaves. It then makes a nest by stitching the leaves together with pieces of grass.

● One of the few birds known to hibernate is the **whippoorwill** (*Caprimulgus vociferus*), a shy nocturnal bird of North America. During hibernation, its body temperature drops from the normal 39°C (102°F) to 18°C (65°F), its breathing stops and its digestive processes cease. American Indians have known about the whippoorwill's curious behaviour for centuries but scientists did not confirm it until the 1940s.

● The **woodcock** (family *Scolopacidae*) has eyes set so far back in its head that it has a 360° field of vision, enabling it to see all round and even over the top of its head.

● American experiments have revealed that the beak of the **red-headed woodpecker** (*Melanerpes erythrocephalus*) hits the bark of a tree with an impact velocity of 20 km/h (13 mph). This means that when the head snaps back, the brain is subject to a deceleration of about 10 g. The force is such that, by the laws of science, the woodpecker's head should fall off.

CRUSTACEANS

● **Barnacles** spend their entire adult lives standing on their heads. The larvae of barnacles are free-swimming but when a larva finds a rocky surface to its liking, it glues itself to the rock by means of a gland on its head. The barnacle then secretes shell plates around its body to protect it for the rest of its stationary life. It used to be thought that, because of their immobile existence, female barnacles released eggs into the sea where they were fertilized at random but in fact the male has an elongated penis which he extends to his nearest neighbour on the rock.

● The **robber crab** (*Birgus latro*) can climb trees. Inhabiting the islands of the south-west Pacific and Indian Oceans, the adult robber crabs can reach 45 cm (18 in) in length and their powerful pincers and long walking legs enable them to tread where other crabs fear to go. They are perfectly capable of climbing coconut palms and, once at the top, will snip off the young coconuts before returning to the ground to eat them.

● Whereas humans become very ill if they lose 10 per cent of their body fluid, the Australian **side-walker crab** (*Holthusiana transversa*) can survive up to 50 per cent dehydration. Thanks to its metabolism and survival techniques, it can cope with years of drought in the arid Australian outback. Its secret is to sit in the draught at the entrance of its burrow in the evenings until its shell is chilled. Then it scurries down into the warm earth so that condensation will form on the shell which has been specially modified to ensure that every drop of moisture on it drains along small channels to the crab's mouth.

FISH

● A small Central American fish called the **four-eyed anablep** (*Anableps anableps*) has movable genital organs. The male's penis can be located either on the left or right side, as can the female's sex organs. So a male with a left penis must mate with a female with a right vagina and vice versa.

● The deep-sea **angler fish** (*Ceratioidei*) lurks

some 5½ km (3½ miles) beneath the surface of the Atlantic Ocean where there is no light. Above its mouth is a bony projection. From this stretches a long, thin line like a fishing rod, the end of which is illuminated by bacteria. The angler fish waves the pole about, causing little fish to investigate in the belief that the moving light is food. Throughout the operation, the angler fish keeps its body perfectly still – until, that is, the tiny fish come within eating distance. The female angler fish is considerably larger than the male, reaching a formidable 0.6 m (2 ft) compared to the male's paltry 10 cm (4 in). There is no doubting who wears the trousers in the angler fish household. In some species of angler fish, once the little male has found a likely mate, he latches on to her and never lets go for the rest of his life. Their vascular systems become united and the male becomes entirely dependent on the female's blood for nutrition. All the male has to offer in return is his sperm.

● The **archer fish** (*Toxotes jaculator*) of South-East Asia has the ability to catch insects even when they are out of the water. The fish uses its tongue like a water pistol and fires a 'bullet' at any unsuspecting insect sitting on a leaf, thus knocking it off the leaf and into the water. The water is squirted up a tube formed between the palate and the tongue and can hit insects at distances of up to 1 m (3 ft 4 in) above the surface.

● A small southern European fish called the **bitterling** (*Rhodeus*) lays its eggs in the body cavity of a mussel. During the breeding season, the female bitterling develops a 4 cm (1½ in) long tube and sets off with her chosen male to seek out a suitable mussel. The search complete, the bitterling positions herself over the mussel's siphon (the tube through which the mussel takes in water), sticks her tube in and lays her eggs inside the mussel. The male bitterling then disperses his sperm over the mussel. After fertilization, the baby bitterlings spend a month inside their mussel incubator before swimming out. The arrangement benefits both parties. For while the female bitterling is laying her eggs, the mussel releases its own larvae which in turn cling to the

bitterling. Eventually, the fish's skin grows over them and they feed on its juices until they are large enough to break away as a young mussel.

● The 6 cm (2½ in) long **copperband butterfly fish** (family *Pontrodontidae*) of the Indo-Pacific is shaped in such a way that an enemy will think its tail is its head and will therefore snap at the wrong end. The butterfly fish even has a false eye near the tail, its real eye being hidden in a dark vertical stripe.

● The male **cichlid** (family *Cichlidae*) of tropical regions changes colour depending on his success with the ladies. A small black fish with orange and white stripes, the male cichlid acquires a coloured throat during the breeding season and proceeds to show it off by opening its mouth to every passing cichlid. If two males meet, there is a battle of wills before one surrenders. The loser skulks away, closing his mouth as he departs and his colourful throat quickly fades. But the winner glows with even more dazzling colours, immediately attracting the attention of the females who are ready for spawning.

● **Clown fish** (*Amphiprion peraila*) of the Indo-Pacific swim in and out of the tentacles of a sea anenome without getting stung. The sea anenome acts as a kind of patron to the clown fish, allowing it to lay its eggs at the base of the anenome's tentacles where they are safe from enemies. The incentive for the anenome is that the presence of the clown fish attracts other fish, eager to attack it, and when the predator falls prey to the anenome's sting, the anenome and the clown fish share the resulting meal.

● **European eels** (*Anguilla anguilla*) swim thousands of miles across the Atlantic to the Sargasso Sea in order to lay their eggs. Having done so, they die. After hatching, the leaf-like larvae drift all the way back across the Atlantic to the rivers where their parents grew up. There they grow and mature for some ten years before they are ready to begin the migration to the Sargasso Sea. The other fish that makes a long, hazardous journey to its breeding grounds is the salmon. Adult king salmon (*Oncorhynchus tshawytscha*) live in the sea but they return to breed in the same clear, upland streams where they hatched, often leaping rapids and waterfalls on their journey upstream – a journey which can be anything up to 3200 km (2000 miles). After the eggs are laid and fertilized, the adult salmon dies.

● **Flying fish** (*Exocoetidae*) glide rather than fly. They rise almost to the surface and swim at top speed, rapidly vibrating their tail fins from side to side at 50 beats per second. The tail fin acts as a propeller, enabling the fish to leap into the air at speeds of up to 55 km/h (34 mph). Using their pectoral fins as wings, the fish usually glide close to the surface where they can flick their tail against the water to gain extra impetus. Flying fish have been known to soar to heights of 6 m (20 ft) and to stay in the air for distances of 200 m (656 ft). They can also change direction in mid-flight.

● The **globe-fish** (family *Tetraodontidae*) gets its common name of sea hedgehog from the sharp spines that appear all over its body when it is frightened or angry. The globe-fish can inflate itself to three times its normal size by filling an air bladder inside its body. It thus takes on the appearance of a prickly ball, an active deterrent to predators. The globe-fish often swims upside down with its air bladder towards the surface.

● The tiny **hatchet fish** (*Gasteropelecus maculatus*) of South America emits from its body ghostly, greenish-white lights which, to the uninitiated, resemble of a row of ferocious teeth. This has the effect of deterring would-be enemies, allowing the hatchet fish to feast in peace on its diet of plankton.

● For the **mouthbrooder catfish** (*Tachysuridae*), which lives off Mozambique, fertilization takes place in the female's mouth. She releases her ova into the water and then turns round and swallows them. When the male swims by, she mistakes the distinctive spots on his anal fin for more eggs. As she opens her mouth to swallow them, she ends up catching his sperm instead. The young fish

remain in the mouth until they have absorbed their egg yolk, before finally venturing out to feed. Even then, they often return to the safety of the mouth at night or if they feel threatened.

● The **mudskipper** (*Periophthalmus*) of the tropical African swamps can leave water to catch insects on land. To get out of the water, it curls its tail against the mud and jerks its body straight. It is able to walk or hop on land for bursts of a few minutes at a time because, although it has no lungs to enable it to breathe in air, it keeps its gill chamber full of oxygenated water. To replenish its supply, it occasionally gulps water from pools. It also absorbs oxygen through its throat and the roof of its mouth. The 25 cm (10 in) long climbing perch (*Anabas testudineus*) from Asia also clam-

One of the few fish to move around on land is the mudskipper which uses its fins as rudimentary legs

bers out of the water in search of food and can spend hours on dry land, travelling considerable distances through mud flats and tangled roots. The climbing perch is an air-breathing labyrinth fish. It breathes with gills but also possesses a supplementary breathing structure called a labyrinth. This apparatus, which is located in a chamber above the gills and is liberally supplied with blood vessels, enables the fish to use oxygen from air gulped through the mouth and so to survive out of water. The perch 'walks' with the help of its tail and by spines on the lower edges of its gill covers.

● **Plaice** (*Pleuronectes platessa*) pick up arsenic from the sea. But it has no adverse effect since their cells are able to bind the arsenic into an inert chemical configuration. The poison is rendered so inactive that it harms neither the fish nor those who eat it. Various other creatures are immune to poisons which can kill humans. Sheep can swallow arsenic while guinea pigs can eat strychnine but will die if given penicillin. Datura and henbane, which are deadly to humans, are common food for snails but parsley is poisonous to parrots. With no ill-effects, a porcupine can swallow enough prussic acid to poison 100 humans.

● The curious **seahorse** (*Hippocampus erectus*) is the only creature where the male becomes pregnant. When ready to breed, the female inserts a nipple-like appendage into the male and releases her eggs into a special pouch in his stomach. He then discharges his sperm over them. Once the eggs are fertilized, the male's belly takes on a familiar rounded shape. When the baby seahorses are big enough, the male releases them into the sea.

● The pain threshold of a **shark** is so high that they feel very little pain. Sharks eating rapaciously have been known to continue feeding even after other sharks have attacked and half eaten them. A shark will also devour parts of its own body which have become detached. Although a shark has gills, it is unable to pump water over them like other fish. So it has to keep swimming in order to push water over its gills. A shark never stops swimming – even when asleep. If it were to, it would sink and drown.

● The male **three-spined stickleback** (*Gasterosteus aculeatus*), common throughout Britain, is a fish which builds a nest. It collects pieces of aquatic plants and glues them together with a cement secreted from its kidneys. It assembles the 5 cm (2 in) plant mass in a small sandy pit under the water and then creates a burrow inside before luring in a female for egg-laying. The nine-spined stickleback (*Pungitius pungitius*) also builds a nest, sometimes on the river bed. In this instance, he will excavate a shallow 'doorstep' at the front of the nest to keep the entrance clear of the mud.

● The **swordfish** (*Xiphius gladius*) has a heater in its brain. The temperature of a fish's body is dependent on that of the surrounding water. Heat is produced by the activity of the fish's muscles and retained in the blood until the blood vessels reach the gills where the heat is lost to the outside. Some fish have developed systems whereby organs which are required to work with ultra-efficiency retain body heat. The swordfish has done that with its head. The swordfish lives in semi-darkness at a depth of around 600 m (2000 ft) by day and returns to the surface at night. In order to keep sufficiently alert during the day to catch food, especially in cold water, the swordfish warms up its eye muscles and brain. Examination of its head reveals that the mass of brown tissue situated close to the brain and one of the eye muscles is packed with parallel rows of small arteries and veins. Instead of being taken away by the veins, the heat is transferred to the arteries and sent back to the brain. Tests have shown that the retina in the swordfish's eye and the brown tissue on the underside of its brain case can be up to 14°C (57°F) warmer than the surrounding seawater.

INSECTS AND ARACHNIDS

● The queen of the **black garden ant** (*Lasius niger*) feeds partly on its own wing muscles. After mating in mid-air in summer, the queen returns to earth and bites off its wings for food. While the male ants, having fulfilled their sexual role, drop to the ground and crawl off to die, the queen hunts out a crevice for a new nest where she proceeds to live on her fat reserves and on the nutrients contained in the now useless wing muscles.

● It has been calculated that a single **cabbage aphid** (*Brevicoryne brassica*) can give birth in a year to a mass of descendants weighing 822 million tonnes, over three times the total weight of the world's human population. Fortunately, the aphid is subject to a high mortality rate.

● Since the female **bedbug** (family *Cimicidae*) has no sexual opening, the male drills his own vagina, using his curved, pointed penis as a drill. The male then inserts his sperm and the blood-sucking female feeds on some of it when blood is in short supply. The female's vagina soon heals over but leaves a nasty scar. Male bedbugs have also been known to drill holes and deposit semen in each other.

THE DANCE OF THE HONEYBEE

✳ An essential factor in the success of the **bee** is the ability of the worker bees to lead colleagues to sources of food. The workers do not leave the hive to look for food at random – they wait for the scouts to report back its precise location. This information is communicated via the dances of the common honeybee. Different species of bee have different dances but each is a symbolic re-enactment of the foraging trip from which it has just returned.

The small honeybee of South-East Asia, *Apis florea*, builds a horizontal platform at the top of its nest, the perfect stage for the worker to perform her dance which consists of a few walking steps in a straight line while shaking her abdomen. The direction that the dancer follows in the straight line of her dance is the direction in which the new source of food lies. The workers indicate the distance of the food by varying the dance. Foragers returning from a food source within 25 m (80 ft) of the hive perform a round dance – a series of circular runs with frequent changes of direction. For distances of over 100 m (330 ft), the worker does a waggle dance, a contracted figure of eight, in which she waggles her abdomen from side to side during the straight run. The distance is indicated by the frequency of the waggles and the duration of the straight run. Distances between 25 and 100 m (80–330 ft) are shown by a routine that is a combination of round and waggle dances.

The common honeybee, *Apis mellifera*, can not only convey the direction and distance of food but also its quality. The more changes of direction in the dance, the higher the sugar concentration in the food source.

With many species of bee, the dance is performed in the darkness of the hive but the worker is still able to give accurate directional information by remembering the position of the sun. She compensates for the ever-changing position of the sun by adjusting the angle from the vertical of her straight runs.

German honeybee expert Dr Martin Lindauer found that a bee which dances for 30 minutes will move the direction of her dance by seven or eight degrees to allow for the change in the sun's position. Common honeybees have different 'dialects'. For example, Italian honeybees change from the round to the waggle when food is about 35 m (115 ft) from the colony whereas Austrian honeybees do so at 80 m (260 ft).

● The male **bee** that mates with the queen dies after sex. Following copulation in mid-air, his penis snaps off inside the queen, serving as a plug to prevent any loss of sperm. He then falls to the ground and bleeds to death.

● The **Necrophorus beetle** (*Necrophorus germanicus*) is nature's undertaker. When a small animal dies, the stench attracts the black and orange beetle. The male beetle lies on his back beneath the corpse, grasps the body with his jaws and pushes the dead animal to a suitable burial place. With the assistance of the female, he then digs a hole and buries the corpse. Using some of the animal's fur as a nest, the female beetle lays her eggs in a tunnel leading from the burial chamber. When the eggs hatch, the grubs feed on the meat from the scavenged body.

● The feet of **blowflies** are covered with special sweet-sensitive taste buds, enabling them to detect traces of sugar millions of times more efficiently than the human tongue.

● The caterpillar of the **king page butterfly** is disguised as bird droppings while the caterpillar of the Costa Rican moth has a rear end that looks like the head of a young viper with two large, scary, black eyes. In both cases, predators are suitably deterred.

● **Cockroaches** can live for up to seven days after having their heads cut off. It seems this is due to clusters of nerve cells in their bodies. Indeed they actually learn faster without their heads than with them.

● The pupa of the **crane-fly** (family *Tipulidae*), which lives in tropical rain forests, camouflages itself as a drop of water. It hangs from the edge of a palm leaf and smothers its body in a transparent mucus called hydroscopic muco-protein. The mucus refracts the light in such a way that the body of the fly becomes virtually invisible, leaving the predator to see what appears to be nothing more enticing than a drop of moisture about to fall from a leaf.

● A **cricket** (family *Gryllidae*) hears through its knees. Its hearing organs are situated near the knees of its front legs. With most animals and humans, the ears are a fixed distance apart, thus enabling sounds to be located by subconsciously comparing the difference in the time it takes to reach each ear. But because a cricket's front legs are always on the move, the distance between its 'ears' is constantly changing. So each of them must act independently as a highly sensitive directional microphone.

The North American daddy-long-legs, the ichneumon fly, has its 'ears' in its feet. It uses them to listen for the sounds made by the larvae of the horntail wasp which are the favourite food of the fly larvae. The female fly locates the wasp larvae by running up and down tree trunks, listening with the hearing cells in her feet for the noises made by the wasp larvae chewing inside.

● The **Javanese leaf insect** (*Phyllium*) does an excellent impression of a real leaf. Its green body has markings which look just like the midrib and veins of a leaf and blotches which resemble leaf holes. The body even has a brown edging to suggest a dying leaf. When resting, the insect settles on a branch and curls its body to form the shape of a leaf.

Leaf insects blend in perfectly with their surroundings

● The female **praying mantis** (*Mantis religiosa*) eats her partner after sex. The female is much larger than the male and during copulation, hooks the deadly arms, which are used for cutting prey in half, around him and begins to nibble away. Sometimes the male has not even finished copulation before she starts gnawing at him but his sex drive is so strong that he can carry on even while gradually being eaten.

● The male **moth mite** (*Pyemotes berfsi*) is a wholly unsavoury character. The male is born as a mature insect and from the moment of birth assists his mother by seizing his sisters as they emerge from the sexual cavity and dragging them out of the birth passage with his hind legs. But no sooner does he pull a female out than he mates with her. The process of birth and mating only takes around four minutes after which the male continues to hover around his mother's birth passage, waiting for the arrival of a new baby sister. While he is waiting, he drills a hole into the side of his mother's body and feeds on her juices.

● The legs of the male **water mite** sometimes double as sex organs, on occasions penetrating the female. While mating, he pins the female to the ground with tiny hooks so that she can hardly move. He also glues himself to her with a special secretion so that even if she manages to free herself from the hooks, there is no escape.

● A **Madagascan moth** (*Xanthopan morgani praedicta*) has a huge tongue some 30 cm (12 in) long which it rolls into a tight coil when not in use. It was Charles Darwin (1809–82) who first hinted at the existence of such an unusual creature. He was intrigued by the discovery in 1862 of an orchid called the Star of Madagascar (*Angraecum sesquipedale*) which has a 30 cm (12 in) spur with nectar at the base. Darwin reasoned that since the orchid existed, there must be a moth with a similarly long tongue to probe deep enough into the flower to collect the nectar and so pollinate the flower. No such insect was known at the time but 40 years later the moth was discovered and called *praedicta* after Darwin's prediction. The reason that the moth had remained undetected for so long was that it only comes out at night and has a very short lifespan. Fortunately, the orchid remains in bloom for several weeks to allow ample opportunity for pollination.

● The male **Indian moon moth** (*Actis selene*) can detect the scent of a female over 5 km (3 miles) away. His tracking system comprises two specially modified antennae which have long hairs, covered in tiny, ultra-sensitive scent-detectors, protruding horizontally from the main stem. To pursue the smell to its source, the male evaluates the strength of the scent and sets off in that direction. He is able to ignore all other scents and can even follow the trail around obstacles.

● The larva of the **polyphemus moth** (*Antheraea polyphemus*) of North America consumes an amount equal to 86 000 times its own birthweight in the first 56 days of its life. In human terms, that is the equivalent of a 3.2 kg (7 lb) baby taking in 273 tonnes of nourishment.

● Some male web **spiders** wrap the female in a cocoon of silk while mating to protect himself from her unfortunate tendency of mistaking suitors for prey. The female is thus rendered immobile, leaving the male to concentrate on copulation, safe in the knowledge that he is not about to be devoured by his partner. By the time she does manage to free herself, he has long gone.

● Few insects are monogamous, but an exception is the **termite** where the royal male and female stay together for life. Sexually mature termites meet on the wing during swarming and, on reaching the ground, shake off their wings and hunt for a suitable location for a nest. Made from watertight balls of earth and plant material cemented together with saliva and excreta, termite mounds sometimes exceed 6 m (20 ft) in height. A mound discovered in Somalia was estimated to be 8.7 m (28½ ft) tall. Once inside the nest, the royal couple mate prodigiously. The female's enlarged abdomen permits, in some species, the laying of an egg every two seconds.

● The male **tick** does not have a penis so instead

he pokes around in the female's vagina with his nose. When her opening is large enough, he promptly turns around and deposits sperm from his rear on to the entrance of her orifice. He then uses his nose to push the sperm deeper into the vagina.

MAMMALS

● The male **swamp antechinus** (*Antechinus stuartii*), a mouse-like marsupial from Australia, is the only mammal which dies after mating. The males dedicate their lives to a round of non-stop copulation until they literally drop dead. The majority die of starvation because they have no time to feed between sex but others are snapped up by predators as they eagerly search for their next mate.

● The **armadillos** (*Dasypodidae*) of South and Central America are unique in the animal world in that they always give birth to quadruplets which are identical right down to the number of hairs on their bodies. Unlike other mammals, where the young in a single litter are usually from different eggs, the armadillo's offspring all come from the same egg. During development, the egg splits and produces identical quadruplets of the same sex. Armadillos have two other unusual characteristics. They can hold their breath for up to six minutes, which is how they can jam their noses into the ground in search of insects; and the male's penis measures one-third of its entire body length.

● The **aye-aye** (*Daubentonia madagascariensis*) is the only living animal to combine the characteristics of a rodent and a monkey. When this shy, nocturnal creature was first discovered on Madagascar in 1780, its incisor teeth convinced experts that it must be a rodent. But scientists were later forced to re-examine their thinking and reclassify the aye-aye as a distant relative of monkeys and human beings since it has one of the most advanced features of primates – an opposable thumb (the thumb can be placed face to face with any of the fingers). Rodents are known to have split from other mammals at a very early stage in evolution and the aye-aye, which has no close relatives, is the only survivor to possess the traits of both classifications.

● **Bats** (order *Chiroptera*), the only mammals truly capable of flight, have an echo-location system to help pinpoint their prey or any obstacles in their way. Most bats can see in twilight but in pitch darkness they rely on emitting high-frequency squeaks, many of which are inaudible to the human ear. As these ultrasonic squeaks are sent out, the bat's enlarged tragus (the small lobe that guards the entrance to the ear) closes the ear which reopens when the squeak has ended so that the ear may pick up its echo reflected back from a solid object. Thus the returning echoes inform the bat of the precise location of any obstacles. Although they fly out of caves in vast numbers, the bats respond only to their own individual echo-signals and are not confused by the sounds of their neighbours.

● In autumn, forest-living **bears** (family *Ursus*) eat dry pine needles which are digested very slowly and finally halt excretion. By plugging its rectum, the bear is able to retain inside itself any food that it subsequently eats. Thus the bear acquires the full benefit of the food's nutritive value during hibernation.

● Domestic **cats** are renowned for their ability to travel long distances in order to find their way home. In 1981, Mehmet Tunc, working in Germany, was on his way back to his native Turkey for a family holiday when his cat Minosch disappeared at the Turkish border. A bedraggled Minosch resurfaced 61 days later at the Tunc home on the island of Sylt in Northern Germany, having covered a distance of some 2400 km (1500 miles).

The Philips family cat, Silky, vanished at Gin Gin, north of Brisbane, Queensland, Australia, in the summer of 1977. On 28 March 1978, thin and 'stinking to high heaven', Silky turned up at the Philips's house in a suburb of Melbourne, Victoria, a journey of 2370 km (1472 miles).

● **Dolphins** can swim at up to 40 km/h (25 mph) despite the fact that the energy necessary to produce such a speed is ten times greater than the dolphin's muscles could be expected to produce. The dolphin attains such speeds because it has a unique method of reducing the friction drag of sea water. The animal's outer skin is a soft, water-logged coating, 1.6 mm (¹⁄₁₆ in) thick, over a fatty, hard inner skin. The coating is composed of a surface diaphragm supported on thousands of tiny pillars with waterlogged spongy material between them. So the tiniest oscillation in the water on any part of the dolphin's body is adjusted to automatically. Tests simulating the dolphin's skin have demonstrated that in air flows of up to 65 km/h (40 mph), the drag is reduced by up to 60 per cent.

● Only two mammals lay eggs – the **duck-billed platypus** (*Ornithorhynchus anatinus*) and the **echidna** (*Tachyglossus aculeatus*), both native to Australia. Also known as the spiny ant-eater, the echidna has a special receptor in its snout, used for detecting electrical signals given off by worms and ants. This is why an echidna always has a runny nose – the nasal secretions create an electrically conductive medium to transport the tiny currents.

● **Elephants** can sniff water 5 km (3 miles) away and other elephants 3 km (2 miles) away. During a period of drought, they can even detect water underground. An elephant needs to drink in the region of 90 litres (20 gallons) of water per day and will dig into a dry river bed at precisely the right spot to find it, often excavating holes up to 3 m (10 ft) deep with their tusks. (Baboons are the only other animals with the ability to locate underground sources of water.) Elephants are also the only animals with four knees and the only ones unable to jump. The Asiatic elephant (*Elephas maximus*) has an average gestation period of 609 days (over 20 months) and a maximum of 760 days – over 2½ times that of a human.

● All the pet **hamsters** in the world today are descended from a single female wild golden hamster (*Mesocricetus auratus*) found with a litter of 12 young in Syria in 1930. The species had been named in 1839 when a solitary animal was found, again in Syria near Aleppo, but there were no further reported sightings for the next 91 years.

● The female **red kangaroo** (*Macropus rufus*) from Australia has evolved a production line which enables it to speed up the development of a foetus if any existing baby kangaroo, or 'joey', dies. The young kangaroo stays in its mother's pouch for some six months. In the meantime, the female mates again, often within a few days of the birth. Although the fertilized egg of this second baby has commenced its development, it remains in a state of suspended animation inside the mother while the first joey grows. When the first joey begins to leave the pouch, the development of the embryo starts up again and the second joey is born at around the time that the first leaves home permanently. But if the first joey dies, the embryo begins developing immediately and is born some 35 days later. Alternatively, the female can reverse the development, reabsorbing the foetus if drought puts the baby's survival in jeopardy.

● Every four years, millions of Scandinavian **lemmings** (*Lemmus lemmus*) go on a mass march of self-destruction. In the first year of life reproduction is slow for this hamster-like rodent but it gathers pace over the next two years so that by the fourth, the females are almost continually with young. At this point, panic seems to set in – the lemmings fear overcrowding and that there will be insufficient food to go round. So they abandon their habitat en masse, following ancient migration paths to the sea, in a bid to find more living space. On the way, many drown trying to cross rivers while others, when they reach the coast, plunge headlong over the cliffs to their deaths.

● A marsupial from Western Australia called the **numbat** (*Myrmecobius fasciatus*) has 52 permanent teeth – more than any other land mammal. Yet it needs none. For its diet consists principally of termites and ants which it swallows

Right Every four years, Scandinavian lemmings march to their deaths on a mass pilgrimage to the sea. Many plunge over cliffs

whole, having scooped them up with its long, thin tongue. The numbat's teeth are believed to be a legacy from an ancestor which needed them to catch and dissect tougher insect prey.

● The North American **opossum** (family *Didelphidae*) is one of the few creatures that can open its mouth wider than 90°. It does this when in combative mood and will hiss at an attacker to try and scare it away, a threatening stance which it can maintain for 15 minutes. If this fails, the opossum adopts a different, somewhat more submissive tactic, and falls down and pretends to be dead. It lies on its side with its eyes closed and tongue hanging out limply. It will even keep up the pretence if the attacker drags it around by the tail. Eventually, with luck, the opossum's adversary will simply wander off.

The hognose snake (*Heteredon platyrhinos*) of North America tries a similar ploy. It rolls on its back and lies motionless with its mouth wide open. If turned over, it will simply flip on to its back again.

● The squeal of a **pig** (*Sus domestica*) often exceeds official noise-pollution levels. The average pig squeal has been measured at between 100 and 115 decibels. Concorde was originally banned from New York's Kennedy Airport because the noise from its engines exceeded 112 decibels at take-off.

● The female **porcupine** (*Erethizon dorsatum*) is only on heat for four hours of the year. Although she feels sexual urges some months earlier and begins pressing sticks against her vulva, all of her sexual activity is crammed into that brief period. Perhaps understandably, she really lets her spines down for those four hours – if only to make copulation less painful for the male. She notches up as many partners as she can – each encounter takes about five minutes – as the woods are alive with the sound of porcupines.

● The tree-climbing **potto** (*Perodicticus potto*) from Africa is the only mammal with part of its backbone outside its body. The actual spinal column is situated internally but each of its vertebrae has a bony spike protruding through a hole in its skin. This forms a row of sharp teeth along the potto's back. The teeth usually remain hidden beneath the fur but when the potto is threatened, it flattens the hairs on either side and tucks its head between its hind legs so that the enemy is confronted with a sharp circle of spikes.

● The **hero** or **armoured shrew** (*Scutisorex congicus*) of central Africa has an unusual spine with bony knobs on it that are designed to prevent the animal from being crushed by rocks and boulders when it is burrowing. The backbone is so strong that the shrew is said to be able to bear the weight of a 77 kg (170 lb) man.

MOLLUSCS

● The **oyster** (family *Ostreidae*) is a hermaphrodite, but its eggs and sperm mature at different times. Thus an individual oyster can be female one week, drawing in sperm-impregnated water through its gills to fertilize its ova, and the following week male, releasing sperm to fertilize a neighbouring female. Oysters are thus able to reproduce at great speed – a single specimen can produce as many as 1 000 000 offspring per year.

● In 1846, two specimens of the **desert snail** (*Eremina desertorum*) were presented to the Natural History branch of the British Museum as dead exhibits. They were glued to a small tablet and duly put on display. Four years later, in March 1850, the museum staff thought that one of the snails might still be alive. Released from its tablet and placed in tepid water, the snail moved and later began to feed. It went on to live for two years.

REPTILES

● The **chameleon** is renowned for its ability to change colour quickly. The 30 cm (12 in) long male Jackson's chameleon (*Chamaeleo jacksonii*) from the mountain forests of East Africa has a range of body colours that can include black, brown, yellow, green, blue and even bright red. Contrary to popular myth, it does not always change colour to match its surroundings. The change can be brought on by its moods or the varying intensity of light. When a chameleon is asleep, it is usually pale green which blends in with its woodland background. When excited, the colours become brighter; when angry, the colours darken; and when frightened, the colours turn paler. In the early morning or late evening, the chameleon is often grey or pale yellow. In bright sunlight, it is usually dark brown.

● If attacked, the **chuckwalla** (*Sauromalus obesus*), at 50 cm (20 in) one of the largest lizards to be found in the United States, will crawl into a space between two rocks and puff itself up with air so that it can not be pulled out. It can inflate its lungs to increase its body size by 50 per cent. If it is caught by its tail, the tail snaps off – a new tail grows within a few weeks.

● After mating, the male **garter snake** (*Thamnophis*) from North America seals up the female's sexual opening with a plug made from kidney secretions. It acts as a type of chastity belt, preventing any further sexual activity, and ensuring that the female is fertilized by the first male to mate with her.

● **Geckos** (family *Gekkonidae*) can run upside down across a ceiling thanks to the ingenious pads on their feet. The pads consist of thousands of fine bristles, covered with even finer hairs which end in Velcro-like hooks. The hairs are so dense that they act as suction pads while the hooks are able to cling to any surface irregularity. Consequently, the little tropical lizard can support several times its own weight hanging upside down.

● The **flying dragon or draco** (family *Agamidae*) from Borneo is an airborne lizard. It has flaps of skin on either side of its body. When it is resting, the flaps are tucked into the body. In order to glide to the next tree, it opens the flaps and hurls itself into the air.

There is also a flying snake (family *Chrysopelea*) which lives in the trees of Asia. When it launches itself from a tree top, it flattens its body, spreads its ribs and drives out all the air from its lungs so that it becomes very thin and flat. This enables it to glide easily. It can also change direction in mid-air by twisting its body.

● In the United States, some **rattlesnakes** (*Crotalinae*) hibernate in the same place each winter, often in groups of up to 300, the total occasionally reaching 1000. They share a site with non-venomous snakes and even prairie dogs, their favourite prey when not in a state of hibernation. A baby rattlesnake is lethal as soon as it is born and a rattlesnake's venom can remain potent for 25 years after its death.

● The **Polynesian skink** (*Eumeces shiltonianus*) has a tail with a life of its own. It is a dull brown colour apart from its bright blue tail. When threatened, the skink sheds its tail which continues to move around of its own accord, its movement sustained by a series of automatic muscle spasms. Distracted by the antics of the tail, the predator often allows the main body of the skink to escape.

● The **tuatara lizard** (*Sphenodon punctatus*), which lives on islands off the coast of New Zealand, has a third eye. The eye, which is situated on top of the lizard's head, has a lens and a retina but no iris, preventing it from focusing on an image. It can only register light and dark. The nerves from the eye run to a gland at the base of the brain and it is thought that the third eye helps the tuatara to get its seasonal timing right for the birth of its young.

WORMS

● After mating, the vagina of the female **bumble-bee eelworm** (*Sphaerularia bombi*) inflates until it is almost 20 000 times larger than she is (she measures 0.3 mm).

The vagina then takes on a life of its own as the main body becomes superfluous and shrivels up and disintegrates. But as soon as the eggs hatch and a new generation of worms emerge, the vagina too dies.

● **Palolo worms** (*Palolo siciliensis*), small bristleworms that inhabit the coral reefs of the Pacific, manage to mate without either party being present. On two nights of the last quarter of the October/November moon, the rear end of each worm, known as the epitoke, detaches itself from the body and rises to the ocean surface along with millions of other epitokes. While the worms themselves remain in their coral homes, at sunrise the epitokes release sperm and eggs into the sea for fertilization.

● A hungry **ribbonworm** (*Nemertea*) has been known to eat 19/20ths of itself over a period of a few months to fend off starvation. The practice of autophagy (self-eating) does not harm the worm which grows back to full size when food once again becomes available.

PLANT KINGDOM

FUNGI

● The **'Lady in the veil' mushroom** (*Dictyophora phalloides*) is one of the fastest-growing organisms in the plant world. It takes just 20 minutes to reach its full height of 20 cm (8 in). It also has the distinction of making a noise as it does so, the rapidly expanding cells emitting an audible cracking sound. A native of the tropical forests of Africa, the 'Lady in the veil' has a shape which bears an uncanny resemblance to a human penis. It derives its name from the flimsy white membrane which forms beneath the cap at full height, a sight reminiscent of a bridal veil. The veil is essential to the survival of the species. It produces a sticky fluid with an odour like rotting flesh, the stench from which attracts carrion flies. As the insects crawl over the fluid, they inadvertently devour the spores contained within it. Flying off after their meal, they proceed to distribute the spores in their faeces.

● Some mushrooms are luminous, possessing the ability to glow in the dark. It is thought that they give off light in order to attract insects which then help disperse the spores.

The fruiting body of *Mycena lux-coeli*, native to the Hachijo Island of Japan, is visible in the dark from a distance of some 15 m (50 ft). From that range, they resemble a group of lanterns and indeed are often used for that purpose in remote jungle regions.

PLANTS

● Some members of the **birthwort** family (*Aristolochia*) are able to control the movement of an insect inside the flower. Native to the tropical regions of America, the birthwort is equipped with inward-facing stiff hairs inside its corolla tube which prevent any visiting insect from escaping. But some have an additional adaptation in the wall of the flower tube – a transparent area which insects wrongly assume is an escape route. In fact, it is a light to lead the insect towards the stigma and thus ensure pollination. Once the stamens have been pollinated, the stiff hairs of the flower wither, allowing the insect to escape unharmed.

● The **bottle gourd** (*Lagenaria siceraria*) is a

tropical climbing plant, the fruit of which is invariably shaped like a bottle. Light and easy to carry and with a tough shell, the fruit is used as a bottle by a number of African tribes, particularly as a container for milk. The Venda tribe of Southern Africa have a different use for the bottle gourd – as a certificate of virginity. When a Venda girl is about to marry, she attends a special school where her virginity is tested by a female teacher. On leaving the school, the girl is presented with a bottle gourd. If she is still a virgin, the gourd's neck remains intact; if she is not, the neck is cut off. And it is not something she can keep to herself for tradition demands that the gourd must be offered by the girl to her groom just before the wedding night . . .

● The **Lithops** genus from the dry region of South Africa are known as living stones. The small, fleshy plants have no stems and consist solely of two succulent, round leaves which are grey or beige in colour. Growing between rocks and pebbles, they are almost indistinguishable from the real stones that surround them. Some grey *Lithops* even have white spots on their surface to match the pebbles. Unlike other plants, the green assimilating tissue of the *Lithops* is not on the surface but is embedded deep inside the leaf structure. Since sunlight is therefore unable to reach the chlorophyll for photosynthesis, the plant has evolved a 'window' of transparent cells through which sunlight can reach the tissue. The plants also have a strange fruit which, when ripe, explodes. The scattered seeds have special air-filled pockets which allow them to float in water, thus assisting their distribution.

● The **pitcher plant** (*Nepenthes mixta*) is a carnivorous plant with a difference. For not only does it eat insects, but it is also capable of devouring small animals, such as the rats and frogs which inhabit the Malaysian forests where it lives. The plant's leaves are shaped to form a pitcher. Its inner wall secretes nectar and this, in addition to a brightly coloured rim, proves irresistible to insects. Once inside the pitcher, the insect falls foul of the slippery, waxy surface and slides down to its death. It can be a long drop. The

The pitcher plant of Malaysia is capable of devouring small animals

largest pitchers can be anything up to 50 cm (20 in) high. The bottom of the pitcher is filled with a liquid and contains special glands which secrete digestive juices. The plant acts as a stomach and is able to digest all the soft parts of the insect's body as well as absorbing its nutritious substances. It would take no more than a few days for the plant to devour completely a piece of meat thrown into the pitcher. The plant also has a less sinister use, the pitchers being ideal receptacles for storing water. Monkeys are frequently seen drinking from them, giving rise to the plant's alternative name of monkey cup.

● Whereas forest fires destroy vast areas of vegetation, the **sugarbush** (*Protea repens*), the national flower of South Africa, depends on them for survival. When its seeds have been fertilized, they are encased inside tough bracts which form around the flowerhead, creating a protective shell that can last for up to 20 years. The bracts, which contain fireproof fibres, do not reopen until they have been scorched by fire. When the fire has passed, the seeds emerge undamaged and are blown away to ground newly fertilized by the fire.

● The **matchbox bean** (*Entada scandens*) is a curious tropical climber with giant pods which can reach 1.5 m (5 ft) in length. Each 9 cm (3½ in) wide pod contains up to 15 reddish-brown seeds which are embedded in separate compartments, resembling a string of matchboxes. In Australia, they were once used as matchboxes. The roasted seeds have fulfilled a variety of functions. Aboriginal women used them as a contraceptive while in Africa they sometimes serve as a coffee substitute.

● The slightest touch causes the **sensitive plant** (Mimosa pudica) of Brazil to collapse in one-tenth of a second. When touched, the cells surrounding the base of the leaflet stalks rapidly lose water, causing the entire leafstalk to collapse. It is thought that this wilting pose deters grazing animals from eating it. Some ten minutes later, the plant returns to its upright position as the cells reabsorb water.

● The rare *Puya raimondii* of Bolivia takes between 80 and 150 years to bloom. And once it has done so, it promptly dies. Although a herbaceous plant, it is built like a tree, with a trunk up to 4 m (13 ft) tall, strong enough to support a man. When in bloom, it produces an inflorescence some 6.7 m (22 ft) tall and 1 m (3 ft) thick, comprising up to 8000 white blooms.

● The largest bloom in the world is that of the **giant rafflesia** (*Rafflesia arnoldii*), native to the tropical jungle of Borneo and Sumatra. Its single red flower can grow to 1 m (3 ft) wide and weigh up to 7 kg (15 lb). A parasite, the plant has no leaves, stem or root and will only grow on the root of one species, the genus *Cissus*. The bud takes nine months to reach full size, the link with the timescale of a human pregnancy leading natives of Malaya to use the buds as a sexual stimulant and fertility charm. The surface of the flower is covered with dirty white patches so that it resembles rotting meat. It also stinks of rotting meat, thus attracting carrion-loving insects. The flower only stays open for four days, after that disintegrating into a slimy mass containing thousands of seeds.

● Two species of **underground orchids** exist in Australia. *Rhizanthella gardneri* was first discovered in 1928 in Corrigin, Western Australia, by a farmer, Mr J. Trott, ploughing his land. A small, leafless plant with a stem just over 2.5 cm (1 in) long, it is completely buried beneath the soil. Even the flower head does not quite reach the surface. The only part of the plant which ever emerges above ground level is a cluster of capsules which are pushed above the surface to disperse the dust-like seeds. The second species of underground orchid, *Cryptanthemis slateri*, was found in New South Wales in 1931.

● Commonly known as the **resurrection plant**, the **Rose of Jericho** (*Anastatica hierochuntica*) has the unique ability to change shape. It grows in arid regions of the Middle East and when there is sufficient moisture in the ground, its branches spread out in a star-like shape with small white flowers. However, after flowering and setting fruit, an operation which always occurs during a drought, the branches curve in to form a ball shape. These balls uproot and are blown across the desert by the wind. When the rain returns, the plant reverts to its spreading habit.

● The **starfish flower** (*Stapelia variegata*) from Africa looks just like a brown and yellow starfish nestling in the sand. It also smells like a dead animal, as a result of which flies, thinking the *Stapelia* is a lump of rotten meat, decide it is the perfect spot to raise a family. As they lay their eggs on the surface, they accidentally pollinate the flower at the same time. The flower is happy but the flies are not. For when the maggots hatch out, there is no rotten meat for them to feed on after all, so they die.

● Among the carnivorous plants are the **sundews** (*Drosera*) and the best known of all, the **Venus fly** trap (*Dionaea muscipula*). The latter, which grows in the bogs and swamps of North America, was discovered in 1760 by Arthur Dobbs, Governor of North Carolina. Each leaf blade has two lobes, at the centre of which are trigger hairs sensitive to an insect's touch. Once the insect lands on the surface of the plant, the lobes shut and the trapped insect is crushed. It takes the plant half an hour to squash and kill a fly and ten days to digest it. The meal over, the leaf blades open again, ready for the next unsuspecting visitor. Each leaf can only catch and digest three insects during its entire life. After that, the leaf blades wither. Fortunately for the plant, it has a number of insect-trapping leaves. Owing to its limited timespan, it is essential that the plant can differentiate between a meal and a drop of rain or a speck of soil. It does not want to waste a valuable closure on such trivia. So if someone or something touches the trigger just once, the plant does not react unless there is another touch within 20 seconds. Only an insect entering the trap can touch the sensitive hairs more than once.

● *Welwitschia mirabilis* can live for over 2000 years yet its central trunk never grows above 1 m (3 ft) in height. Instead, the energy is transmitted to its two huge leaves which never fall and continue growing throughout the plant's life. The leaves are often as long as 6 m (20 ft) and are thick and leathery. Over the years, they become frayed at the ends, ripped to shreds by the wind and scorched by the desert heat. The plant was discovered by Dr Frederic Welwitsch in 1859 during his journey through the Namibian desert in south-west Africa. When it was first taken to England, the head of Kew Gardens described it as 'the most wonderful plant ever brought to this country, and the very ugliest'. Dr Welwitsch has the plant engraved on his tombstone at London's Kensal Green cemetery.

Welwitschia mirabilis has two giant leaves which never fall. The plant can live for hundreds of years

TREES

● The **banyan tree** (*Ficus benghalensis*) of India has more than one trunk. When the tree reaches a certain size, it sends down rope-like roots which, on reaching the soil, take root and then thicken to form additional trunks. Thus the tree can spread outwards almost indefinitely. A 200-year-old specimen in Calcutta Botanic Gardens has over 1700 trunks. During Alexander the Great's Indian campaign (327–325 BC), 20000 soldiers are said to have sheltered under a single banyan tree.

● The **boojum tree** (*Idris columnaris*) can be found growing in arid, semi-desert areas of California. Its base measures aproximately 1 m (3 ft) in width, but as the trunk, which can exceed a height of 20 m (65 ft), reaches upwards, it gradually reduces to a series of long, tentacle-like protuberances. Sometimes these flexible extensions droop down to the ground and root so that the tree forms a complete arch. To add to the curious effect, the boojum tree has no branches, being covered instead with thorny stems. The tree does have a practical use, however, since old boojums are often hollow at the base, thus making an ideal location for a beehive. Indeed, American Indians considered the boojum tree to be an important source of honey.

● The **grapple tree** (*Harpagophytum procumbens*) of South Africa produces a fearsome fruit called the 'Devil's Claw' which has been known to kill a lion. The fruit, which measures about 6 cm (2½ in) across, is covered in fierce hooks which latch on to passing animals. In trying to shake the fruit off, the animal disperses the seeds but as it does so, the claw's hooks sink deeper into the creature's flesh. If the animal touches the fruit with its mouth, the fruit will attach itself to the animal's jaw, inflicting considerable pain and preventing it from eating. Whilst antelope are the usual victims, lions have been reported as starving to death after an encounter with the Devil's Claw.

● When the fruit of the South American **sandbox tree** (*Hura crepitans*) is ripe, it explodes with such force that the seeds can be scattered up to 14 m (46 ft) from the main trunk. The explosion

is so loud that people experiencing it for the first time have been seen cowering in fear.

● The **traveller's tree** (*Ravenala madagascariensis*), a tropical plant found in Madagascar, is a remarkable source of water, up to 1½ litres (2½ pints) being stored in a single tree. The tree, which can attain heights of 30 m (98 ft), has a leaf formation resembling a giant fan. At the base of each leaf stalk is a kind of cistern. During the rainy season, water collects on the leaf's ribbed surface and flows down a groove to the 'cistern' where it is stored. If the thick end of the leaf stalk is pierced, the water gushes out, to the relief of many a thirsty traveller – hence the plant's common name.

● There are few stranger sights in Africa than the **sausage tree** (*Kigelia africana*), the fruits of which, some 60 cm (2 ft) long and 10 cm (4 in) thick, look just like sausages. To complete the illusion, they dangle from the main body of the tree on long stems as if hanging in a butcher's shop window. The fruits have a different connotation to the Ashanti people of Ghana. They call the tree '*nufatene*' which means 'hanging breasts', likening it to old tribeswomen whose life of unremitting breastfeeding results in very long breasts.

Left One of the world's strangest trees – the sausage tree of tropical Africa

PLACES

● The **Arches National Park**, 40 km (25 miles) north of Moab, Utah, USA, features dozens of arches, each sculpted by nature. The arches are the result of erosion, formed by the disintegration of the weakest part of the sandstone. The area's formation began around 150 million years ago when layers of Entrada sandstone were formed from the sand and sediment of an inland sea. The salmon-tinted type of sandstone is especially susceptible to the formation of arches. The park

is home to the longest natural arch in the world. The Landscape Arch has a span of 88.7 m (291 ft) and is set some 30 m (100 ft) above the canyon floor. In one place, erosion has narrowed its section to 1.8 m (6 ft).

● No woman or female animal has knowingly been allowed to set foot on **Mt Athos** in Macedonian Greece since a special decree was issued in AD 1060. Yet the 2033 m (6670 ft) high mountain is dedicated to a woman. It is the holy mountain of the Eastern Orthodox Church and dedicated to the Virgin Mary but, because Mary is supposed to have visited Athos, no other female has been considered fit to set foot on it. The mountain's principal inhabitants are monks.

● The largest block of stone in the world is **Ayers Rock** in Australia's Northern Territory which rises to a height of 348.4 m (1143 ft) above the surrounding plain. Made of red sandstone, it is 2.4 km (1½ miles) long and 1.6 km (1 mile) wide. Two-thirds of the rock is believed to be below ground. The setting sun turns the rock a series of deeper reds before it fades into grey. The reverse performance takes place at dawn each day.

● The **Dead Sea** on the Israel–Jordan border is not a sea at all but a large inland salt lake some 80 km (50 miles) long and 15 km (9 miles) wide. Its shore, 392 m (1286 ft) below sea-level of the eastern Mediterranean, makes it the lowest place on the Earth's land surface. The Dead Sea is some seven times more salty than seawater. Nearly one-third of it consists of dissolved salt and other minerals including potash and magnesium compounds. The salt content enables bathers to float on the surface but no fish can survive there, the only lifeforms which can exist being salt-loving micro-organisms.

● Some 50 million years ago in north-east Wyoming, USA, a mass of molten rock forced its way through a layer of sedimentary rocks laid down on the bed of an ancient inland sea millions of years earlier. The molten rock cracked as it cooled, forming a number of columns. Over the centuries, the softer sedimentary rocks have been eroded by the weather and the Belle Fourche river, leaving a stunning flat-topped mountain called the **Devil's Tower**. Standing like a huge tree stump, it is 265 m (869 ft) high and its summit is 85 m (279 ft) across. In 1906, it was named the first national monument in the US and more recently was used as the landing strip for extra-terrestrials in the film *Close Encounters of the Third Kind* (US 77). There are 80 different routes to the top, a fact borne out by over 1000 eager climbers each year.

The statues on Easter Island have puzzled experts for centuries

● Among the great mysteries of the world are the statues of **Easter Island** in the South Pacific. Over 1000 giant statues, carved from volcanic rock, are scattered across the island. Many weigh 20 tonnes, but the largest which is 9.7 m (32 ft) tall tips the scales at 90 tonnes. With their elongated heads, it is thought that the statues are images of Polynesian chiefs who probably reached the island from the west some 2000 years ago. Transportation has long puzzled experts but it is believed that the statues once stood upright on stone platforms, having been hauled into position on wooden sledges pulled by teams of men.

● The deepest recesses of the ocean are usually too cold to support any form of life. But where there are cracks in the Earth's crust, heat from the interior escapes to warm the water and make life possible. One such hot spot was discovered about 800 km (500 miles) west of Ecuador and 2400 m (8000 ft) below the surface of the Pacific by explorers aboard the scientific submarine *Alvin* in 1977. There they found a densely populated colony of crabs, clams and fish.

● Situated 24 km (15 miles) north of Scone in the **Hunter Valley** region of New South Wales is the fire that never goes out. At first geologists thought the mysterious column of smoke came from a volcano but it transpired that the cause was a burning seam of coal 150 m (500 ft) below the surface. The belief is that some 2000 years ago a tree, possibly set on fire by lightning, fell on to the exposed face of the coal seam. This set the coal alight and the fire has slowly smouldered.

● The 383 sq m (148 sq miles) of the **Petrified Forest** in Arizona, USA, features one of the most remarkable landscapes on Earth – fossilized trees of stone in reds, yellows and rainbow colours, sparkling like gems.

Two million years ago, in the late Triassic Period of the Early Mesozoic era, the area was rife with tall conifers. When they fell, they were transported by rivers and coated by mud and sand from the mountains. Everything was then covered with layers of volcanic ash while water, rich with silica, permeated the tissue of the trees, cutting off the supply of oxygen, preventing decay and forming various types of quartz crystals. Molecule by molecule, silica replaced cellulose and made a faithful reproduction of the wood. Every part of the tree absorbed varying amounts of trace minerals, such as iron or sulphur, which stained the silica in the diverse colour shades.

● At Hyden, 350 km (217 miles) south-east of Perth in Western Australia, is **Wave Rock**, a 15 m (49 ft) high rock, shaped like a huge wave. It has been shaped over hundreds of years by the wind, sand and weather.

10

COINCIDENCE

THE ARTS

● As a schoolboy, French poet Emile Deschamps (1791–1871) tasted plum pudding for the first time, at the suggestion of his fellow diner, a M. de Fortgibu, who had acquired a taste for the dessert in England. Ten years later, Deschamps was passing a restaurant when he saw a plum pudding being prepared inside. On asking for a slice, he learned that the pudding was reserved . . . for M. de Fortgibu. Many years later, Deschamps was attending a dinner party and about to have his third encounter with plum pudding. As Deschamps was entertaining guests by recounting the restaurant story, M. de Fortgibu arrived at the door. He too had been invited to the dinner but had got lost. Deschamps recalled: 'My hair stood up on my head!'

● In the early 1970s, Welsh actor Anthony Hopkins agreed to star in a film version of George Feifer's *The Girl From Petrovka* and scoured the bookshops of London in search of a copy of the original novel. His quest was unsuccessful until, on his way home, he spotted a copy lying on a seat at Leicester Square underground station, obviously having been forgotten by a traveller. Two years later, Hopkins was working in Vienna on the film when he received a visit from Feifer. The

author lamented that he had no copy of his own book – he had given the last one to a friend who had lost it in London. 'Is this the one,' asked Hopkins, producing the copy he had found, 'with the notes scribbled in the margins?' It was indeed George Feifer's own copy.

● *Black Abductor* was the title of a 1972 novel from Harrison James (James Rusk Jr's pen name) in which a group of terrorists, with a black ringleader, kidnapped the daughter of a wealthy public figure with right-wing leanings. The daughter, a student named Patricia, was snatched near her college campus. Her boyfriend, who was with her at the time, was beaten up by kidnappers and briefly became a suspect. In the book, Patricia eventually became sympathetic to her kidnappers' cause. Two years later, on 22 February 1974, 19-year-old Patricia Hearst (student daughter of wealthy, right-wing Randolph Hearst) was kidnapped from her apartment near the University of California's Berkeley campus by members of the Symbionese Liberation Army, a terrorist group whose leader was black. Miss Hearst's former boyfriend, Steven Weed, who had been with her when she was seized and had been badly beaten up, was an early suspect. So too was James Rusk

175

Jr – the FBI had read his novel. The final coincidence occurred on 15 April 1974 when Patricia Hearst was photographed taking part in a bank robbery – initially seen as evidence that she had succumbed to her kidnappers' ideology.

● Hungarian author Arthur Koestler was imprisoned for three months by Franco's nationalists as a suspected spy during the Spanish Civil War in 1937, and threatened with execution. In search of comfort, he recalled Thomas Mann's novel *Buddenbrooks* in which a character, facing up to the fact that he is about to die, gains strength from a book by Schopenhauer that contains certain metaphysical speculations about death. The day after his eventual release, Koestler wrote to Thomas Mann, whom he had never met, and thanked him for giving him the inspiration to carry on. Mann wrote back to say that he had not read that passage of Schopenhauer's for over 40 years, but the day before he had been sitting in his garden when he felt a sudden urge to read it once more. He had gone indoors to fetch the book from his library, only to be interrupted by the postman ringing the doorbell. The postman handed him Koestler's letter.

● When American novelist Anne Parrish first visited Paris in the 1920s, she decided to browse among the secondhand bookstalls that line the banks of the River Seine near the Île de la Cité. There she found an old volume of *Jack Frost and Other Stories*, a book which she had loved as a child in Colorado Springs but had never seen a copy of since. She opened it and peered in disbelief at the inscription on the flyleaf. It read: 'Anne Parrish, 209 N. Weber Street, Colorado Springs'.

● On 28 October 1884, *The Times* carried a story about a boat called the *Mignonette* which had foundered that summer. Four survivors had been cast adrift in an open boat, the three senior crew members eventually eating the cabin boy, Richard Parker. In 1838, Edgar Allan Poe had written a story entitled *The Narrative of Arthur Gordon Pym of Nantucket* which also featured a shipwreck and the eating of a seaman. The name of Poe's unfortunate sailor was Richard Parker.

> ✱ Horror film stars Vincent Price, Peter Cushing and Christopher Lee were all born on 27 May – but in different years, 1911, 1913 and 1922 respectively.

● English novelist, J.B. Priestley (1894–1984) described how his wife, archaeologist Jacquetta Hawkes, once purchased three large lithographs by Graham Sutherland. That night, she left them leaning against a chair in her bedroom, prior to putting them up in the morning. The lithograph on the outside, face up, and thus the only visible one, was of a grasshopper. As she climbed into bed, Jacquetta Hawkes felt a movement and pulled back the sheets. There was a grasshopper in the bed. No grasshopper had ever been seen in that room before or after nor anywhere in the house.

● Russian poet Alexander Pushkin (1799–1837) forecast his own death in his poetic novel *Eugene Onegin*, published in 1831. The book sees Onegin, bored with the social life of St Petersburg, visiting a country estate where he rejects the advances of a teenage girl who falls in love with him. He then challenges a young poet named Lenski (based on Pushkin himself) to a duel and kills him. In 1831, Pushkin married a teenage girl, 17-year-old Natalia, but she became infatuated with a guards officer, Baron Georges d'Anthes. The jealous Pushkin insulted the officer and his family, causing the Baron to challenge him to a pistol duel in January 1837. In the duel, Pushkin was fatally wounded.

> ✱ American writer Mark Twain was born in 1835, the year of Halley's comet. Twain remarked that as he had come into the world with the comet, so he would pass from the world with it. Halley's comet returned in May 1910 and Twain died on 21 April that year, aged 74.

JULES VERNE'S SPACE PREDICTIONS

✳ French author Jules Verne (1828–1905) had an uncanny knack of predicting the future. His stories *From the Earth to the Moon*, published in 1865, and the sequel, *Round the Moon*, both accurately foretold the events surrounding space missions which were undertaken over 100 years later. *From the Earth to the Moon* was mirrored by the *Apollo 11* lunar flight of 1969. Verne's spacecraft was launched from Cape Town, Florida, a site near the present launch pad at Cape Canaveral. Verne's ship was called the *Columbiad* and contained three astronauts. There were three men in the *Apollo* command module, named *Columbia*. Verne's craft travelled at around 40 000 km/h (25 000 mph) and reached the Moon in four days, one hour. *Apollo* travelled at 38 600 km/h (24 000 mph) and made the journey in four days, six hours. Verne's writings also forecast the near disaster suffered by *Apollo 13* in 1970. In Verne's story, an oxygen explosion prevented the spaceship *Columbiad* from landing on the Moon and it had to use a complicated 'slingshot' manoeuvre to catapult itself back to Earth. It crashed into the Pacific where the crew were picked up by ship. *Apollo 13*, whose command module was again the *Columbia*, was also prevented from landing on the Moon by an oxygen tank explosion. The crew were forced to use a 'slingshot' tactic to fly around the Moon and catapult the craft back to Earth. Like the astronauts on Verne's *Columbiad*, they ignited rockets to get out of orbit and landed in the Pacific where they were rescued by ship. Perhaps *Apollo 13* was doomed to failure. It was launched at 13.13 (American time) and the explosion occurred on 13 April.

Right A man ahead of his time – Jules Verne possessed an uncanny ability to prophesy the future of the world

CRIME

● After refusing to pay alimony to his wife, John Blackman of Eastbourne, Sussex, was sent to jail in April 1922. Shortly afterwards, one of the magistrates who had sentenced him, John Duke, died. Still refusing to pay, Blackman received a further sentence. Following the hearing, another of the magistrates, Major Molineux, was taken ill and soon died. A few minutes after sentence was passed at Blackman's third court appearance on the same charge, magistrate H.D. Farnell suffered a seizure and died without regaining consciousness. In October 1923, the stubborn Blackman appeared at Eastbourne Crown Court before Judge MacKarness and was again sent to prison. He finished his sentence just in time to attend the judge's funeral. In July 1924, Blackman received his fifth custodial sentence. By September of that year, J.T. Helby, one of the magistrates at that hearing, was dead.

● In 1799, an American private ship, the *Nancy*, was being pursued by a British warship in the Caribbean. Prior to capture, the *Nancy*'s skipper, Thomas Briggs, managed to throw the ship's American papers overboard and replace them with Dutch forgeries. Charged in Jamaica with running a British blockade during wartime, Briggs seemed set to go free for lack of evidence. But, during the trial, another British ship, the HMS *Ferret*, arrived in port and produced the damning papers. The *Ferret* had captured a large shark off Haiti and when the shark's stomach had been opened up, the American papers had been found inside.

● On 13 February 1746, Frenchman Jean Marie Dubarry was executed for the murder of his

> ✳ On 17 October 1678, English politician Sir Edmund Berry Godfrey was found murdered, his body left in a ditch on London's Greenberry Hill. Three men were arrested and tried – Robert Green, Henry Berry and Lawrence Hill.

> ✳ A French assassin named Claude Volbonne murdered Baron Rodemire de Tarazone in 1872. The baron's father had also been murdered 21 years previously – by a Claude Volbonne. The two killers were not related.

father. Exactly 100 hundred years later, on 13 February 1846, another Frenchman called Jean Marie Dubarry was also executed for killing his father.

● Accused of cheating in a poker game at the Bella Union saloon, San Francisco, in 1858, Englishman Robert Fallon was shot dead. Since the $600 he had won had been obtained by such dubious means, it was considered unlucky merely to split it among the remaining players. So they called in a passer-by to take the dead man's place, confident that they would quickly win back their money. But the new player turned the $600 into $2200. When the police arrived, they asked the stranger for $600 so that they could pass it on to Fallon's next of kin. The mystery player turned out to be Fallon's son – he had not seen his father for seven years.

● Early in 1938, playwright A.J. Talbot penned a one-act comedy, *Chez Boguskovsky*, in which a man called Boguskovsky steals a painting from the Louvre in Paris. On 15 August 1939, a painting was stolen from the Louvre. The thief turned out to be a man named Boguskovsky.

● In 1883, Henry Ziegland of Honey Grove, Texas, jilted his sweetheart who, in despair, killed herself. Her brother attempted to avenge her by shooting Ziegland. Although the bullet only grazed Ziegland's face and lodged in a tree, the brother was convinced that he had killed him and promptly took his own life. In 1913, Ziegland decided to dynamite the tree with the bullet in it. The force of the explosion fired the old bullet through Ziegland's head, killing him.

DISASTERS

● Residents of the small farming town of Beatrice, Nebraska, USA, were renowned for being religious and punctual. So when choir practice was set for 7.20 p.m. on 1 March 1950, everyone was expected to be there. But the minister was late. His wife and daughter (both members of the choir) and he waited while the daughter's dress was being ironed. Another girl member of the choir was also delayed – by her geometry homework – while two others fell prey to a faulty car engine and two more wanted to hear the end of a radio programme. In fact, all 15 members of the Beatrice choir were late that night, none arriving before 7.30. It was indeed a blessing since at 7.25 an explosion destroyed the entire church.

● On 23 May 1939, the recently built American submarine *Squalus* sank off the eastern seaboard. A sister ship, the *Sculpin*, managed to rescue over half of the 56-man crew. The *Squalus* was salvaged and renamed the *Sailfish*. In 1943, the *Sculpin* was sunk by the Japanese who took 42 men prisoner, placing half of them on board the aircraft carrier *Cuyo*. Approaching Japan, the *Cuyo* was torpedoed by the *Sailfish* and everyone on board was killed. Thus the crew of the *Sailfish* had killed half of the survivors of the submarine that had come to their rescue four years previously.

● In 1898, retired Merchant Navy officer Morgan Robertson wrote a novel, *The Wreck of the Titan*, about a huge 'unsinkable' British liner which, on its maiden voyage from Southampton to New York with 3000 passengers on board, struck an iceberg in the North Atlantic and sank. Many lost their lives because of a shortage of lifeboats. On 15 April 1912, the supposedly unsinkable *Titanic*, on its maiden voyage from Southampton to New York with 2340 passengers, struck an iceberg in the North Atlantic and sank. A total of 1513 perished, the majority because there were too few lifeboats.

In April 1935, a ship named the *Titanian*, carrying coal from Newcastle to Canada, almost suffered the same fate as the *Titanic* when encountering an iceberg in that same area of the North Atlantic. Luckily, crewman William Reeves had a premonition of impending disaster and yelled 'Danger ahead!' to the navigator shortly before the iceberg became visible in the darkness. Reeves was born on 15 April 1912, the day the *Titanic* sank.

On 15 April 1987, the memorial service was held for those lost on the *Herald of Free Enterprise* ferry which had capsized at Zeebrugge, Belgium, the previous month. Also on 15 April 1987, memorabilia from the *Titanic* came up for auction.

Seven weeks after the *Titanic* sank, her sister ship, the *Olympic*, nearly went aground off Land's End, Cornwall. Seven weeks after the *Herald* disaster, another ferry, the *Hengist*, collided with a French trawler which capsized.

The sinking of the *Titanic* formed part of a chain of curious coincidences

● On 5 December 1664, a boat sank while crossing the Menai Strait, off North Wales. Only one of the 81 passengers survived – Hugh Williams. On 5 December 1785, another boat sank in the same place. The sole survivor was named Hugh Williams. Then on 5 August 1820, 24 passengers drowned in a third disaster. The only survivor went by the name of Hugh Williams.

✳ In 1975, a Bedfordshire family were shaken when a huge chunk of ice fell out of a clear sky and smashed through the roof of their house. At the time they were watching a film on television about the sinking of the *Titanic*.

PAST COINCIDENCES

● Ancient Aztec priests taught that the bearded wind god Quetzalcoatl had been forced into exile across the eastern sea and had vowed to return in the year One Reed of the Aztec calendar. Spaniard Hernan Cortés, who was also bearded, happened to arrive on the Atlantic coast to begin his conquest of Mexico in 1519 – the Aztec year of One Reed. So the invading Cortés was hailed as a god by the Aztecs whose chiefs fell on their knees in awe of him. This greatly hastened the Spanish conquest of the entire Aztec empire.

● On 25 January 1787, Jabez Spicer of Leyden, Massachusetts, was killed by two bullets during an attack on the federal arsenal at Springfield. He was wearing the same coat that his brother Daniel had been wearing when he too was killed by two bullets on 5 March 1784. The bullets which killed Jabez passed through the holes made by the bullets which had killed Daniel.

● In 1812, Eugénie, wife of French Marshal Oudinot, was eagerly awaiting delivery of a bust of her husband, modelled by an artist from Berlin. When it finally arrived, one of the plaster shoulders was badly damaged, about to drop off. A few days later, her husband had his shoulder smashed by grapeshot during the Russian campaign.

● Princess Maria del Pozzo della Cisterno was unlikely ever to forget the day of her wedding to Amadeo, the Duke D'Aosta, son of the King of Italy, in Turin on 30 May 1867. Her wardrobe mistress hanged herself; the place gatekeeper cut his throat; the colonel leading the wedding procession collapsed from sunstroke; the stationmaster was crushed to death under the wheels of the honeymoon train; the King's aide was killed by a fall from his horse; and the best man shot himself!

● The Prince of Wales (the future Edward VII) was a keen fox hunter and numbered among his hunting companions the actor Edward A. Sothern. One day, the Prince presented his friend with a golden matchbox, designed to be attached to a watch chain. Sothern kept the matchbox with him at all times, only to lose it after being thrown from a horse. Mourning its disappearance, he had a duplicate made and gave it to his son Lytton, also an actor. During a tour of Australia, Lytton Sothern gave the duplicate to a friend named Labertouche. Back in England, Lytton's brother George was out hunting when a farmer handed him the golden box which had been lost 20 years earlier but had been found only that morning by a ploughboy. Lytton and George's brother, Edward H. Sothern, was on a theatre tour in the United States when the box was found. George notified him of the find by letter which he read while travelling by train with fellow actor Arthur Lawrence whom he had met for the first time that day. Edward H. Sothern related the story to Lawrence and wondered what had become of the duplicate box. At that point, Lawrence dangled a chain in front of him. On it was the duplicate given to Lawrence by Labertouche.

● Seven of the eight US Presidents who have died in office – either through illness or assassination – were elected at exactly 20-year intervals. The seven were: William Harrison (elected 1840), Abraham Lincoln (1860), James Abraham Garfield

(1880), William McKinley (elected for second term 1900), Warren Harding (1920), Franklin Roosevelt (elected for third term 1940) and John F. Kennedy (1960). The eighth was Zachary Taylor, elected in 1848 and died in office 1850.

● A series of coincidences links the assassinations of Abraham Lincoln and John F. Kennedy. Lincoln was elected in 1860, Kennedy in 1960; both were assassinated on Fridays in front of their wives; their successors as President were both named Johnson; Andrew Johnson was born in 1808, Lyndon Johnson in 1908; both assassins, John Wilkes Booth (born 1839) and Lee Harvey Oswald (born 1939), were killed before coming to trial; Lincoln's secretary, whose name was Kennedy, advised him against going to the theatre and Kennedy's secretary, whose name was Lincoln, advised him not to go to Dallas; Booth shot Lincoln in a theatre and ran to a warehouse, Oswald shot Kennedy from a warehouse and ran to a theatre; the surnames of both Presidents have seven letters; and the names of both assassins have 15 letters.

● A few months before Lincoln's assassination, John Wilkes Booth's elder brother Edwin had been standing on a crowded Jersey City railway platform when he saw the crush push a young man into the path of an oncoming train. Risking his own life, Booth snatched the stranger to safety. The young man was Abraham Lincoln's son, Robert. Incredibly, Robert Lincoln was to be at the scene of three presidential assassinations. On 14 April 1865, he rushed to Ford's Theatre where his father lay fatally wounded. In 1881, he was at James Garfield's side seconds after the President had been shot. And 20 years later, he was on the point of joining President McKinley at the Pan American Exhibit when he learned that McKinley had been shot dead.

● Having arrived in Monza earlier that day, King Umberto I of Italy and his aide visited a restaurant on the evening of 28 July 1900. There the King noticed that he and the restaurant owner were virtual doubles, both facially and physically. The King remarked on this and in conversation with the padrone it emerged that both men were called Umberto and both had been born in the same town on 14 March 1844. Both had been married on 22 April 1868, to a woman called Margherita, and each had named his son Vittorio. On the day of Umberto's coronation, the other Umberto had opened his restaurant. The day after their meeting, the King was dismayed to learn that his double had died in a shooting accident. As he asked his aide to find out about the funeral details, three shots rang out from an assassin's gun. King Umberto was shot dead.

● At the outbreak of the First World War, French intelligence agents arrested a suspected German spy, Peter Karpin. For the next three years, the French kept his arrest a secret, sending fake reports to his superiors and intercepting all funds sent to France on his behalf. These funds were used to buy a car which, in 1919, two years after Karpin had finally managed to escape, killed a man in the Ruhr, at that time still occupied by the French. The victim of the road accident was Karpin, the escaped spy.

✳ Franz Richter, a 19-year-old volunteer in the Austrian Transport Corps at the end of the First World War, was admitted to the corps hospital suffering from pneumonia. In the same hospital was another patient named Franz Richter, also 19, also suffering from pneumonia, and also a volunteer in the Transport Corps. Both men had been born in Silesia.

● David Page, an English soldier in 1940, discovered that the wedding photographs which he had been anxiously awaiting had been accidentally opened by a soldier in another troop. The confusion was understandable – one man was Page no. 1509321, the other was Pape no. 1509322. At the end of the war, Page became a bus driver with London Transport at the Merton depot, Colliers Wood. One day, he noticed that more tax than usual had been deducted from his wages and queried it. He discovered that his pay had been mixed up with those of a driver who had recently transferred to the garage. The other driver was the same Pape. Furthermore, Page's PSV licence no. was 29222, Pape's was 29223.

● One of the most remarkable series of coincidences surrounded the Allied preparations for D-Day in 1944. The code name for D-Day was 'Operation Overlord' and each stage had its own individual code name. Neptune was the naval initiative, Omaha and Utah were the code names for two French beaches where landings were to take place, and Mulberry was the code name for the artificial harbours to be used for beachhead supply.

Thirty-three days before the scheduled invasion date, these names started to appear as answers in *The Daily Telegraph* crossword puzzle. On 2 June, just four days prior to D-Day, 'Overlord' appeared as an answer – the solution to the clue 'some big-wig like this has stolen some of it at times'. This was too much for the security forces who descended on *The Telegraph*'s Fleet Street offices expecting to find a German spy. Instead they found bewildered schoolteacher Leonard Dawe, the newspaper's crossword compiler for 20 years. The fact that five of his clues had matched the carefully guarded code names had been nothing more than pure chance.

SPORT

● The evening before the 1946 FA Cup Final between Charlton Athletic and Derby County, the match referee, answering a question from the BBC, had stated that the chances of the ball bursting for the first time in a final were a million to one. But the following day, the ball did burst as Derby centre-forward Jackie Stamps shot for goal. And when the two clubs met in a Football League match five days later, the ball burst again.

The following year, Charlton were back at Wembley for the Cup Final, this time their opponents being Burnley. And amazingly yet again the ball burst!

● Brothers Jack and Frank Taylor were full-back partners with Wolverhampton Wanderers before the Second World War. In June 1952, within a week of each other, both entered football management for the first time, Jack at Queens Park Rangers, Frank at Stoke City. During season 1960–61, they both lost their jobs – Jack at Leeds United, Frank at Stoke.

● For three successive seasons between 1956 and 1958, Leeds United were drawn at home to Cardiff City in the third round of the FA Cup. On each occasion, Cardiff won 2–1.

● Identical twins John and Desmond Rosser scored holes-in-one in consecutive rounds at Auckland Golf Club, New Zealand. Playing in a medal competition on Saturday 15 March 1975 with his brother and two other members, John, the elder twin, holed-in-one at the 10th hole with his wedge. In their next game the following Wednesday, the twins were again playing in a fourball when Desmond holed-in-one at the 13th using his driver.

TWINS

● Michael Chisholm and his twin brother Alex from Coatbridge, Scotland, were inseparable, even to the point of dressing alike. In 1955, Michael joined the Merchant Navy as a cabin boy and on 28 December that year, Alex, who was the older twin by a matter of minutes, went to see him off as he sailed from the Clyde for Egypt. Four days later, Alex was celebrating New Year's Day with friends near Glasgow when he suddenly complained of tiredness. Although he was a strapping, healthy young man of 17, he died soon afterwards from a heart attack. Michael was in the Bay of Biscay when he heard the news. That night, Michael, just as well-built as his twin, died in his sleep. It was less than 48 hours after Alex had died.

...an troop... naked, in sea at Terracina, enjoying their first bath for many days.

8th ARMY OVER MELFA RIVER

esterday's communiqué from diterranean Advance H.Q. said: LAND.—Both Fifth and Eighth rmies have made further progress. he Eighth Army has now broken the Hitler Line and has established a bridgehead beyond the Melfa River, although some enemy units are offering stiff resistance, and are still holding out on the flanks of the advance.

The Fifth Army, after having gained contact with the patrols of the Allied bridgehead force, have continued offensive operations on both fronts. Littoria has been occupied and Cisterna has been captured after heavy fighting. More than 12,000 prisoners have been taken since the start of operations.

AIR.—Yesterday fighter-bombers of the First Tactical Air Force further intensified their onslaught against enemy troop concentrations, guns, tanks and motor transport. In a cord day's operations they destroyed damaged many hundreds of vehicles. Medium bombers attacked bridges and viaducts in the essential Italian railway system.

Deep in Southern France escorted heavy bombers attacked important rail centres in the Lyons and Grenoble districts. Other heavy bombers attacked the airfields at Piacenza, Monfalcone harbour and the oil stores at Porto Marghera.

Last night medium and heavy night bombers attacked roads in the Viterbo area. Over 80 enemy aircraft were active during daylight hours and 20 of them were destroyed. Twelve of ours are missing. The Mediterranean Allied Air Force flew well over 3,000 sorties.

NAVAL.—In further support of the Army's thrusts enemy targets in the Anzio area were again bombarded from the sea on May 24 and 25. Good results were reported. Fires and explosions were seen, occupied buildings destroyed and gun positions and bivouac areas were covered.

MINISTER'S TRIBUTE

After apologising for his late arrival at a Press conference at the Ministry of Information yesterday, Mr. Brendan Bracken, Minister of Information, said: "Before I came here the Prime Minister showed me a little information about our campaign in Italy.

"There is no doubt that Gen. Alexander, who has the noble qualities of courtesy and competence which remind one of Gen. Lee, is conducting one of the greatest campaigns in the history of warfare in Italy."

VATICAN'S FOOD PROBLEM

From Our Special Correspondent
BERNE, Friday.

The only oasis in German-occupied Italy to-day appears to be the Vatican. There life is described as "almost normal."

The inhabitants of the Vatican now have enough milk and small rations of meat it is stated. This relative luxury while 2,000,000 Romans go hungry is obviously worrying the Papal authorities, who cannot feed the entire city.

PRIZE COMPETITION No. 5,797

Three prizes of books to a value of thirty shillings, to be selected by the winners from advertisements in THE DAILY TELEGRAPH on Fridays, will be awarded to the senders of the first three correct solutions opened. Solutions must reach THE DAILY TELEGRAPH, 135, Fleet Street, E.C.4, not later than first post on Thursday. Envelopes must bear 2½d. stamp, and be marked Prize Competition in top left-hand corner. Winners' names appear on Friday.

NAME ....

ADDRESS ....

ACROSS

1 No half-baked praise (two words—4, 4)
5 The county of firm personnel (6)
9 Incog. (two words—3, 5)
10 Not apparently very high-class land (6)
11 —but some bigwig like this has stolen some of it at times (8)
13 They may send one's temperature up, oddly enough (6)
14 It serves its turn in the opening episode (8)
16 Scattered in-road to order (6)
19 He has his duty to master (7)
20 "Die a V.C." (anag.) (Improving words to a soldier?) (6)
21 It needs Erse to slander (3)
26 Need to come to signify (6)
27 When to change to the 31 across? (8)
28 To show grief about a lady is not fruitless (6)
29 What separates the novice from the adept (8)
30 No enemy allowed a bed (6)
31 Remote tering minus don't mix around here (two words—5, 3)

DOWN

1 Cut out the chaff and do not delay victory (6)
2 The one that was left at the post? (6)
3 Hang up more than a corner (6)
4 They are probably prepared for floods in this English town (6)
6 Not prolonged enough to bade the torso hot (two words—3, 5)
7 Not a strange spirit, apparently (8)
8 Entertainment that tells one what to do at it (8)
12 This Eastern is often in a whirl (7)
15 Is familiar with the cells from birth (3)
16 Reversed in 26 across (3)
17 Sounds a useful thing to wear, but no help (8)
18 There's no list for the ships on this (two words—4, 4)
19 Of secret composition and not taxed (two words—4, 4)
22 What a girl may expect if a sailor gives her the bird? (6)
23 Cool place to work in? (6)
24 Figure of speech is turned on quite a way (6)
25 Asked for convalescent patient's meal (6)

Y'DAY'S SOLUTION.—ACROSS: 1, Bread sauce; 9, Trio; 10 Snail's pace; 11, Squail; 12. Contact; 15. Britain; 16, Table; 17, Arum; 18, Brad; 19, Stamp; 21, Orifice; 22, Periwig; 24, Ashore; 27, Eliminator; 28, Mink; 29, High and dry. DOWN: 2, Rank; 3, Alight; 4, Suspect; 5, Upas; 6, Eyesore; 7, Broad arrow; 8, Howling dog; 12, Coat of arms; 13, Nourishing; 14, Taste; 15 Blimp; 19, Screech; 20, Perdita; 23, In hand; 25, Ling; 26, Tour.

QUICK CROSSWORD

ACROSS

1 Sphere
8 Airman
9 Car
11 Sage
12 Parts of ears
14 Chessmen
15 Stairs
17 Gaelic
19 Counsel
21 Food plant
24 Part of window
27 Puts to flight
29 Channels
31 Wild beasts
32 Totter
33 Regretful
34 Violent behaviour
35 Repairs

DOWN

2 Wild beast
3 Colour
4 Fondle
5 Walk like a crab
6 Wounds
7 Alloy
10 Gets up
13 Frank
16 Relate
18 Repose
20 Metal
22 Fairies
23 Taken no notice of
25 Jacob
26 Fierce light
27 Apartments
28 Normal
30 Run away

Y'DAY'S SOLUTION.—ACROSS: 1. Trail; 4. Discard; 8 Unaided; 9, Blind; 10, Piece; 11, Cremate; 15, Rife; 15, Truest; 17, Append; 20, Earl; 22, Redeems; 24, Agate; 26 Bring; 27, Efforts; 28, Degrees; 29, Loses. DOWN: 1 Trumpet; 2, Adage; 3, Ladders; 4, Deduct; 5, Sabre; 6 Animate; 7, Dodge; 12, Rear; 14, Item; 16, Undying; 18, Playful; 19, Dresses; 21, Assess; 22, Rapid; 23, Eagle; 25, Parts

Printed and Published by THE DAILY TELEGRAPH Ltd., 135, Fleet-street, London, E.C.4; and at Withy Grove, Manchester, 4.

The Daily Telegraph crossword puzzle containing the 'Overlord' answer – the code name for the D-Day operation in 1944

✱ Dorothy Collins lived in Brighton, Sussex, and her twin sister Marjorie lived in South Africa. In April 1961, Dorothy died from an accidental overdose of sleeping pills only a few hours before a cable arrived at her house bringing the news that Marjorie had died.

● Twin sisters Terry Connolly and Margaret Richardson were born on St Valentine's Day, 1943, in Leicester. Margaret was adopted at six weeks old, Terry at eight months so that neither was aware of the other's existence until 1978. Yet a number of coincidences linked their separate lives. They had married on the same Saturday of the same year (1960) within an hour of each other. Both planned to have four children who were conceived and born at approximately the same time. When the twins were reunited in 1980, Margaret's son Luke was 11½, Terry's daughter Beth was 11; Margaret's Ruth was 9, Terry's Tim was 10; Margaret's Ben was 4, Terry's Matt was 5; and Margaret's Jim and Terry's Meg were both 3. Terry had wanted to name her first daughter Ruth but had been dissuaded because unpleasant neighbours had a daughter of the same name.

● Identical twins Bridget Harrison of Leicester and Dorothy Lowe of Blackburn, Lancashire, were separated only weeks after their birth in 1945. They did not meet again until 1979. Neither woman had known she was a twin but their lives had formed remarkable parallels. They had married within a year of one another – Bridget had named her son Andrew Richard while Dorothy had called hers Richard Andrew. Dorothy's daughter was called Catherine Louise and Bridget's Karen Louise (Bridget had wanted to call her daughter Catherine but had changed it to Karen to please a relative). Both Bridget and Dorothy had cats called Tiger and both had studied the piano to the same grade, stopping after the same exam. Both women had suffered from meningitis and both were avid readers of historical novels — Dorothy of Catherine Cookson, Bridget of Caroline Marchant, Cookson's other pen name. When reunited, both had seven rings on their hands and both wore the same favourite perfume. But

perhaps the biggest coincidence was that both women had kept diaries for one year only – 1960. The two diaries were of the same make, type and colour, and Bridget and Dorothy had each faithfully made entries for exactly the same number of days before stopping.

● Twin sisters Tuula and Marietta Jaavaara from Borgå, Finland, did everything together. If they were separated for any length of time as children, they would fall asleep – sometimes for days on end – until they were back together. On one occasion when they were apart, both girls developed abscesses under their chins. In December 1970, the twins were an apparently healthy 23 years old. Suddenly Tuula collapsed at home, and shortly afterwards Marietta collapsed too. Both were taken to hospital where doctors, mystified by their illness, tried to revive them by heart massage. But within an hour, Tuula was dead. Ten minutes later, Marietta also died.

● On 19 August 1939 at the Memorial Hospital in Piqua, Ohio, twin brothers were born to an unmarried mother. They went on to be adopted by different families and grew up not knowing of each other's existence. Adoptive parents Jess and Lucille Lewis of Lima, Ohio, called their new son James, unaware that 130 km (80 miles) away in Dayton, the other adoptive parents, the Springer family, had also called their new son James. It was another 39 years before James Lewis and James Springer were reunited but the list of coincidences regarding those missing years is astonishing. Both had grown up with adoptive brothers called Larry and had owned dogs called Toy. At school, both excelled at mathematics but hated spelling. Both had put on 4.5 kg (10 lb) in their late teens for no obvious reason before losing the weight later. Both started having headaches when they were 18 which would begin in the late afternoon and develop into migraines. Both had married women called Linda, divorced them and subsequently remarried women named Betty. One first son had been named James Alan, the other James Allan. Both men had been part-time deputy sheriffs, employed by McDonald's and worked as pump attendants in petrol stations. Both enjoyed carpentry and technical drawing. Both liked stock-car racing but hated baseball. Both had had vasectomies. And each year, both twins had taken their families to the same small Florida holiday resort of St Petersburg, driving there in the same make of car (a Chevrolet) and staying at hotels on the same beach.

● At 12.15 p.m. on 13 November 1958, precisely the time that Keith Main was undergoing an exploratory operation for a hole-in-the-heart at Newcastle-upon-Tyne General Hospital, his twin brother Kenneth ran sobbing to their mother, complaining of pains in his chest. A few days later when Keith had his stitches removed, Kenneth was again stricken with such pain that his mother took him to the doctor. Medical staff could find no sign of anything physically amiss.

● Twins Jim and Arthur Mowforth, who were inseparable as boys and had led almost identical RAF careers, died on the same day in April 1975, aged 66. Jim died from a heart attack in Bristol and Arthur died from the same cause at Windsor, 150 km (93 miles) away.

● Separated as babies in Trinidad in 1933, Jack Yufe and Oscar Stohy were raised in the most diverse manner imaginable. Jack stayed in Trinidad where he was brought up by the father, a Jewish merchant, while Oscar was taken to Germany by the mother and became a junior member of the Hitler Youth. Jack spoke only English, Oscar spoke only German.

Yet when reunited 46 years later at an airport in Minnesota, they were almost identically dressed. Both wore wire-rimmed rectangular spectacles, blue shirts with epaulettes and both sported short clipped moustaches. Both read magazines in the same unusual way, beginning with the back cover and finishing at the front, both liked to dip buttered toast into their coffee and both fidgeted with elastic bands round their wrists. They even shared the same favourite practical joke of pretending to collapse in a sneezing fit in a crowded lift.

BIBLIOGRAPHY

Album of Curious Houses, An, Lucinda Lambton, Chatto & Windus, 1988

Arthur C. Clarke's World of Strange Powers, John Fairley and Simon Welfare, Collins, 1989

Astonishing Britain, Anthony Burton, David & Charles, 1990

Automania, Julian Pettifer and Nigel Turner, Collins, 1984

Benson and Hedges Golfers' Yearbook

Beyond Explanation, Jenny Randles, Robert Hale, 1985

Bizarre Architecture, Charles Jencks, Academy Editions, 1979

Bizarre Leisure Book, The, Stephen Jarvis, Robson, 1993

Book of Beasts, The, John May and Michael Marten, Hamlyn, 1982

Book of Lists, The, David Wallechinsky and Amy Wallace, Aurum Press, 1994

Britain's Living Folklore, Roy Palmer, David & Charles, 1991

Butter Side Up, Dr Magnus Pyke, John Murray, 1976

Christo: The Running Fence, Werner Spies, Thames & Hudson, 1977

Compleat Birdman, The, Peter Haining, Robert Hale, 1976

Concise Guide to Kings and Queens, The, Peter Gibson, Webb & Bower, 1985

Converted into Houses, Charles A. Fracchia and Jeremiah O. Bragstad, Thames & Hudson, 1977

Cricket's Strangest Matches, Andrew Ward, Robson, 1990

Curious Customs, Martin Green, Impact, 1993

Dictionary of Superstitions, A, edited by Iona Opie and Moira Tatem, Oxford University Press, 1989

Drunken Goldfish, The, William Hartson, Unwin Hyman, 1987

Encyclopaedia of Modern Architecture, edited by Gerd Hatje, Thames & Hudson, 1963

Events in Britain, Bernard Schofield, Blandford Press, 1981

Festivals of Europe, Gordon Cooper, Percival Marshall, 1961

Follies, Gwyn Headley and Wim Meulenkamp, Jonathan Cape, 1986

German Festivals and Customs, Jennifer M. Russ, Oswald Wolff, 1982

Great Eccentrics, Peter Bushell, George Allen & Unwin, 1984

Great Theatrical Disasters, Gyles Brandreth, Granada, 1982

Guinness Book of Almost Everything You Didn't Need to Know About the Movies, The, Patrick Robertson, Guinness, 1986

Guinness Book of Military Anecdotes, The, Geoffrey Regan, Guinness, 1992

Guinness Book of Military Blunders, The, Geoffrey Regan, Guinness, 1991

Guinness Book of Movie Facts and Feats, The, Patrick Robertson, Guinness, 1988

Guinness Book of Music, The, Robert and Celia Dearling, Guinness, 1986

Guinness Book of Rail Facts and Feats, The, John Marshall, Guinness, 1981

Guinness Book of Records, The, (various)

Guinness Book of Theatre Facts and Feats, The, Michael Billington, Guinness, 1982

Guinness Book of Weather Facts and Feats, The, Ingrid Holford, Guinness, 1977

Irish Eccentrics, Peter Somerville-Large, Lilliput Press, 1990

Laws of the Earliest English Kings, The, F.L. Attenborough, Cambridge University Press, 1922

Living World, The, Michael Bright, Robson, 1987

Ned Sherrin's Theatrical Anecdotes, Virgin, 1991

Peter the Great, Henri Troyat, Hamish Hamilton, 1988

Prophecy and Prediction in the 20th Century, Charles Neilson Gattey, Aquarian Press, 1989

Reader's Digest Book of Facts 1985

Reader's Digest Mysteries of the Unexplained 1982

Secrets of the Royals, Gordon Winter and Wendy Kochman, Robson, 1990

The Strangest Plants in the World, Prof. S. Talalaj, D. and J. Talalaj, Robert Hale, 1992

Timpson's England, John Timpson, Jarrold, 1987

Timpson's English Eccentrics, John Timpson, Jarrold, 1991

Troughs and Drinking Fountains, Philip Davies, Chatto & Windus, 1989

20th Century American Architecture, Sydney Le Blanc, Whitney, 1993

Twins, Peter Watson, Hutchinson, 1981

Vision of the Brain, A, Semir Zeki, Blackwell, 1993

Wild Sex, Susan Windybank, Virgin, 1992

World's Greatest Cranks and Crackpots, The, Margaret Nicholas, Octopus, 1990

World's Greatest Mistakes, The, Nigel Blundell, Hamlyn, 1984

World's Greatest Mysteries, The, Gerry Brown, Hamlyn, 1989

INDEX

Abercrombie House 94
Adventures of Chatran, The 74
Adventures of William Tell,
  The 80
Aellopedes, The 121
Aeroplane House 95
Agate, James 16
Albatross, wandering 154
Alexandros I, King of Greece
  113
Alfonso XII, King of Spain 108
Allworth Triplet Tandem, The
  122
Almotamid, King of Seville 109
Ammerdown Park Column,
  The 90
Anableb, four-eyed 156
Andorra, war with Germany
  114
Angler fish 156–7
Ant, garden 160
Antechinus, swamp 163
Antoine, André 75
Aphid, cabbage 160
Arbuckle, Roscoe 'Fatty' 78
Archer fish 157
Arches National Park 172
Armadillo 163
  racing 41
Arman 68, *68*
Arnold, Malcolm 72
'Aromarama' 74
Ates, Roscoe 77
Augustus II, Elector of Saxony
  110
Aurorae 148
Axolotl 154
Aye-aye 163
Ayers Rock 173
Ayres, Dr W.O. 121, *121*
Aziz, Abdul 57

Baba, Lotan 52, *52*
Bacall, Lauren 77, *77*
Bacqueville, Marquis de 119,
  120
Bag 79
Balloon Velocipede 122
Bandama Rally 61–2

Banyan tree 171
Barathon, François *118*, 130
Barnacle 156
Bartel, Josef 54
Bat, echo-location system of
  163
Bathtub Race, Vancouver 41
Bean throwing night 42
Bears, eating habits of 163
Beckford, William 12, 91
Bedbug, mating habits of 160
Bee, dance of the 160, 161
Beer Can Regatta 43
Beetle, Necrophorus 161
Behind the Great Wall (US 59)
  74
Behra, Jean 61
Bensley, Harry 52
Bentham, Jeremy *6*, 20
Benzene, discovery of 134
Bernhardt, Sarah 16–17
Berwick-upon-Tweed, war with
  Russia 114–15
Bessemer, Sir Henry 128
BEST stores 87
Beswick, Hannah 12–13
Biffin, Sarah 65
Big Banana 87
Big Deal at Dodge City (US
  66) 76
Big Lobster 87
Big Merino 87
Big Pineapple 87
Big Red One (US 80) 74
Birch, Thomas 26
Birthwort 168
Bitterling 157
Black Abductor 175–6
Blanc, Mel 77
Blanchard, Jean Pièrre 120
Blessing the Fields 44
Blowfly 161
Blue moon 147–8
Boat, collapsible 128
  whale-shaped 131
Bogan Club 79
Bollée, Léon 122
Bone House, The 96
Boojum tree 171

Book, smallest 71
Booth, David 32, *33*
Booth, Richard 11
Bottle gourd 168–9
Bottle Kicking and Hare Pie
  Scrambling 44
Bow, Clara 17
Bower-bird 154
Bowles, Thomas Gibson 13
Bramble Bank 58
Brick throwing 43
Brighton and Rottingdean
  Electric Tramroad 126, *127*
Brighton Pavilion 94
Brummell, George 'Beau' 29
Buckland, Frank 22
Burry Man's Day 44
Bustard, Kori 154
Butterfly, king page 161
Butterfly fish, copperband 157

Cadillac Ranch 65, *67*
Cats, homing powers of 163
Caesar, Julius 109
Cahn, Sir Julien 26–7
Calcio 49
Campbell, Donald 33
Cappadocia, churches in 84
Captain Cook's Cottage 94
Carlin, Ben 52
Carpio, Lope de Vega 79
Caruso, Daniel 56
Casa Batlló 96
Casa Milà 96
Catherine the Great, Empress
  of Russia 7
Cavendish, Henry 19
Cazotte, Jacques 33–4
Censorship, film 75
Chameleon 167
Chander, Jagdash 53
Charlemagne 109
Charles I 70, 110
Charles VI, King of France 7, *8*
Charles VIII, King of France
  109, 113
Charles, Jacques 120
Cheese-rolling 44–5
Chemosphere 96

Chesterfield, Parish Church of
  Our Lady and All Saints 84
Chevalier, Maurice 77
Chewing gum, invention of
  134
Child rulers 111–12
Christian, Prince of Schleswig-
  Holstein 112
Christina, Queen of Sweden
  38
Christo, Javacheff *64*, 66–7
Chuckwalla 167
Churchmobile 125
Cichlid 157
Clam shell pitching tournament
  41
Clarabelle Cow 75
Clarke, Marguerite 77
Cleopatra (US 34) 76
Clinton, Clifford E. 87–8
Clown fish 157
Cockerel, death sentence
  passed on 116
Cockroaches, headless 161
Coffee, drinking of outlawed
  115
Coker, John 56
Colbert, Claudette 77–8
Colburn, Zerah 31
Coleman, Johannes 54
Collyer, Homer and Langley
  19
Connector 129, *129*
Conrad, Joseph 70
Convulsions, cure for 39
Coober Pedy 96
Cook, Robert 29
Cooke, Adolphus 21–2
Coombs, Pat 80
Cope, Fred 63
Cope, Henry 29
Cope, Kenneth 81
Coriolis effect 147
Cornbury, Lord 29
Corrigan, Douglas 121
Cortés, Hernan 180
Couture, Al 57
Cow-pat tossing 41, *48*
Crab

robber 156
  sidewalker 156
Crane-fly 161
Creasey, John 70
Creative Salvage 68
Creighton, Charles 53
Cricket
  hearing organs of 161
  iguana stopped play 58
  on ice 57
  on a sandbank 58
  one-legged versus one-
    armed
Cristo Rey 85
Crocodile Hotel 88
Crossword puzzle, longest to
  solve 71
Crotch, William 31
Crystal Cathedral 85
Cugnot, Capitaine Nicolas-
  Joseph 123

D-Day, coincidences
  surrounding 182, 183
Dadaism 65
Dad's Army 80–1
Dala horse, world's biggest 90
Davidson, Rev. Harold 25, 26
Davies, Marion 76, 97
Da Vinci, Leonardo 68
Dawson, Stan 58
Day of the Dead 41
Dead Sea 173
De Groof, Vincent 120
De Gusmao, Father
  Bartolomeu 119
Del Cano, Sebastian 109–10
DeMello, Andragone 31
DeMille, Cecil B. 76
Dempsey, Jack 'Nonpareil' 56,
  57
Denby Dale Pie 150
de Nerval, Gérard 18
Denham, Father 26
Deschamps, Emile 175
Desforges, Canon 119–20
Devil's Tower 173
Devon Loch 60–1
Dexter, Timothy 96
Dimbleby, Richard 81
Dolphin 164
Doo Dah Parade 41–2
Dover, Dick 62

Dowie, John Alexander 12
Drepana, Battle of 103
Drop City 97
Duchamp, Marcel 65
Dunmow Flitch 45
Durante, Jimmy 77
Dymaxion House 97

Eagle Rock 97
Earth, curiosities of 147–9
Easter Island 173, 173
Edison, Thomas Alva 134
Edmund Ironside 113
Edward I 113
Edward II 114, 114
Edward VI 110
Edward VII 38, 180
Eel, European 157–8
Eelworm, bumblebee 168
Egerton, Francis Henry 22–3
Egg-throwing 45
Egremont Crab Fair 45
Egyptian House 94
Eiffel Tower Bicycle 122, 122
Elephant, water detection
  ability of 164
Elephant Hotel 88, 88
Elfego Baca Golf Tournament
  60
Enchanted Hill, The 97
Episcopalian Church, The 94
Erikstrup, Henning 63
Esha Ness 61
Evans, John 40, 53
Ewell, Richard S. 24
Excalibur Hotel 87, 88
Eyre, Ned 29–30

Facsimile machine, invention
  of 132, 133
Faringdon Folly 90
Ferdinand II, King of Sicily 7–8
Ferriëm, Madame de 34
Festival of Candles 50
Festival for Grandmothers 50
Fibonacci sequence 142
Fields, W.C. 78
Fish, showers of 138–9, 139
Fishlock, Laurie 57–8
Flettner, Anton 130
Floating Church of the
  Redeemer 85

Floating cinema 89
Flying Cat Ceremony 50
Flying dragon 167
Flying fish 158
Fonthill Abbey 12, 91
Ford, Arthur 34
Ford, Henry 13
Foulke, William 'Fatty' 27, 27
Francis, Dick 60–1
Freston Tower 100
Freud, Sigmund 38
Friar Park 90
Frog
  American tree 153
  Darwin's 153
  flying 153
  paradoxical 153
Frogs, showers of 138, 140
Fuller, 'Mad Jack' 93
Fuller, Richard Buckminster 97
Fuller, Samuel 74, 76

Gable, Clark 78
Gadfly 71–2
Gadsby 71
Galton, Sir Francis 134
Garland, Judy 78
Garson, Greer 76
Garter snake 167
Gaudi, Antonio 86, 96
Gecko 167
Geddes, Dr Auckland 37
George II 110
George III 8
George IV 110
George V 112
Ghan Railway 126
Gladstone, William Ewart 20–1
Gleave, Sidney 59
Globe-fish 158
Goddard, Sir Victor 34
'God Save the King' 72–3
Goebbels, Josef 75
Goetheanum 87
Goff, Bruce 97–8
Goldfish, inebriated 146
Golf
  along streets of London 59
  balls, shower of 141
  cross-country 59
  endurance 59–60
  night-time 59
  on ice 60

  on moon 60
  on mountain 60
  unusual holes-in-one 59, 60
  versus a fisherman 58–9
Gonder, Harry 59–60
Goodman, Dickie 72
Gotmaar Festival 43
Goupil, Monsieur A. 120–1
Grace, W.G. 27
Grant, Cary 75
Grant, Julia 34
Grapple tree 171–2
Great Klondike Outhouse
  Race 42
Greb, Harry 57
Grenfell, Joyce 78
Grishin, Seriozha 31–2
Grofé, Ferde 72
Grundtvig Church 85
Guiseux, Count de 121

Haakon VII, King of Norway
  113
Hajianestis, General 24
Haldane, John Burdon
  Sanderson 21
Hamlet 80
Hamster 164
Happy End (Cze 68) 74
Harford, Henry Charles 24–5
Hargis, James 53
Harris, 'Bumper' 126
Hatchet fish 158
Hatfield, Charles 141–2
Hats, the compulsory wearing
  of 115
Hawker, Robert 26, 99
Haxey Hood Game 46
Head, Ellen 36
Hearst, William Randolph 76,
  94, 97
Heaviside, Oliver 19
Heiligenschein 143–4
Helium, properties of 144
Hemingway, Ernest 37
Henley-on-Todd Regatta 43
Henry I 113
Henry Christophe, King of
  northern Haiti 8
Hepburn, Katharine 38
Her Twelve Men (US 54) 76
Heygate, H.J. 57
High Country Golf Club 60

Hirst, James 30
Hoatzin 154–5
Hocktide 46
Hollywood Wives 81
Hopkins, Anthony 175
Hornbill, Great Indian 155
Horse racing, on ice 51
Hoskins, Allen Clayton 78
House
  paper 99
  rotating 99
  shark in roof 98
House in the Clouds *82*, 91
Howard, Rev. Geoffrey 53
Howland Green, Hetty 13–14
Huescar, war with Denmark
  115
Hughes, Howard 19–20
Hummingbird, ruby-throated
  155
Hurling 46
Hurlinger, Johann 53
Hypocrites, The (US 15) 75

Ice blocks, falls of 138–9,
  180
Ice Hotel 88–9
Ichikawa, Kon 74
Inca empire, conquest of 104
Incredible Mr Limpet, The (US
  64) 74
Ingalls Hockey Rink 89
Insects, as delicacy 149
Intimate Revue, The 79
Inventions, failed 136
Ireland cricket team 58
Isles of Scilly, war with
  Netherlands 115

Jackson, General Thomas
  'Stonewall' 25
James, Duke of Monmouth
  110
Janssen, David 35
John, King 109
Jonathan Livingston Seagull
  (US 73) 74
Jones, Ken 124
Juana, Queen of Spain 8
Jules Undersea Lodge 89
Jumping frog contest 42
Jungle, The 91
Jupiter 146

Kahakura, Jamie 62
Kangaroo, red 164
Karansebes, Battle of 105–6
Karvonen, Veikko 54
Kean, Edmund 17
Keaton, Buster 123
Keene, Brian 53
Kennedy, John F.,
  assassination of 181
Kerak, Siege of 103–4
Kessler, George A. 14
Key, Francis Scott 73
Kickball race 42
Kid Creole and the Coconuts
  71
King Alfred's Tower 91
King of the Mountain Festival
  43
Kirby Muxloe Castle 83
Kirk, Herbert 54
Kirwan, Richard 21
Kite fighting 43
Kittow, Mr Stuart 61
Kiwi 155
Knaresborough Bed Race 46
Knighthood of the Old Green
  46–7
Koestler, Arthur 176
Kolberg (Ger 45) 75
Konigin Luise, the sinking of
  106
Krakatoa, East of Java (US
  68) 76

Ladd, Alan 78
'Lady in the veil' mushroom
  168
Lady of Lyons, The 79
Lalibela, churches of 85
Language, curiosities of 71
La Tomatina 50
Laughing, outlawed 115
Laurie, John 80–1
Lawn Mower Championships
  50
Laws of America, bizarre 116
Leaf insect, Javanese 161,
  161
Leavenworth 94–5
'Le Bateau' 66
Lee, John 117
Le Mans 24-Hour Race 61
Lemmings 164, *165*

Lenard, Professor Philipp 38
Lennon, John 38–9
L'Eolienne 123
Lepanto, Battle of 104
Lewson, Jane 20
L'Hirondelle et la Mésange
  (Bel 20) 75
Liberace 124
Library books, overdue 70–1
Life Begins at Forty 81
Light, curiosities of 143
Lilliput organ 72
Lincoln, Abraham,
  assassination of 180–1
Lincoln, Elmo 76
Lisboa, Antonio 68
Lithops 169
Llama dung, as railway fuel
  126
Lloyd, Harold 78
'Long Term Parking' 68, *68*
Lotito, Michel 17
Louis XIV, King of France
  110
Lowe, Arthur 80–1
Lowrey, Tommy 60
Ludwig II, King of Bavaria 8–9,
  83–4
Luis Filipe, Crown Prince of
  Portugal 112
Lully, Jean Baptiste 72
Lyons, Lewis Melville 65

Macaulay, Thomas Babington
  32
Macbeth, curse of 80
Macready, William Charles
  17–18
McCaig's Folly 91–2, *92*
McGuire, Pat 12
McInnes, Maud 58
McQuone, Anthony 32
Madame Butterfly (US 32) 75
Maggots, shower of 141
Maharajah's Well 95
Mallee fowl 155
Manley, Norman L. 60
Manning, Matthew 36–7
Mantis, praying 162
Marbles, outlawed 115
Margaret, 'Maid of Norway'
  113–14
Margaret, Princess 39

Marie Antoinette, Queen of
  France 9
Martin, Mrs Paddy 60
Matchbox bean 170
Matisse, Henri 66
Mayer, Louis B. 76–7
Meat, shower of 140
Melgarejo, General Mariano
  108
Mello, Rosemary 63
Melu, Joan 72
Mendes, Gilberto Ambrosio
  Garcis 72
Menlek II, Emperor of
  Abyssinia 117
Mercury 147
Merry-Go-Round, The (US 23)
  77
Mice, shower of 140
Mini, multi-seat 124
Mirages 148–9
Mite
  moth 162
  water 162
Mithridates VI, King of Pontus
  113
Molard, Hubert 72
Moles, trial of 116
Monroe, Marilyn 79, 80
Moose Dropping Festival 42
Moran, Robert 72
Morwenstow, vicarage at 26,
  99
Mosse, Claude 53
Moth
  Indian moon 162
  Madagascan 162
  polyphemus 162
Motor car
  collapsible 125
  grass-covered 124
  swan-shaped 124
  swimming pool 125
Mt Athos 172–3
Mouthbrooder catfish 158
Mozart, Wolfgang Amadeus
  32, *32*
Mudskipper 158–9, *158*
Museum of the Mousetrap 69
Musical instruments
  bizarre 72
  largest 73
Mussolini, Benito 75

Mustapha III, Sultan of Turkey 110
Mütter Museum 70
Mytton, Jack 14, *15*

Najork Foot Motor Boat 130
Naked racing 47
Nell Gwynn (GB 34) 75
Neuschwanstein Castle 83–4
Nitro-cellulose, invention of 134
Nixon, Robert 35
Noailles, Comtesse de 14–15
'No Art' movement 66
Noctilucent clouds 148
Norberg, Bengt 53
Norton, Joshua 11
Notre-Dame-du-Haut, Chapel of 85–6
Novarro, Ramon 79
Numbat 164–6

O'Connor, Donald 79
O'Higgins, Bernardo 105
O'Keefe, John 80
Onoda, Lt Hiroo *102*, 112
Opossum 166
Orton, Richard 72
Otto, King of Bavaria 9
Oyster 166

Pack o' Cards 89
Paganini, Niccolò 73
Painshill 92
Palais Idéal 84
Palio 50–1
Pancake racing 47
Pandya, Arvind 53
Panorama 81
Parrish, Anne 176
Pathan, Sir Mahabat Khan Babi 23
Peel, Bobby 27–8
Penguin, Emperor 155
Penny-Farthing Championships, Australian 43
Pepi II, King of Egypt 109
Perky Bat Tower 101
Peter the Great, Tsar of Russia 9–10, *10*, 110
Petrified Forest 174
Philip, Prince of Calabria 110

Philippe, Duke of Orleans 110
Phillips, Conrad 80
Phillips, Sir Thomas 15
Phobias, unusual 38
Pig, noise of 166
Pig War, The 108
Pigeons, the musical appreciation of 146
Piggy Bank Museum 69
Pineapple, The 92–3
Pisa, Leaning Tower of 101
Pitcher plant 169, *169*
Pius V, Pope 35
Pizarro, Francisco 104
Plaice, arsenic content of 159
Plover, Egyptian 155
Poe, Edgar Allan 176
Polley, George Gibson 53
Pompidou Centre 89
Porcupine 166
Portmeirion 95
Postman Pat 81
Potter's Museum of Curiosity 69, *69*
Potto 166
Pozzo, Andrea 66
Priestley, J.B. 176
Prime numbers 143
Prussian army, failings of 104–5
Purvis, Will 117
Pushkin, Alexander 176
Puya raimondii 170

Quarters, The 95
Quetzal 155

Race against the Train 47
Rafflesia, Giant 170
Railway highest 126–8 smallest 128
Ramdarie, Dookie 95–6
Randall and Hopkirk (Deceased) 81
Rarijipari 42
Rats, trial of 116–7
Rattlesnake 167
Reagan, Johnny *56*, 57
'Red rain' 141
Renoir, Pierre-Auguste 65
Resolute, The 130
Ribbonworm 168

Richards, Gordon 60
Richardson, Sir Ralph 18
Ridding, Bill 63
Rin Tin Tin 76, 79
Rivers, Joe 57
Roberts, Steve 122
Roller skates, early demonstration of 133
Rolling-pin throwing 43
Rooke, Sir George 104
Rose of Jericho 170
Rosendahl, Peter 54
Rossetti, Gabriel Charles Dante 70
Rothschild, Baron Lionel 23–4
Roubillac, Louis François 68
Round House, The 95
Roundup Time in Texas (US 37) 76
Running of the Sheep 42

St Anthony of Padua 37
St Anthony's Day 42
St Enodoc Church 85
St George, Church of 85
St Ignazio, Church of 66
St John, Church of 95
St Moritz 51
St Patrick's Day Parade, World's Shortest 42
St Petersburg Ice Palace 83
Sackville, Lady 15–16
Sagrada Familia, La 86
Salmon 158
Salut, Jean-Pierre 62
Sandbox tree 172
San Fedelino, Church of 85
Santa Anna, General Antonio Lopez de 25
Santa Isabel de Hungria, chapel of 86
Satie, Erik 18, 73
Sausage tree 172, *172*
Scent of Mystery (US 60) 74
Schumann, Robert 18, 38
Seahorse 159
Secretary bird 155–6
Segal, Vivienne 77
Sellers, Peter 76
Sensitive plant 170
Setsubun 42
Sham castles 90, 93
Shark 159

Shaw, Percy 16
'Shell House' 99
Shepard, Alan 60
Shepherds' Race 51
Ship House 96
Shrew, armoured 166
Shrovetide football 47–8
Sidney, Sylvia 75
Singing Dogs 73
Singing Sheep 73
Sistiaga, Jose Antonio 76
Skink, Polynesian 167
Slocum, Captain Joshua 130
'Smallest Theatre in the World' 79
'Smell-O-Vision' 74
Smith, Ernest 59
Snail, desert 166
Snakes, shower of 140
Snuff-Taking Championships, UK 48
Soccer
  curious abandonments 62–3
  game of three halves 62
  least competitive league 62
  on stilts 63
  outlawed 115
Soor, Battle of 104
Spencer, Herbert 21
Spiders 162
Spinach, myth of 150
Stamford Bridge, Battle of 103
Stanhope, Lady Hester 30
Starfish flower 170
Star Floating Palace 89
'Star Spangled Banner' 73
Steiner, Marcel 79
Stendhal Syndrome, The 65–6
Stephen II, Pope 109
Stephenson, George 125
Stethoscope, invention of 133
Stickleback, three-spined 159
Stockhausen, Karlheinz 72
Stoke Newington Pumping Station 89
Strike, Hilda 54
Struth, William 30
Sugarbush 169–70
Sugar Loaf 93
Sullivan, Roy C. 142, *142*
Swabian War 104
Swinging the Fireballs 48

Swordfish 159
Symmes, John Cleves 28

Tailorbird 156
Taivallahti Church 86
Tanabata Matsuri 43
Tanga, Battle of 106
Tar-barrel rolling 48
Tarzan of the Apes (US 18) 76
Tattingstone Wonder 93
Tchaikovsky, Peter Ilyich 73–4
Teeth, false 136
Templeton Carpet Factory 89
Temppeliaukio Church 86
Tennis, outlawed 115
Termite 162
Thicknesse, Captain Philip 123
Thirteen Women (US 32) 76
Thomas, Clive 62
Thompson, William 16
Thornton, Spencer 35
Tick, mating habits of 162–3
Titanic, sinking of 179, *179*
Toad
  common *152*, 153
  fire-belly 153–4
  Surinam 154
Todd, Michael Jr 74
Toe-wrestling 48
To Have and Have Not (US 44) 77
Toutschkoff, Countess 35
Tracked by the Police (US 27) 76
Traffic lights, exploding 123
Tragedy in US History Museum 70
Trail of the Pink Panther, The (GB 82) 76
Train, George 28
Tram, horse-shaped 123

Traveller's tree 172
Traynor, Jack 37
Triangular Lodge 99–100, *100*
Tricycle, dog-powered 122
Trobridge, Ernest *98*, 99
Tuatara 167
Turpin, Ben 77
Twain, Mark 36, 176

Ubu Roi 79
Ulster Road Bowls 48
Umberto I, King of Italy 181
Unbuilt structures 101
'Unchained Melody' 74
Underground
  church 85, 96
  hotel 96
  orchid 170
Underwater
  art 66
  ballroom 93
  hotel 89
  race walking 43
  statue of Christ 66
Uranus 146–7
Urine, as mouthwash 150
US Air Force Academy Chapel 84–5, *85*

Vacuum cleaner, invention of 134–5, *135*
Van Butchell, Martin 29
Van Drebbel, Cornelius 128
Vareilles, Gaston 62
Velez, Lupe 79
Venable, Evelyn 77
Venus 146
Venus fly trap 170–1
Verdun, capture of 106–7
Verheylewegen, Jamy 66
Verne, Jules 177, *177*
Victoria, Queen 112, *112*

Voliva, Glenn Wilbur 12
Volkswagen Beetle, customised 124–5, *125*
Von Blücher, Prince Gebhard 24
Von Hülsen, General 113
Von Stroheim, Erich 77

Wagner, Richard 74
Walsh, Stella 54, *55*
Walton, Ralph 57
Wang Ching Chang 54
War of Jenkins' Ear 107
War of the Worlds, The 81
Water, properties of 144
Watermelon Day 42
Waterton, Charles 24
Wave Rock 174
Wedding ceremonies, German 51
Wedding, naked 39
Wedding of the Giants 51, *51*
Wedding Tower 100
Welbeck Abbey 84
Welch, Jack 57
Welles, Orson 80, 81
Welwitschia mirabilis 171, *171*
Whippoorwill 156
White, John 61
White Bread Runners 48–9
White Dog (US 84) 76
Whooping cough, cure for 39
Whuppity Stourie 49
William I, King of Würtemberg 36
William of Orange, statue of 68–9
Williams, Andy 77
Williams, John 36
Williams, Kenneth 18–19, 80
Williams, Wallace 56
Williams-Ellis, Sir Clough 95

Winchester, Sarah 16
Wingo, Plennie L. 54
Witley Park 93
Wolgast, Adolph 57
Wonder Dogs 73
Wood, Natalie 38
Woodcock 156
Woodpecker, red-headed 156
World Black Pudding Knocking Championships 43–4
World Bog Snorkelling Championships 44
World Elephant-Polo Championships 43
World Flounder Tramping Championships 45
World Gurning Championships 45, *45*
World Peashooting Championships 47
World Veterans' Championships 54
World Worm-Charming Championships 49
Worms, experiments on 146
Worms, Palolo 168
Wortley, Alexander 100
Wright, Ernest Vincent 71
Wright, James 53
Wright, Lawrence 39
Writing on the Wall, The (Fra/Bel 82) 74

Yashin, Lev 62

Zanzibar, defeat of 108
Zion City 12
Zizka, General Jan 109
Zugspitze Tower 101
Zuider Zee, Dutch surrender at 105, *105*

PICTURE CREDITS

Allsport/Hulton Deutsch 55; Ann Ronan at Image Select 121, 127, 129, 132, 135, 139, 179; Associated Press 102; Colorsport 27; Cricklewood Library and Archives 98; FLPA 152; Gamma Presse 64, 68, 87; Hulton Deutsch 8, 10, 26, 114, 125; Image Select 23, 32, 77; John Frost Newspapers 183; Mary Evans Picture Library 15, 120, 122, 165, 177; Peter Newark's American Pictures 56; Peter Newark's Historical Pictures 107, 118; Peter Newark's Military Pictures 105; Planet Earth Pictures 154, 158, 161, 171, 172; Popperfoto 33, 45, 51, 52, 88, 92, 112, 140, 169, 173; Rex Features/Globe Photos Inc. 48; Stefan Richter (all rights reserved) 69; Spectrum Colour Library 82, 100; University College London 6.